Vol. LXXXVI

Bible Expositor and Illuminator

SPRING QUARTER   March, April, May 2014

Looking Ahead 2
Editorials 3

Jesus' Fulfillment of Scripture

UNIT I: Jesus and the Davidic Covenant

Mar.   2—An Eternal Kingdom—II Sam. 7:4-16 4
Mar.   9—Son of David—Ps. 89:35-37; Isa. 9:6-7; Matt. 1:18-22a 18
Mar.   16—An Everlasting King—Ps. 110:1-4; Acts 2:22-24, 29-32 32
Mar.   23—Worthy Is the Lamb—Rev. 5:6-13 46

UNIT II: What the Prophets Foretold

Mar.   30—The Entrance of the King—Zech. 9:9; Matt. 21:1-11 60
Apr.   6—The Cleansing of the Temple—Isa. 56:6-7; Jer. 7:9-11; Mark 11:15-19 74
Apr.   13—The Suffering of the King—Jer. 23:5-6; Zech. 6:9-15; John 19:1-5 88
Apr.   20—The Resurrection of the King (Easter)—Hos. 6:1-3; Luke 24:1-12 102
Apr.   27—From Suffering to Glory—Isa. 53:5-8; Luke 24:25-27, 44-47 116

UNIT III: Jesus' Use of Scripture

May   4—Victory over Temptation—Deut. 6:13-16; Matt. 4:4-11 130
May   11—Jesus' Mission on Earth—Luke 4:14-21 144
May   18—Jesus' Teaching on the Law—Matt. 15:1-11, 18-20 158
May   25—The Greatest Commandment—Lev. 19:18; Deut. 6:4-7; Mark 12:28-34 172
Topics for Next Quarter 188
Paragraphs on Places and People 189
Daily Bible Readings 190
Review 191

Editor in Chief: Grace M. Todd

Edited and published quarterly by
THE INCORPORATED TRUSTEES OF THE
GOSPEL WORKER SOCIETY
UNION GOSPEL PRESS DIVISION

Rev. W. B. Musselman, Founder

Price: $4.55 per quarter*
$17.00 per year*
*shipping and handling extra

ISBN 978-1-936898-88-6

Lessons based on International Sunday School Lessons; the International Bible Lessons
for Christian Teaching, copyright © 2010 by the Committee on the Uniform Series and used
with permission. Edited and published quarterly by The Incorporated Trustees of the Gospel
Worker Society, Union Gospel Press Division, 2000 Brookpark Road, Cleveland, Ohio
44109-5812. Mailing address: P.O. Box 6059, Cleveland, Ohio 44101-1059. www.union
gospelpress.com

LOOKING AHEAD

One of the fascinating proofs for the inspiration of the Bible is the fulfillment of prophecy, and the central focus of biblical prophecy is Jesus Christ. Through a combination of Old and New Testament texts, this quarter's lessons examine how Jesus fulfilled—or will yet fulfill—what the prophets foretold.

The first four lessons examine Jesus' fulfillment of the Davidic covenant. This covenant is first studied, with special emphasis on the eternal nature of the kingdom promised. Next, we observe how Jesus fulfilled prophecies related to the messianic Son of David and the eternal kingdom over which He will rule. This unit ends with a glimpse of the future worship He will receive as the glorified Lamb of God.

Lessons 5 through 9 focus on specific events in Jesus' earthly experience that the prophets foretold. One of these was Jesus' triumphal entry, as prophesied by Zechariah. Another was the cleansing of the temple, as foreseen by Isaiah and Jeremiah. The King's sufferings, as foretold by Jeremiah and Zechariah, were another theme fulfilled in the unjust trials Jesus endured.

Jesus' resurrection, intimated by Hosea and other prophets, is the theme of our Easter lesson. And this second unit ends with Jesus' own exposition of various Old Testament prophecies that foretold how He would turn His sufferings into glory.

Our third unit brings together several examples of how Jesus used Old Testament Scripture during His earthly life. One such occasion was when He was tempted. He turned away Satan's thrusts with timely reminders from the law. Another was during a synagogue service in Nazareth, when He revealed His messianic mission through a passage from Isaiah.

A third occasion for its use came when critics faulted His disciples for not ceremonially washing their hands. Jesus set such traditions over against the true teaching of the law and exposed His critics as hypocrites. A final example was His answer to the question of which commandment was greatest. In doing so, He confounded the legalists, who had overlooked the essence of God's will.

These lessons show not only how minutely prophecy was fulfilled in Christ but also how much He revered and used it. This should stimulate us to follow His example and embrace the Word of God in life and service.

—*Robert E. Wenger.*

PLEASE NOTE: The Incorporated Trustees of the Gospel Worker Society, Union Gospel Press Division, most earnestly endeavors to proclaim fundamentally sound doctrine. The writers are prayerfully selected for their Bible knowledge and yieldedness to the Spirit of Truth, each writing in his own style as enlightened by the Holy Spirit. At best we know in part only. "They received the word with all readiness of mind, and searched the scriptures daily, whether those things were so" (Acts 17:11).

Jesus: Our Living Example

JOYCE M. SIMON

Giving someone an example of how to do something plays an important role in the learning process, whether it is learning to fly a kite, bake a cake, drive a car, or solve a problem in algebra. The example can be visual, demonstrating how something is done, or it can be in the form of written instructions.

As children of God, we now have the benefit of both methods. We have the Scriptures, our instruction manual that gives us all the information we need in order to live successful and fulfilled lives. And although Jesus is no longer walking among us in human form, God's Holy Spirit dwells with every baptized believer to instruct, to comfort, and to tell us when we are on the wrong path.

Before the advent of Jesus, God attempted to use the people of Israel as an example. The hope was that by obeying His laws and, as a consequence, reaping the benefits of protection and prosperity, they could influence the heathen nations around them. The people of Israel failed—miserably.

To atone for their sins, the Israelites were required to offer an unblemished animal as a sacrifice.

In time, the cycle of sin, repent, obey for a while, and then sin again wearied the Lord. He told the Prophet Jeremiah to tell them, "Thou hast forsaken me, saith the Lord, thou art gone backward: therefore will I stretch out my hand against thee, and destroy thee; I am weary with repenting" (Jer. 15:6).

We are no different from the people of Israel. Many of us get caught in that same cycle. We obey for a while; then we fall prey to some temptation, which causes us to sin. We repent fervently and obey for a while; then we fall prey to Satan again, and the cycle is repeated. The level of our belief and our willingness to obey determine how long this cycle will continue.

Failure by the Israelites was no surprise to the Lord. He knew they would fail. To that end, He had already prepared a built-in fail-safe provision—Jesus. He would be the final sacrifice. He was the only lamb without spot or blemish (cf. I Pet. 1:19) acceptable to God as complete atonement for the sins of all who are willing to believe and accept God's offer of salvation.

The proclamation of Jesus' birth, mission, death, and triumphant resurrection was foretold by the Prophet Isaiah. "For unto us a child is born, unto us a son is given: and the government shall be upon his shoulder: and his name shall be called Wonderful, Counsellor, The mighty God, The everlasting Father, The Prince of Peace. Of the increase of his government and peace there shall be no end, upon the throne of David, and upon his kingdom, to order it, and to establish it with judgment and with justice from henceforth even for ever. The zeal of the Lord of hosts will perform this" (Isa. 9:6-7).

Jesus' mission was twofold. As the final sacrifice, He opened the door of salvation to every individual willing to accept God's offer. This gave us direct access to the Lord. Jesus is also our example of how we can live lives that

(Continued on page 186)

Scripture Lesson Text

II SAM. 7:4 And it came to pass that night, that the word of the LORD came unto Na'than, saying,

5 Go and tell my servant Da'vid, Thus saith the LORD, Shalt thou build me an house for me to dwell in?

6 Whereas I have not dwelt in *any* house since the time that I brought up the children of Is'ra-el out of E'gypt, even to this day, but have walked in a tent and in a tabernacle.

7 In all *the places* wherein I have walked with all the children of Is'ra-el spake I a word with any of the tribes of Is'ra-el, whom I commanded to feed my people Is'ra-el, saying, Why build ye not me an house of cedar?

8 Now therefore so shalt thou say unto my servant Da'vid, Thus saith the LORD of hosts, I took thee from the sheepcote, from following the sheep, to be ruler over my people, over Is'ra-el:

9 And I was with thee whithersoever thou wentest, and have cut off all thine enemies out of thy sight, and have made thee a great name, like unto the name of the great *men* that *are* in the earth.

10 Moreover I will appoint a place for my people Is'ra-el, and will plant them, that they may dwell in a place of their own, and move no more; neither shall the children of wickedness afflict them any more, as beforetime,

11 And as since the time that I commanded judges *to be* over my people Is'ra-el, and have caused thee to rest from all thine enemies. Also the LORD telleth thee that he will make thee an house.

12 And when thy days be fulfilled, and thou shalt sleep with thy fathers, I will set up thy seed after thee, which shall proceed out of thy bowels, and I will establish his kingdom.

13 He shall build an house for my name, and I will stablish the throne of his kingdom for ever.

14 I will be his father, and he shall be my son. If he commit iniquity, I will chasten him with the rod of men, and with the stripes of the children of men:

15 But my mercy shall not depart away from him, as I took *it* from Saul, whom I put away before thee.

16 And thine house and thy kingdom shall be established for ever before thee: thy throne shall be established for ever.

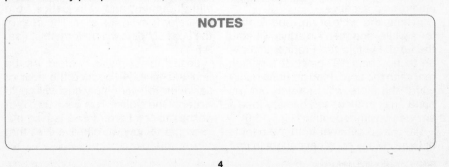

NOTES

An Eternal Kingdom

Lesson: II Samuel 7:4-16

Read: II Samuel 7:1-17

TIME: about 1000 B.C.   PLACE: Jerusalem

GOLDEN TEXT—"Thine house and thy kingdom shall be established for ever before thee: thy throne shall be established for ever" (II Samuel 7:16).

Introduction

There are many remarkable evidences that the Bible is the inspired Word of God, but one of the most striking is the fulfillment of Old Testament prophecies.

Among the multitude of fulfilled prophecies are those related to the first advent of Jesus Christ. The Gospel writers and apostles have pointed out numerous ways He fulfilled prophecy given from the time of Adam and Eve to the book of Malachi. Our lessons this quarter will examine a number of these prophecies, along with New Testament records of fulfillment.

Our first unit, consisting of four lessons, relates to Jesus' fulfillment of the Davidic covenant. Jesus was not only the divine Son of God but also the human son of King David. For centuries the Jewish people longed for the reign of the Davidic Messiah.

These hopes were based on a covenant God had made with David and his offspring. This covenant was given by the Lord at the height of David's reign, and its terms were repeated in numerous psalms and prophecies thereafter. This week's lesson examines the original promises God made.

LESSON OUTLINE

I. DAVID'S OFFER DECLINED— II Sam. 7:4-7

II. DAVID'S FORTUNES PROTECTED—II Sam. 7:8-11a

III. DAVID'S DYNASTY ESTABLISHED—II Sam. 11b-16

Exposition: Verse by Verse

DAVID'S OFFER DECLINED

II SAM. 7:4 And it came to pass that night, that the word of the LORD came unto Nathan, saying,

5 Go and tell my servant David, Thus saith the LORD, Shalt thou build me an house for me to dwell in?

6 Whereas I have not dwelt in any house since the time that I brought up the children of Israel out of Egypt, even to this day, but have walked in a tent and in a tabernacle.

7 In all the places wherein I have walked with all the children of Israel spake I a word with any of the tribes of Israel, whom I commanded to feed my people Israel, saying, Why build ye not me an house of cedar?

The Lord's question for David (II Sam. 7:4-5). David was by this time well established as king (vs. 1). He had earned the approval of all the tribes of Israel, had defeated his major enemies, and was living in his own house in Jerusalem. He had also assigned the ark of the covenant a place in the city.

But David was not satisfied with this. He thought the ark deserved a better dwelling place (II Sam. 7:2). His own house was a luxurious dwelling of cedar, while God's ark was only surrounded by curtains. Curtains had been fine for the nomadic life of the wilderness, but surely the ark deserved a better place now.

David implied to Nathan the prophet that he intended to build a proper house for God, and Nathan hastily agreed (II Sam. 7:2-3). He was touched by the sincerity of David's intentions. But he had not consulted the Lord about the matter, and that night the Lord spoke to him and corrected his hasty advice (vs. 4). The rest of our passage, then, is God's revelation to David through Nathan.

This revelation began with a question: "Shalt thou build me an house for me to dwell in?" (II Sam. 7:5). This question anticipated a negative answer (cf. I Chron. 17:4). It implied that the initiative for building a temple should come from God Himself, not a king. This is evident from the verses that follow. If He had needed or wanted a temple, He would have asked.

The question also implied that if a temple was to be built, David was not the one to do it. The Lord was not opposed to the idea (cf. II Sam. 7:13), but He reserved the right to designate both the person and the time to do it. David was unsuitable for building a temple

because he was a man of war who had shed much blood (I Kings 5:3; I Chron. 22:7-8; 28:2-3). God wanted it to be a house of peace; so Solomon, a man of peace, would build it in a tranquil time.

The Lord's previous dwelling (II Sam. 7:6-7). The Lord reminded David that He had been satisfied with the place of worship already designated. More than four hundred years had passed since the Exodus from Egypt. Shortly after this, He had given specific instructions about the place He wanted for worship (Deut. 12:5-14). There He would live among His people.

"In a tent and in a tabernacle" (II Sam. 7:6) can be translated "in a tent as a dwelling." There God "walked" with Israel as they traversed the desert. He went wherever they went, giving guidance, protection, provision, and discipline. And after they had reached their land, His ark of the covenant remained with them, though no temple then existed.

In light of this history, the Lord asked another question: In all the places He had accompanied them, had He ever asked why the tribes of Israel had not built Him a house of cedar? David was invited to review every location in which God had walked with them. He would look in vain for any command to build a luxurious temple.

There is some question about the words "the tribes of Israel, whom I commanded to feed my people Israel" (II Sam. 7:7). We have no record that God ever assigned a shepherding role to the tribes of Israel. The passage parallel to this in I Chronicles 17:6 uses the word "judges" instead of "tribes." There is a difference of only one letter in these two Hebrew words, so perhaps our text originally read "judges." The tribes, of course, could have acted as shepherds through the judges who arose from within them.

In any case, the Lord made it clear that He had never demanded of former leaders that they build Him a temple. He had been satisfied with the tabernacle, and He still was. The time for a temple had not yet come. He had a dwelling among His people, and that was the most important thing. It is worthwhile for us today to reflect on this when considering whether imposing structures are significant to God.

DAVID'S FORTUNES PROTECTED

8 Now therefore so shalt thou say unto my servant David, Thus saith the LORD of hosts, I took thee from the sheepcote, from following the sheep, to be ruler over my people, over Israel:

9 And I was with thee whithersoever thou wentest, and have cut off all thine enemies out of thy sight, and have made thee a great name, like unto the name of the great men that are in the earth.

10 Moreover I will appoint a place for my people Israel, and will plant them, that they may dwell in a place of their own, and move no more; neither shall the children of wickedness afflict them any more, as beforetime,

11a And as since the time that I commanded judges to be over my people Israel, and have caused thee to rest from all thine enemies.

The Lord's care for David (II Sam. 7:8-9). The Lord now began to reveal what He really had in mind for David and Israel. He had something even better for him and his descendants—an eternal covenant. Though this passage does not use the word "covenant," other texts that refer to these promises do (cf. II Sam. 23:5; Ps. 89:3).

God first reviewed all He had done for David to bring him to this point. He referred to him as "my servant" (II Sam. 7:8)—a title reserved for a select few, such as Abraham, Moses, and Caleb. Thus, although it appears to be a humbling title, it actually was a term of honor. To raise him to this position, God had tak-

en him from the "sheepcote" (pasture), where he had been caring for the sheep.

From that humble status, the Lord had promoted David to be "ruler over my people, over Israel" (II Sam. 7:8). "My people" emphasizes that Israel was not an ordinary nation; it belonged to God. And David was chosen to shepherd this chosen people. What a contrast to watching over the sheep— and what an honor!

Since the day Samuel anointed David, the Lord had been with him wherever he went. He not only preserved him from his enemies; He had defeated them all. The Amalekites, Philistines, Jebusites, Saul, and all other foes had been removed or subdued. For many years, David's anointing might have appeared meaningless, but the One who promised him the kingdom preserved him until he had actually obtained it.

Now the Lord promised to increase David's stature even more. "Have made thee a great name" (II Sam. 7:9) should probably read "*will* make thee a great name." David's name would come to be honored among "the great men that are in the earth." He would be remembered as one of the giants of history. Unlike Saul, David never sought this reputation for himself. His promotion had come about solely through the sovereign will of God.

The Lord's care for Israel (II Sam. 7:10-11a). God's promotion of David was part of His larger purpose to preserve and bless Israel. He would "plant them, that they may dwell in a place of their own, and move no more." There they would be secure; their enemies would not "afflict them . . . as beforetime." "Beforetime" refers to the chaotic time of the judges, when foes had attacked relentlessly.

The promise of a land for Israel had been a prominent feature of God's covenant with Abraham (Gen. 15:7-21). David's conquests had secured much of this territory, but peace was

7

still not a reality. It would remain for Solomon to achieve this promised goal (cf. I Kings 4:21-25).

But our text implies that Israel's rest in their own land would be permanent: they would move no more, and their enemies would afflict them no more (II Sam. 7:10). This was not achieved in Solomon's day. Since then they have been exiled twice, and enemies still threaten them to this day. Later prophets continued to tell of a final restoration and peace for Israel (cf. Jer. 32:37-44; Ezek. 39:25-29; Zech. 10:6-12), and this has not yet been completed. It remains for the Messiah to accomplish.

DAVID'S DYNASTY ESTABLISHED

11b Also the LORD telleth thee that he will make thee an house.

12 And when thy days be fulfilled, and thou shalt sleep with thy fathers, I will set up thy seed after thee, which shall proceed out of thy bowels, and I will establish his kingdom.

13 He shall build an house for my name, and I will stablish the throne of his kingdom for ever.

14 I will be his father, and he shall be my son. If he commit iniquity, I will chasten him with the rod of men, and with the stripes of the children of men:

15 But my mercy shall not depart away from him, as I took it from Saul, whom I put away before thee.

16 And thine house and thy kingdom shall be established for ever before thee: thy throne shall be established for ever.

The promise of a ruling house (II Sam. 7:11b). There is now a play on the word "house." David wanted to *build* a house for the Lord (a temple), but the Lord declared that He would *make* David a house (a ruling dynasty). Not content to make David a great king personally, He would guarantee the continuation of the throne to his posterity as well. And the promise was unconditional, an exhibition of sheer grace.

The promise of an approved heir (II Sam. 7:12-15). God now looked beyond David's lifetime. He promised, "I will set up thy seed after thee, which shall proceed out of thy bowels, and I will establish his kingdom." The Lord would install an heir who had not yet been born. David knew by this that none of his existing sons, who at that time numbered at least six and possibly even nine (cf. I Chron. 3:1-9), would succeed him. As revealed later, Solomon would be his heir.

"I will establish his kingdom" (II Sam. 7:12) uses a verb that speaks of bringing something into being and making it certain. It is especially used of God's works, such as Creation, which stand firm (cf. Pss. 24:1-2; 119:90; Prov. 3:19). But it also is used of His direction in establishing kingdoms, kings, and dynasties (cf. I Sam. 13:13; II Sam. 5:12; Ps. 89:4). So here God committed Himself to making the kingdom of David's heir certain and steadfast (cf. I Chron. 17:11; 22:10).

The Lord declared that this heir "shall build an house for my name" (II Sam. 7:13). Here "house" is used of a literal building, and it would be a temple for the Lord. In Scripture, "name" usually signified the person himself. Thus, a house for God's name was one in which His very presence dwelled. Though He is omnipresent, He condescended to live in a special way among His people.

Solomon fully understood the role the Lord had given him. When negotiating with Hiram of Tyre for materials for building the temple, he recalled God's promise to his father (I Kings 5:2-5). And when he dedicated the completed structure, he recalled before all the people the covenant that had prepared the way for this joyous day (8:15-20).

The Lord also promised David that He would "stablish the throne of his (Solomon's) kingdom for ever" (II Sam. 7:13). Although Solomon would eventually die, his "throne," or dignity and power, would never end. The right to the Davidic throne would continue to the rest of David's descendants perpetually and, eventually, eternally, in Christ (cf. Luke 1:31-33). This was possible because Christ Himself is eternal.

Regarding Solomon, the Lord also promised, "I will be his father, and he shall be my son" (II Sam. 7:14; cf. I Chron. 22:9-10). With all the tenderness of a father, God would establish an intimate relationship with him. Yet as a father has to chastise a son when he goes astray, so God promised to chastise Solomon. He would use other men to discipline him for his sin.

The paternal relationship of God to Solomon finds application in the New Testament to Christian believers (II Cor. 6:18). But as with Solomon, it demands of us filial obedience (vss. 14-17). Disobedience will bring chastening (Heb. 12:5-11).

Solomon did, indeed, suffer "the stripes of the children of men" (II Sam. 7:14) when he sinned (I Kings 11:14, 23, 26). But the Lord also vowed, "My mercy shall not depart away from him, as I took it from Saul" (II Sam. 7:15). Saul had been rejected and his dynasty cut off because he disobeyed God (I Sam. 13:13-14; 15:22-28). But God promised He would not reject Solomon—though he might have deserved it. Solomon's son did, indeed, lose most of Israel's tribes (I Kings 12:19-20), but his father's line survived.

The promise of an eternal kingdom (II Sam. 7:16). On this note of covenant faithfulness, the Lord concluded His message to David through Nathan. His "house," "kingdom," and "throne" would be established and remain fixed forever. Because of apostasy there were long stretches during which no king occupied David's throne. But there was always a Davidic descendant *available* to occupy it. David's dynasty lasted until Jesus,

God's Son and David's son, appeared and claimed the kingdom.

Jesus claimed the legal right to the throne through His legal father, Joseph, who had descended from David through Solomon (Matt. 1:6-16). But He claimed lineal descent from David through His mother, Mary, who had descended from another son of David, Nathan (Luke 3:23-31). Through Him alone could the kingdom be eternal, as Gabriel told Mary (1:32-33).

Thus, the climax of Jesus' reign is still future, awaiting His return (cf. Isa. 11:1-10; Dan. 7:13-14; Rev. 19:11-16). But its fulfillment is just as certain as His first advent, for it is based on the covenant faithfulness of the God of David.

—Robert E. Wenger.

QUESTIONS

1. Why did David want to build a temple for the Lord? Why was he not the right person to do so?

2. How had God lived among His people before David's time?

3. Summarize what the Lord had done for David to this point.

4. What did God plan to do in the future for David and Israel? When will Israel's goal be reached?

5. What did God mean when He promised to make David a house?

6. How do we know David's heir was not one of his older sons?

7. What work did God say David's heir would accomplish?

8. What would happen to David's heir if he should go astray?

9. How was it possible for David's dynasty to be eternal?

10. Has Jesus yet fulfilled the Davidic covenant? Explain.

—Robert E. Wenger.

Preparing to Teach the Lesson

The prophecies of Israel's coming Messiah picture Him as Israel's anointed King. A vital element in this role is that He would be of the lineage of King David. In this lesson your class should gain an understanding of how this promise began.

We will also examine how this future King will reign forever on David's throne. In future lessons we will see how Christ will fulfill this promise.

TODAY'S AIM

Facts: to show that when David sought to build a temple for God, God instead promised to build a dynasty for him—an eternal kingdom ruled over by His Son, the eternal King.

Principle: to show that the coming of Christ was in keeping with God's covenant with David, providing one more step in making the Messiah's arrival recognizable for Israel.

Application: to show that as God prepared for the coming of Christ by means of His covenant with David, we can be assured that He is in control of history and that all that He has promised will come to pass.

INTRODUCING THE LESSON

David was secure in his kingdom. He had successfully transported the tabernacle and the ark of the covenant to Jerusalem. He was living in his royal residence. Jerusalem could now officially be recognized as the capital of Israel.

As David enjoyed this time of peace, he expressed his desire to replace the tabernacle with a permanent temple. God used this opportunity to establish one more step in His plans to send the Messiah. By making His covenant with David, He established that the lineage of David would be the line through which the Messiah would come and upon whose throne He would sit.

DEVELOPING THE LESSON

1. God's response to David's plan (II Sam. 7:4-7). Nathan the prophet was initially in agreement with David's desire to build a temple for the Lord. David was a godly man who had repeatedly exhibited faith and dependence on the Lord and upon whom the Lord's blessings had been clearly evident. Nathan had no reason to dissuade the God-centered plans of a godly king. He encouraged David to pursue his plans.

Discuss what God revealed to Nathan. What was God's main point? Even though David's plans were well intentioned, what do we need to learn about God's greater plans and will? What does this tell us about our own plans?

God began His message with a rhetorical question on the order of "Can you build a house for God?" It is not possible to build a structure that can contain God. David's intention was to build a proper, permanent building for the worship of God that would replace the tabernacle, which was temporary and portable in nature. His own house was more sturdy and permanent than that within which the priests ministered. However, God's intention was to narrow even further the human lineage through which He would fulfill His promises.

David lived until 971 B.C. The Exodus from Egypt took place in 1445 B.C., with the construction of the tabernacle taking place in 1444 B.C. God told Nathan that He had met and led Israel by means of the tabernacle. At any point in that period, God could have instructed His people to build a more permanent structure. However, the tabernacle had served His purposes.

Draw a time line on the board. First, track the time from the Exodus to David. Next, track the time from David to the birth of Christ, around 6 B.C. Finally, track the time from Christ to the present, noting that the fulfillment of the Davidic covenant with Christ reigning on David's throne is yet future.

2. Appointment of kings for God's people (II Sam. 7:8-11a). God reminded David of his humble beginnings as a poor shepherd. He had raised David to be the king over Israel, God's chosen people. God also had continually watched over him. Since the days of the judges, God had placed His leaders in position. He was about to reveal to David His plans for His future King, who would come through David's line.

Point out to your class that God orders history to fulfill His plans. When He told David through Nathan that He was now going to build a house for David, He was further laying in place His plans for the coming of Christ.

Long before He had given directions to Moses about the construction of the tabernacle and its furnishings, God had made His covenant with Abraham, promising to make him a blessing to all the world (Gen. 12:1-3; 13:14-17; 15:18-21; 17:1-8).

From the beginning God had promised to send His Messiah, who would redeem mankind (Gen. 3:15). Over time, the prophecies of the Messiah became more specific and narrow. First God selected Abraham. He then narrowed the promise through Isaac and then through Jacob (Israel). Next, He narrowed the promise to the tribe of Judah, and now, by Nathan's prophecy, to David.

3. An eternal covenant with David (II Sam. 7:11b-16). God's covenant with David extended far beyond his own life. His seed, or descendant, would inherit an eternal throne. God promised him a dynasty on the throne. From here on, the Messiah would be identified as the Son of David. This term became synonymous with the Messiah (Matt. 1:1; 9:27; 12:23; 15:22; 20:30-31; 21:9; 22:42). Have your students look up these verses.

Gabriel revealed to Mary that her unborn son, Jesus, would be called the "Son of the Highest" to whom the Lord would give "the throne of his father David" (Luke 1:32).

Isaiah wrote that the Messiah would reign "upon the throne of David" (Isa. 9:7). The coming millennial kingdom will be ruled over by a Davidic king (Jer. 30:4-11; Ezek. 34:23-24; 37:24-25; Amos 9:11-15).

David's final words recalled God's promise (II Sam. 23:1-5).

ILLUSTRATING THE LESSON

When God reveals that He has a plan for us, He will fulfill that plan. Count on it.

GOD WILL FULFILL HIS PROMISES

God's Promises

COUNT ON THEM

CONCLUDING THE LESSON

God revealed to David a narrowing of His focus for sending the Messiah. The coming Redeemer would be a King of David's descent and would reign from his throne forever.

ANTICIPATING THE NEXT LESSON

In the next lesson we will examine the unfolding of God's covenant with David through the birth of Christ, the King who will one day reign from His eternal throne.

—*Carter Corbrey.*

PRACTICAL POINTS

1. The Lord is always ready to guide us if we allow Him to do so (II Sam. 7:4-7).
2. God's perfect character means He provides everything we need, since we can do nothing on our own (vss. 8-9).
3. We trust our Heavenly Father more when we realize how He fulfills His promises to us (vss. 10-11).
4. The Lord provides for us in even the smallest ways (vss. 12-13).
5. If God disciplines us, it is because, as His children, we have a family relationship with Him (II Sam. 7:14; cf. Heb. 12:6).
6. The Lord's consistent care for us provides stability in an unstable world (II Sam. 7:15-16).

—Anne Adams.

RESEARCH AND DISCUSSION

1. Was David disappointed when God did not allow his temple plans? Why or why not? Have you ever felt God's leading to cancel your plans in favor of His? How did you feel? What did you learn?
2. Is God's power restricted geographically? How does that affect your Christian life? Does God's great power reassure you or frighten you?
3. In II Samuel 7:10, God promised that Israel would never again be troubled by evil men or displaced from their land. Has this promise been kept? Discuss.
4. God's promises concerned David's spiritual heritage. How do you define your spiritual heritage?

—Anne Adams.

ILLUSTRATED HIGH POINTS

Shalt thou build me an house?

Sometimes God overrules our plan to bless Him with His own plan to bless us. As a new Christian, I wanted to reach my community for Christ. I set out to start a dial-a-prayer line.

Thankfully, my plan failed. Weeks later, I felt a strong desire to walk our city's streets and tell strangers about Jesus. God's plan began to unfold for me. I met Christians who helped me organize and expand the street ministry. Three decades later, I direct Reach and Rescue Ministries, an evangelistic outreach to the homeless.

King David sincerely desired to build God a house. But God had plans to build David a house—an eternal lineage that would include the Messiah Himself.

Shall be established for ever

A fifth-grade class in Medina, Ohio, planted a time capsule in 1968 to commemorate the town's sesquicentennial. It was ceremoniously buried in the lawn of the town square, to be opened at the bicentennial in 2018. Pictures, newspaper articles, and the personal writings of the ten-year-olds will be revealed then.

Multiple changes have occurred since the time capsule was buried. Hairstyles and fashions have morphed over the decades. The lawn of the town square has been transfigured, becoming a meeting place for festivals, markets, and art shows. And untold transformations have occurred in the minds and bodies of those fifth-graders, now nearing sixty.

Everything on earth undergoes change. But the Word of God does not alter at all. God's promise to David established his kingdom forever. It was fulfilled in Jesus Christ, whose throne will endure throughout eternity.

—Beverly Jones.

Golden Text Illuminated

"Thine house and thy kingdom shall be established for ever before thee: thy throne shall be established for ever" (II Samuel 7:16).

The words of God in our golden text were not an answer to David's request. Rather, they were the answer to David's heartfelt desire to honor the Lord.

David wanted to build a temple for the Lord (II Sam. 7:1-3). The building of such a magnificent structure was not wrong, even though God had not ordered its construction (vss. 5-7). But in God's plan, David was not the right person for this job. It would be left for his son Solomon to build the temple, for unlike his father, Solomon was not a warrior and a man of bloodshed (cf. I Chron. 22:8).

While David was not permitted to build a house for the Lord, the Lord promised to build a "house" for David. In fact, the Lord promised to establish David's house, kingdom, and throne forever.

This promise to David is known as the Davidic covenant. It is essentially an expansion of the Abrahamic covenant. The Lord had promised Abraham a land, many descendants, and divine blessing (cf. Gen. 12:1-3). The promise to David concerned Abraham's descendants—particularly the descendants, or "house," of David. David's royal line would continue forever. Also, his "kingdom" would be established forever; and his "throne," which speaks of authority to rule over a kingdom, would continue forever too.

This promise was unconditional, and it clearly looked far beyond the reign of David and his son Solomon (II Sam. 7:12-13). We know from history that David's descendants did not rule in unbroken succession, but this is not what was promised. The promise was that the kingdom—that is, Israel—and the throne and house of David would continue to exist and one day be established forever. The Jewish people themselves understood this and looked forward to the coming reign of the Son of David.

Jesus Christ, the Son of David, came to reign over an eternal kingdom. The angel told His mother, Mary, that He would be given the "throne of his father David: . . . and of his kingdom there shall be no end" (Luke 1:32-33). And while Israel rejected their Davidic King, He still lives, and He will return one day to reign over a restored kingdom that will last forever.

Throughout the years of Israel's apostasy, exile, and repeated subjugation to other nations, the promise to David was never withdrawn. His kingdom will be established forever, and from his throne, his descendant will reign eternally. The only descendant of David who could fulfill such a promise is Jesus Christ.

It is a testimony to King David's faithfulness that God would honor him with such a far-reaching promise. It is a testimony to the faithfulness of God that He would keep that promise despite the later sins of David himself (II Sam. 11), as well as the faithlessness of the Jewish people through the centuries. God's Word is true, and He is true to His word. His plan is not altered, even by the unfaithfulness of His people (cf. II Tim. 2:13).

—Jarl K. Waggoner.

Heart of the Lesson

"On November 25, 1895, a cornerstone of ice was laid in Leadville, Colorado—the beginning of the largest ice palace ever built in America. In an effort to bolster the town's sagging economy, the citizens staged a winter carnival.

"On New Year's Day of 1896, the town turned out for the grand opening. The immense palace measured 450 x 320 feet. The towers that flanked the entrance were 90 feet high. Inside was a 16,000-square-foot skating rink. But by the end of March the palace was melting away, along with the hopes of Leadville. The thousands of visitors had spent very little" (*Today in the Word,* August 4, 1993).

The temporal nature of life on earth always tempers any fascination that the Christian may have to even the best this world has to offer. In this week's lesson, we become fascinated with God's promise to David because of its eternal nature.

1. God's communication with Nathan (II Sam. 7:4-7). King David had established a luxurious home in which to live and experienced a season of comfortable peace (vs. 1). In the midst of this, David was concerned that the worship of the Lord was centered in the tabernacle, a temporary, tent-like structure.

King David then called in Nathan the prophet and shared his concern (II Sam. 7:2). Nathan encouraged King David to fulfill the desires of his heart (vs. 3). That night the Lord corrected Nathan, reminding him that He had never commanded anyone to build Him an earthly house.

The struggle that the Christian experiences on earth between temporal, earthly desires and eternal, spiritual realities is incredibly tenacious. What is even more tenacious is God's intervention in this struggle as He lovingly and tenderly challenges the believer to embrace His eternal nature and live with an energetic passion fueled by eternal hope.

2. God's covenant with David (II Sam. 7:8-16). The remainder of this week's lesson text summarizes God's unconditional covenant promise to King David, which included the following provisions: (1) David would have a son who would succeed him on the throne; (2) the earthly house that David desired to build would be constructed by his son; (3) the throne of David's kingdom would be continued forever.

In summary, Nathan revealed God's words that King David's house, kingdom, and throne would be established forever. God's covenant promise was partially fulfilled in Solomon, David's son. But the covenant promise goes far beyond Solomon in that King David's kingdom, throne, and house were established forever. The ultimate fulfillment of God's covenant promise to King David is satisfied in the Person and work of the Lord Jesus Christ.

God's Word reveals that followers of Jesus Christ experience life on the earth as foreigners in a strange and temporary place (cf. Heb. 11:13; I Pet. 2:11). God's Word also reveals that followers of Jesus Christ have received mercy that has extracted them from a life of evil darkness and transferred them into a life of spiritual light. With this comes the responsibility to proclaim the excellent character of their Saviour (cf. I Pet. 2:9-10).

Fulfilling this holy responsibility demands that the follower of Jesus Christ prioritize the eternal above the temporal. Christians should joyfully seek first God's eternal kingdom (cf. Matt. 6:33).
—*Thomas R. Chmura.*

World Missions

It is easy for us Christians to forget that we are part of a great covenant between God and man. God always keeps His word, but as sinful human beings, we tend to forget to keep our part, and often we break it. This breaks the heart of God as He waits for us to return to Him. A covenant is more than a contract; it is a binding promise. When our good God is part of this plan, we can be sure that all parties will benefit. This week He reminds us of what lies ahead for the faithful.

Church history is dotted with many martyrs who gave up their lives for their faith in Jesus. One such man was the bishop of Smyrna named Polycarp. When he was told that he would soon be burned at the stake for his faith in Jesus, he replied, "But why do you delay? Come do what you will." One must then ask what gave this ordinary man such courage in the face of death. The simple answer in our lesson this week is that he was living for an eternal kingdom. This life was just a bridge to that eternal kingdom.

As believers in Jesus, it is so important for us to realize that our stay on this earth is only temporary and that we have a destination of more importance beyond this life. Sometimes, despite its hardships, this world glitters a little too much, and we easily lose sight of that greater goal. We are called to give this message to the world. We are to show them that the hardships of this world hardly compare to the glory that lies ahead of us that God has already prepared for us (Rom. 8:18).

We will remember the idea of covenant that we mentioned at the beginning. This has to do with the character of our God, who loves us so much and, yes, keeps His promises. When God tells us something, we can trust Him. We cannot see what He is preparing for us in the future, and we may ask ourselves whether it is worth waiting for. Those who have already trusted Him have been fully satisfied. It is now our task to spread the good news of this gospel to the rest of the world so that they know this too.

Only this past weekend, I took a group of adult students to observe how people of some other religions worship. What strikes me is that although they are truly committed to what they believe, they often have no hope and no assurance like what we receive when we believe in our Lord Jesus. Our task in this world, once we have trusted in Jesus, is to provide to others the news of that hope in the covenant-keeping God who loves us so much. He is preparing that eternal kingdom for us. It is worth telling others about it.

Before his execution for his faith, Polycarp, bishop of Smyrna, stated, "Eighty-six years have I served [Christ] and He has done me no wrong. How can I blaspheme my King and my Saviour?" Such an example of courage and conviction, of experiential faith in our Lord, may fan the world's desire to know our Lord Jesus.

As followers of Jesus, we are part of this great mission to share the gospel with a world that is hurting. The discovery of a God who keeps covenant with His people is worth dying for. After all, did not Jesus die on the cross for us? He was God in the flesh, incarnated for us. It is this unique and selfless act that makes it all very worthwhile. Now we must share with the world the good news of an eternal kingdom that is prepared for us. He will soon take us home.

—A. Koshy Muthalaly.

The Jewish Aspect

Saul, Israel's first king, was a miserable failure. He had done the unthinkable. He had offered a priestly sacrifice—a ceremony restricted to Aaron's sons. The Prophet Samuel had to tell Saul he was finished as ruler, for "the Lord hath sought him a man after his own heart" (I Sam. 13:14).

The man God sought was David. Many a Sunday school teacher has had to grapple with the story of a shepherd boy who became a king—a king who murdered a faithful soldier and friend, stole his wife, and suppressed his enemies with bloodshed.

Thomas Carlyle, no friend of godly righteousness, had this to say about David: "All earnest souls will ever discern in it (David's life) the faithful struggle of an earnest human soul towards what is good and best. Struggle often baffled, sore baffled, down as into entire wreck; yet a struggle never ended; ever with tears, repentance, true unconquerable purpose, begun anew" (*On Heroes, Hero-worship, and the Heroic in History,* Bibliolife).

David was certainly a man after God's own heart, for through David's family line God gave an eternal King, a throne for that King, and an imperishable kingdom. If David came back today, he would be shocked at how cold and indifferent the Jewish people are to the great covenant promises we find in this week's text.

Most Jews have no expectation of a ruler on David's throne. Some Jews believe the kingdom is underway right now. Some Orthodox Jews even believe that one of their rabbis is the Messiah.

How did the Jews lose sight of the promises made to David? About forty years after the Lord went back to glory in the ascension (Acts 1:9-11), Jerusalem came under siege by the Roman army (A.D. 70). Local Christians had been warned in Luke's Gospel that a siege was coming (chap. 21). Jewish historians tell us that the "Nazarenes, that is, those who accepted Jesus of Nazareth as the Messiah, indifferent to the national cause, sought safety in flight from Jerusalem; the small community settled in Pella beyond the Jordan" (Margolis and Marx, *A History of the Jewish People,* Jewish Publication Society of America).

Rabbi Ben Zakkai, a Pharisee, was persuaded that Jerusalem and the temple were doomed. He boldly asked the Romans for the privilege of opening a Jewish center for studying the Torah in peace. The wish was granted.

The new faith was based on a forced misreading on sacrifices in Hosea 6:6. "For I desired mercy, and not sacrifice; and the knowledge of God more than burnt offerings" (Margolis and Marx).

The way was opened to change Old Testament texts that spoke of a Messiah who would come to sit on David's throne. The prophecies of the coming King-Messiah go untaught. The Talmud (the often disturbing sayings of the rabbis) has taken the place of Old Testament history and prophecy. The result is religious Jews who do not know much of what was promised to their fathers and who seem unwilling to listen to the truth.

This blind indifference does not prevent Jews from coming to the Saviour-Messiah. A new report tells of 14 Jewish missionaries in the land of Israel who have won 112 Jews to the Messiah. Good numbers are also being reached in our own country.

A recent conference of missionaries to the Jews of North America had ninety-two workers in attendance. Every possible way of reaching Jews is under way today. God will indeed fulfill His promises to David.

—Lyle P. Murphy.

Guiding the Superintendent

How is it that the finite mind of man thinks that he can help our infinite God? We conceive grandiose plans, thinking they will excite God, when living a life of faith and obedience to His holy commandments is what gets God's attention. From this week's lesson we can learn that there are good ideas and then there are God's eternal purposes and plans for His covenant people.

DEVOTIONAL OUTLINE

1. David's plan to build God a temple (II Sam. 7:4-7). Considering how mightily the hand of God was at work in his life, it is commendable that David desired to provide the best place for the ark of the covenant, the dwelling place of God. Perhaps this was the Prophet Nathan's rationale for encouraging David to proceed without having consulted God.

David lived and rested from war in a magnificent royal palace that had been built for him. He wanted no less for God, whose ark remained in a tent. But God revealed through Nathan that from the Exodus until then, He had had no desire to reside in an extravagant cedar house; nor had He asked the earlier Israelite leaders why they had not built Him such a house.

2. God's plan to make David a kingdom (II Sam. 7:8-11). A close study of the Bible will confirm that from the beginning of time, God was preparing a people for Himself—as what He did for David and the Israelites exemplifies. God elevated David from following sheep to shepherding His chosen people. The nation praised David and sang songs about his conquest, but the reality was that God put David's enemies in his hands. It was God who gave rise to David's legacy, which would live on long after his demise.

God gave these same people the land of Canaan for a permanent possession and kept Israel's enemies at bay. God has many mansions prepared for the weary Christians who are in constant warfare with the evil one.

3. God's plans lead to everlasting life (II Sam. 7:12-16). God chastises those He loves, and He reproved Nathan for his nod to David's desire to build God a temple. God proceeded to outline how He would execute His greater plan for the building of the temple. Although David was a man after God's own heart, he was also a man of unclean hands; therefore, God chose Solomon, the seed of David, to build the temple. God would guide, direct, and chide him as a father loves and nurtures his son.

God rejected David's sins, but He did not reject David. He committed to establishing David's dynasty, and this was accomplished with the coming of our Lord Jesus.

As Nathan told David the full account of his encounter with God, so every believer must share God's plan to extend the gift of eternal life through the shed blood of Jesus Christ, His only begotten Son.

AGE-GROUP EMPHASES

Children: Teach the children that heaven is God's home and that by faith they can go to live with Him in His eternal kingdom.

Youths: Caution the young people that even a good idea can become a distraction that blinds them to seeing God's greater plans and blessings for their lives.

Adults: Challenge your adults to search themselves to ensure that they have prepared themselves to live in the house that God has provided for them.

—*Jane E. Campbell.*

Scripture Lesson Text

PS. 89:35 Once have I sworn by my holiness that I will not lie unto Da'vid.

36 His seed shall endure for ever, and his throne as the sun before me.

37 It shall be established for ever as the moon, and *as* a faithful witness in heaven. Se'lah.

ISA. 9:6 For unto us a child is born, unto us a son is given: and the government shall be upon his shoulder: and his name shall be called Wonderful, Counsellor, The mighty God, The everlasting Father, The Prince of Peace.

7 Of the increase of *his* government and peace *there shall be* no end, upon the throne of Da'vid, and upon his kingdom, to order it, and to establish it with judgment and with justice from henceforth even for ever. The zeal of the LORD of hosts will perform this.

MATT. 1:18 Now the birth of Je'sus Christ was on this wise: When as his mother Ma'ry was espoused to Jo'seph, before they came together, she was found with child of the Ho'ly Ghost.

19 Then Jo'seph her husband, being a just *man,* and not willing to make her a publick example, was minded to put her away privily.

20 But while he thought on these things, behold, the angel of the Lord appeared unto him in a dream, saying, Jo'seph, thou son of Da'vid, fear not to take unto thee Ma'ry thy wife: for that which is conceived in her is of the Ho'ly Ghost.

21 And she shall bring forth a son, and thou shalt call his name JE'SUS: for he shall save his people from their sins.

22a Now all this was done, that it might be fulfilled which was spoken of the Lord by the prophet.

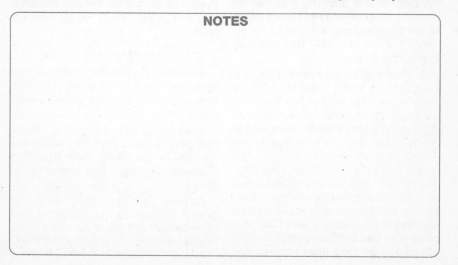

NOTES

Son of David

Lesson: Psalm 89:35-37; Isaiah 9:6-7; Matthew 1:18-22a

Read: Psalm 89:3-14, 30-37; Isaiah 9:1-7; Matthew 1:18—2:6

TIMES: unknown; about 733 B.C.;
7 or 6 B.C.

PLACES: unknown; Jerusalem;
Nazareth

GOLDEN TEXT—"She shall bring forth a son, and thou shalt call his name JESUS: for he shall save his people from their sins. Now all this was done, that it might be fulfilled which was spoken of the Lord by the prophet" (Matthew 1:21-22).

Introduction

Promises that are not fulfilled quickly are often forgotten. The longer a promise goes unfulfilled, the harder it is to believe it will be kept. Parents who make light promises to their children hazard the loss of their trust if they do not keep them. Many are cynical about politicians because campaign promises are often unfulfilled. Many have come to believe that promises are made to be broken.

Some of God's promises were fulfilled in a short time, some were fulfilled after many years, and some still have not been fulfilled. Not understanding God's timing, some have become cynics. Peter wrote of scoffers who said, "Where is the prom-ise of his (Christ's) coming? for since the fathers fell asleep, all things continue as they were" (II Pet. 3:4). A two-thousand-year delay leads many to discount Jesus' promise. This week's lesson examines some of God's key promises.

LESSON OUTLINE

I. CONFIRMING THE COVENANT
—Ps. 89:35-37

II. FORESEEING THE KINGDOM—
Isa. 9:6-7

III. FULFILLING THE PROMISE—
Matt. 1:18-22a

Exposition: Verse by Verse

CONFIRMING THE COVENANT

PS. 89:35 Once have I sworn by my holiness that I will not lie unto David.

36 His seed shall endure for ever, and his throne as the sun before me.

37 It shall be established for ever as the moon, and as a faithful witness in heaven. Selah.

The firmness of God's oath (Ps. 89:35). Psalm 89 was written at a difficult time in Israel's history. It is attributed, in its title, to Ethan the Ezrahite, a man renowned for his wisdom in Solomon's time (cf. I Kings 4:31). If this ascription is correct, the psalm must have been written shortly after Solomon's death, when the kingdom split due to Rehoboam's arrogance (chap. 12). The psalmist may have been lamenting the loss of ten tribes by David's house or Rehoboam's later humiliation at the hands of Shishak (14:25-26).

In any case, the latter part of Psalm 89 (vss. 38-52) speaks of the humiliations suffered by the Davidic king and his kingdom. In the midst of these circumstances, the psalmist reminded the Lord of His promises, especially those in the covenant with David (cf. vss. 3-4). The passage in our lesson (vss. 35-37) speaks of its firmness and reliability.

"Once have I sworn by my holiness that I will not lie unto David" (Ps. 89:35) affirms God's oath to fulfill all He had promised to David's house. "Once" could be taken to mean "once for all," or "one thing"—the one promise He had made to preserve David's descendants in power (vss. 30-34). So firm was this promise that God had sworn by His own holiness (cf. Amos 4:2). The implication is that His very holiness was at stake in the oath's fulfillment.

The nature of God's oath (Ps. 89:36-37). God had sworn to David that "his seed shall endure for ever." In fact, He now added, "His throne [shall endure] as the sun before me." The sun is reliable in its rising each day, and God declared that it would be a permanent part of His creation (Gen. 1:16-18; 8:22). In the same way, God's covenant with David's seed will be reliable and permanent (cf. Jer. 33:20-26).

David's throne, God declared further, "shall be established for ever as the moon" (Ps. 89:37). The moon, like the sun, had been ordained to mark light and darkness, and it was just as permanent. So David's throne, in spite

of any appearances to the contrary, will continue permanently. So also will the people of Israel, over whom David's seed will rule (Jer. 31:35-36; 33:25-26).

The phrase "and as a faithful witness in heaven" (Ps. 89:37) may be considered a further enlargement on the illustration of the sun and the moon. Since "heaven" can also be translated "sky," it may mean that as long as these heavenly bodies remain there, they are a witness of God's faithfulness in fulfilling His covenant with David. Some, however, take this witness to be God Himself. In any event, His promise is sure.

FORESEEING THE KINGDOM

ISA. 9:6 For unto us a child is born, unto us a son is given: and the government shall be upon his shoulder: and his name shall be called Wonderful, Counsellor, The mighty God, The everlasting Father, The Prince of Peace.

7 Of the increase of his government and peace there shall be no end, upon the throne of David, and upon his kingdom, to order it, and to establish it with judgment and with justice from henceforth even for ever. The zeal of the LORD of hosts will perform this.

The character of the King (Isa. 9:6). The circumstances in which Isaiah wrote this passage, like those of Psalm 89, were not encouraging for the ruling line of David. Judah had been threatened by an alliance between Israel and Syria (II Kings 16:5-6). In spite of assurances from Isaiah that this threat would fail (Isa. 7:3-9), King Ahaz appealed to the king of Assyria for help (II Kings 16:7-9). This exposed him to an even greater threat—the rapidly expanding Assyrian Empire (Isa. 8:5-8).

But in those days of darkness, the Lord gave Isaiah a message of light and hope for His people (Isa. 9:1-7). Our lesson text (vss. 6-7) is the culmination of this message. It portrays the coming Messiah and the eternal glory of His kingdom.

The word "for" in Isaiah 9:6 connects this statement with the prophecy of joy and blessing in the preceding verses. These will come only because of the perfect Ruler he now described. "Unto us" makes it clear that He will come specifically to Israel, and He is said to be both a "child" who will be "born" and a "son" who will be "given."

As a child, the messianic King will enter the world like any other child, albeit through a miraculous virgin birth (Isa. 7:14; Matt. 1:23). He will thus identify with the needs of mankind. As a son, He is given by a gracious God. "Son" in Isaiah 9:6 could refer to this King as the Son of David, whose kingdom is described in verse 7. But more likely it means He is the Son of God (cf. Ps. 2:6-7). So Israel's coming King will be both human and divine.

This One, said Isaiah, will have the government "upon his shoulder" (Isa. 9:6). Many take this to mean that the weight of governing will rest on His shoulders. But the singular "shoulder" may suggest a different meaning— showing the authority of His rulership as an insignia on His shoulder (cf. 22:22). In either case, it is clear that supreme authority belongs to Him.

"His name shall be called" (Isa. 9:6) refers not to proper names but to attributes of the coming King. In our Authorized Version, it appears that five attributes are listed, but many Bible scholars believe there are only four. They take "Wonderful" and "Counsellor" together as one characteristic. Either interpretation is acceptable. "Wonderful" is really the Hebrew noun for "wonder," which refers to something that excites astonishment because it is beyond human understanding. Jesus Christ is a wonder in every aspect of His being and accomplishments. If "wonder" is taken with "Counsellor," it means that He is a wonder of a Counselor.

In His role as a counselor, this Ruler both formulates plans and advises others to carry them out. Every king should be a counselor (cf. Mic. 4:9), and the Messiah will be the greatest counselor of all. He will be endowed with "the spirit of wisdom and understanding, the spirit of counsel and might, the spirit of knowledge and of the fear of the Lord" (Isa. 11:2; cf. Col. 2:3). Other rulers need counselors to guide them; He will not. He will never make an unwise decision.

This King also is "The mighty God" (Isa. 9:6). It may seem strange that one described as a "child" should have this title. Yet this is a title Isaiah used elsewhere for the Lord (10:21), and he had already alluded to His union with humanity in the term "Immanuel" (7:14).

"The everlasting Father" (Isa. 9:6) means, literally, "the Father of eternity." Being God, the Messiah is eternal by nature and gives eternal life to those who trust Him. His rule also will be eternal (cf. vs. 7). He is depicted here as the fatherly Ruler of His subjects.

Finally, He is the Prince of Peace. He will cause all wars to cease during His reign, and this peace will be based on a deeper peace between God and man that He procures through His death on the cross (Rom. 5:1, 11).

The duration of His kingdom (Isa. 9:7). Isaiah's messianic prophecy climaxes with a description of Messiah's eternal kingdom. Though He sits on "the throne of David," He will not die as the rest of David's descendants have. Founded on justice and righteousness and characterized by perpetual peace, His kingdom will conclude mankind's history on earth and continue into eternity (Dan. 7:14; Luke 1:33).

FULFILLING THE PROMISE

MATT. 1:18 Now the birth of Jesus Christ was on this wise: When as his mother Mary was espoused to Joseph, before they came together, she was found with child of the Holy Ghost.

19 Then Joseph her husband, being a just man, and not willing to make her a publick example, was minded to put her away privily.

20 But while he thought on these things, behold, the angel of the Lord appeared unto him in a dream, saying, Joseph, thou son of David, fear not to take unto thee Mary thy wife: for that which is conceived in her is of the Holy Ghost.

21 And she shall bring forth a son, and thou shalt call his name JESUS: for he shall save his people from their sins.

22a Now all this was done, that it might be fulfilled which was spoken of the Lord by the prophet.

Joseph's dilemma (Matt. 1:18-19). The entrance of the divine Son of David into the world occurred in a way only God Himself could have planned and executed. The child Isaiah foresaw would be born as any human being, except that He would be miraculously conceived by a virgin. The Angel Gabriel informed Mary, the chosen virgin, of this, and Mary accepted her role humbly (Luke 1:26-38). But it would bring complications.

At this time, Mary was "espoused (betrothed) to Joseph" (Matt. 1:18), but it was "before they came together." Jewish betrothals were as legally binding as marriage, and the couple were considered husband and wife (cf. vs. 19). During the year-long betrothal period, they would not live together; their faithfulness would be tested. The betrothal could be ended only by marriage or divorce.

During this time, Mary "was found with child of the Holy Ghost" (Matt. 1:18). Mary, of course, knew the unique nature of her pregnancy, and Matthew reports here that it had come about through the power of the Holy Spirit. But until this time, she had not revealed this to Joseph (cf. vs. 20), and he was left to draw other conclusions when her pregnancy became evident. She had visited Elisabeth for about three months (Luke 1:39-40, 56) and now had returned to Nazareth.

Joseph's dilemma was this. First, he was "a just man" (Matt. 1:19) who in good conscience could not marry Mary, since he concluded that she had been unfaithful. On the other hand, he was "not willing to make her a publick example." The law had prescribed the death penalty (Deut. 22:23-24), but this was rarely carried out. He could have divorced her publicly, thus shaming her, but he wanted to avoid this.

The alternative Joseph was considering was to hand Mary the letter of divorce privately in the presence of witnesses without stating his reasons. He thus would have been conforming to the law and at the same time showing compassion.

The angel's reassurance (Matt. 1:20-21). While Joseph was still considering his course of action, "behold, the angel of the Lord appeared unto him in a dream." "Behold" calls attention to the unusual and striking event. Angels are prominent in the narratives of Jesus' birth and early life. Prior to this, angels had appeared to Zacharias and Mary, and they later would bring messages to the shepherds and twice to Joseph. They always appeared in their usual role of messengers of God.

The angel's message to Joseph was crucial. Had Joseph divorced Mary, Jesus would have been born out of wedlock, and His claim to be the Messiah would have seemed questionable. But the message to Joseph averted this and was reassuring in several ways.

First, the angel addressed Joseph as

"thou son of David" (Matt. 1:20). Joseph was in the royal line (cf. vs. 16), and although he would not be Jesus' biological father, he would provide the legal basis for Jesus to claim Davidic kingship. Second, the angel told him not to be afraid to take Mary as his wife, explaining that her unborn child had been supernaturally conceived. This tells us that Mary probably had not told Joseph this before. And even if she had, he would have considered her explanation too fantastic to believe.

The angel continued: "And she shall bring forth a son" (Matt. 1:21). It is significant that he did not say, as to Zacharias, that she "shall bear thee a son" (Luke 1:13). The angel commanded that His name be "Jesus" (Matt. 1:21), the Greek equivalent of the Hebrew "Joshua."

Mary also had been told that this should be His name (Luke 1:31). But Joseph was now given the reason behind it—He would "save his people from their sins" (Matt. 1:21). The name Jesus itself means "Yahweh is salvation," and it signified the saving work He would accomplish through His death and resurrection. In the Greek sentence, "he" is emphatic, implying that Jesus alone would accomplish this. Joseph likely assumed "his people" meant Israel, but Scripture shows that these are all who trust in the Messiah.

The expectation of the Messiah was currently at a high point among the Jews, but the Messiah most of them expected was a political and military figure who would save them from the Romans. Apart from a brief period from 142 B.C. to 63 B.C., they had been under foreign power since the Babylonian Captivity, and the iron fist of Rome stimulated messianic hopes. But few of them expected the Messiah to give Himself as a ransom for their sins (cf. Matt. 20:28; John 11:51).

The prophecy's fulfillment (Matt. 1:22a). "Now all this was done" gives the impression that the angel's words were now ended and that Matthew was commenting on what they meant prophetically. But the usual translation of the verb tense would be "Now all this has been done," and it is possible that the words that follow are still the angel's. He may have been saying that all that has happened, including Mary's miraculous conception, was the fulfillment of prophecy.

Though our lesson text ends at this point, we do well to note what this prophecy was. It was Isaiah's word to Ahaz (Isa. 7:14) assuring him of Israel's deliverance through the house of David. Now this virgin-conceived Son of David was about to appear, and He would be, in the true sense, "Emmanual" (Matt. 1:23).

—Robert E. Wenger.

QUESTIONS

1. What were the circumstances under which Psalm 89 was written?
2. Why did the psalmist liken the seed of David to the sun and moon?
3. Why did the house of David need encouragement when Isaiah gave his messianic prophecy?
4. In what sense is the promised Messiah a "son" (Isa. 9:6)?
5. What names did Isaiah use to describe the Messiah's attributes?
6. Why could Isaiah say that the Messiah's kingdom would be eternal?
7. What was the relationship between Joseph and Mary when the angel appeared to Joseph?
8. What was Joseph considering doing in his relationship with Mary?
9. What does "Jesus" mean? Why was Mary's child to have this name?
10. In what way was the Jews' vision of the Messiah distorted?

—Robert E. Wenger.

Preparing to Teach the Lesson

In the previous lesson, we examined how God made His covenant with David to establish David's throne forever through the Messiah.

In this week's lesson we will look at confirmation of this covenant and learn that Jesus is the Son of David.

TODAY'S AIM

Facts: to show that Jesus is the Son of God and the Son of David.

Principle: to show that God kept His promises to send a Saviour who is both God and man.

Application: to show that the Son of God, our Saviour, came into the world as promised.

INTRODUCING THE LESSON

In our lesson this week we will examine how God confirmed His promises made in the Davidic covenant and revealed more fully through Isaiah how the Messiah would be God Incarnate.

We will also study how the prophecies of the coming Messiah and King were fulfilled with the birth of Christ.

DEVELOPING THE LESSON

As a reminder, make a copy of the text of the Davidic covenant from II Samuel 7:16, and post it where the class can refer to it.

1. A psalmist's confirmation of the Davidic covenant (Ps. 89:35-37). Ethan the Ezrahite, the Levite author of Psalm 89, praised God for His faithfulness, which was demonstrated in His unconditional, eternal covenant with David. God's past faithfulness was evidence that He would honor His covenant promises to David for the future. Ethan understood that there would be a span of time before the true Davidic King would arrive. The sinful actions of David's descendants during this time would not cancel the original covenant. God had made His promise, and He would not lie to David.

Discuss with your students why God's holy and righteous nature makes it impossible for Him to lie or deceive. Since His covenant promise to David is irreversible, Israel could have confidence that the Messiah would come as promised. To illustrate His promise, God compared it to the reliability of the sun and the moon.

What would the dangers and consequences be for us today if God were unreliable? What if He could lie to anyone? Discuss this with your class, and help them understand that we depend on the holy and unchangeable character of God.

The psalmist reaffirmed the eternal nature of the Davidic covenant in Psalm 89:36, stating that "his seed shall endure for ever." Regardless of what would happen between the time of David's personal reign and the coming of the One who would ultimately occupy the throne, God's covenant would not be changed.

2. Isaiah's confirmation of the Davidic covenant (Isa. 9:6-7). Isaiah's prophetic ministry to the southern kingdom of Judah began after the fall of the northern kingdom in 722 B.C. and ended sometime after 686 B.C. His book contains some of the most significant messianic prophecies in the Bible. One of these prophecies is in our Scripture text for this lesson.

Isaiah 7:14 had foretold that a virgin would bear a son. In 9:6-7, the prophet gave further details about this unique child.

First, this child would have a human ancestry, that of Adam, Abraham, and, most significant for our lesson, David (Matt. 1:1; Luke 3:31, 34, 38). While this would be a human child born of a virgin, He would also be God in the flesh. Isaiah gave several characteristics and qualities that defined the identity of the King who will rule from the throne of David, thus fulfilling the Davidic covenant.

Isaiah described the coming Son as a government ruler. He is a King, in keeping with God's promises to David. He next described the various names of this King.

List these names on the board. Discuss how they refer to the Son who would be God Incarnate, just as Isaiah 7:14 foretold, with the name Immanuel, which means "God with us."

Isaiah 9:6 first identifies Him as "Wonderful, Counsellor." There is disagreement as to whether the names should be separate or joined, but it seems best to combine them. The wisdom of Solomon will be displayed in an even greater way in the Messiah.

The second title or name is "mighty God" (Isa. 9:6), or *El Gibbor. Gibbor,* a Hebrew word often associated with prowess in warfare, pictures the strength and power of God. The combined name would be blasphemous if given to a mere human. It clearly reflects God Incarnate and the descriptions of Christ found in John 1:1-18 and Philippians 2:5-11.

The Davidic King's third name further emphasizes His dual nature, being both human and divine. The Son and King would be called "everlasting Father" (Isa. 9:6). This reflects His eternal nature and His close connection to His Father, God, in the Trinity. As the "Prince of Peace," He would bring peace between God and man.

3. The arrival of the Davidic Son (Matt. 1:18-22a). Matthew wrote to a Jewish audience and emphasized how Jesus was the fulfillment of the messianic prophecies and the Davidic covenant, beginning with His genealogy.

After introducing Jesus as the Son of David, Matthew described His birth. The careful wording of Matthew's account in both the genealogy and the description of the conception make it clear that Jesus was born of a virgin and that Joseph, who was also of the line of David, was not His biological father. However, Jesus' legal claim to the throne of David is evident. Everything was in agreement with Isaiah's prophecies.

Discuss with your class how these prophecies were fulfilled in a literal way. God is not vague in His promises.

When the angel visited Joseph, he greeted him as "thou son of David" (Matt. 1:20), tying him with David's lineage. This established Jesus' legal claim to be Israel's King and ultimately the final Heir to David's throne.

ILLUSTRATING THE LESSON

God sent Jesus, Son of God and Son of David.

GOD IS FAITHFUL

HE SENT JESUS

CONCLUDING THE LESSON

God is faithful to keep His promises. His covenant with David and the prophecies of a Saviour were fulfilled with the birth of Christ.

ANTICIPATING THE NEXT LESSON

In the next lesson we will discover more about the Messiah's role as both King and Priest.

—*Carter Corbrey.*

PRACTICAL POINTS

1. God's reliability is reassuring in an unreliable world (Ps. 89:35).
2. The sun and the moon are temporary compared to God's eternal promises to preserve His people (vss. 36-37).
3. It is comforting to know that the One who rightly carries the most exalted titles grew up as a child in a human family (Isa. 9:6).
4. As David's spiritual descendants, we share in God's plans (vs. 7).
5. God carefully planned Jesus' human family to provide the right environment for Him (Matt. 1:18-20).
6. We are truly humble when we follow God's will but do not expect or demand any special treatment from Him (vss. 21-22).

—Anne Adams.

RESEARCH AND DISCUSSION

1. Is it possible for God to be deceitful? If it is, what would that mean for your salvation and faith? Could you depend on God's Word?
2. Which characteristic of Christ in Isaiah's description is most meaningful for you? Why? How does knowing these traits affect your spiritual life?
3. What character traits enabled Joseph to support Mary? Did they allow him to also be a good father to Jesus? Was Joseph reassured or relieved when he learned the truth about Mary? Discuss.
4. God had specific plans for His Son's birth and name. Was it important that all these be followed? Why?

—Anne Adams.

ILLUSTRATED HIGH POINTS

Unto us a son is given

A couple had been married for three years and were celebrating a quiet Christmas in their modest home. After they exchanged and unwrapped all the gifts from under the Christmas tree, the young wife sank back in her overstuffed chair. With tea in hand, she waited while her husband started working on his traditional Christmas breakfast. Then she set the table as he brought the cooking to a conclusion.

As they sat down to begin eating, she robustly announced, "I have one more gift for you. We're going to have a baby!" That Christmas morning erupted in joy and celebration. The upcoming birth would change their lives forever.

The birth of Jesus would change the world forever. Foretold by the Prophet Isaiah centuries before, His birth was a joy-filled occasion for those who believed the Scriptures.

Save his people from their sins

A young man entered his father's brick masonry business when he was fourteen years old. He had always been interested in his father's work and had preferred building blocks to other toys even as a toddler. So it was no surprise when he enthusiastically accepted his father's invitation to learn the masonry business.

Father and son shared the same goal. Their mutual objective was to build a successful business that would carry on through the family line.

Jesus and His Father worked together to create the most vital enterprise in human history—the redemption of mankind. The miraculous birth, sinless life, agonizing crucifixion, and victorious resurrection all were fashioned by the Father, foretold by the prophets, and performed by Jesus.

—Beverly Jones.

Golden Text Illuminated

"She shall bring forth a son, and thou shalt call his name JE-SUS: for he shall save his people from their sins. Now all this was done, that it might be fulfilled which was spoken of the Lord by the prophet" (Matthew 1:21-22).

As Joseph contemplated what he should do about his impending marriage to Mary now that he had discovered she was pregnant, an angel appeared to him in a dream and brought a reassuring message. The angel informed Joseph that Mary had miraculously conceived by the power of the Holy Spirit and that he should not fear taking her as his wife (Matt. 1:20). The angel then revealed to Joseph what had already been revealed to Mary: she would bear a son, and this son was to be named Jesus (cf. Luke 1:31).

By all indications, Joseph was a godly Jewish man, a "just man" (Matt. 1:19), and a descendant of King David (vs. 20). The very appearance of the angel, along with the various elements of the angel's message, quickly convinced Joseph that the child Mary carried was in fact Israel's Messiah.

A godly Jew such as Joseph would have connected Mary's supernatural virginal conception with Isaiah's prophecy (Isa. 7:14). And the name Jesus, given to Him because He would "save his people from their sins" (Matt. 1:21), clearly pointed to the prophesied Messiah's work.

"Jesus," or *Yēsous,* was the Greek equivalent of the Hebrew name Joshua, *Yehoshua,* or *Yeshua.* The name means "the Lord is deliverance" or "the Lord is salvation." Such a name was appropriate for Israel's Messiah, for His work would be one of saving, or delivering, people from their sins. The prophets spoke of the deliverance provided by the Lord's Servant (Isa. 61:1-2). His salvation, in fact, would bring deliverance from "the guilt, pollution, power, and punishment of sin" (Hendriksen, *Exposition of the Gospel According to Matthew,* Baker).

Even Jesus' disciples did not initially grasp the magnitude of the Messiah's work, so it is unlikely that Joseph fully understood what the angel's message meant. But it is certain he understood that Mary's son was Israel's long-awaited and prophesied Messiah. This would soon be confirmed when he compared notes with Mary. However, assuming that Joseph, as a godly Jewish man, had a good knowledge of the Old Testament Scriptures, he must have quickly concluded that the child was the fulfillment of the messianic prophecies of old.

Like other Jews, Joseph understood from Daniel's prophecy that the Messiah's coming was very near (Dan. 7:24-27). He also knew that the Messiah must be a descendant of David (Jer. 23:5), and both he and Mary were of the Davidic line.

Matthew then pointed out that "all this was done, that it might be fulfilled which was spoken of the Lord by the prophet." The reference is to the prophecy of the virgin birth in Isaiah 7:14 (cf. Matt. 1:23). Only the virgin-born Son of God (Luke 1:35), free of the taint of human sin, could deliver His people from their sins.

Joseph could not foresee all that Jesus would do, but he grasped the fact that this One was the Messiah, who would save His people. He responded in obedience by immediately taking Mary as his wife (Matt. 1:24).
—*Jarl K. Waggoner.*

Heart of the Lesson

A minister of God once said, "As I look ahead, far ahead, two to three years down the road, I do see God doing it, even though I may not know all of the details today. That's what vision is. Vision is not a crystal ball or hearing audible voices. It is the belief in one's heart that God is going to do something that is consistent with His Word and consistent with His will, and believing that what God is going to do will have an amazing impact on your life. Having vision is having the confident belief that the promises of God are going to be realized in the future of our church" (www.sermoncentral.com).

King David must have been a man of great vision. God made a covenant with David that included a promised son. King David's confident belief that God's promise would be realized helped shape him to become a man after God's own heart, one who would fulfill His will (Acts 13:22).

1. God's oath (Ps. 89:35-37). Confident belief that engenders vision comes not merely from promises made but from promises made in a context of holiness and honesty. The psalmist Ethan the Ezrahite restated God's promise to King David that his seed and throne would endure forever.

King David did not realize that God's covenant promise would have its ultimate fulfillment in Jesus, the Son of David. God's followers today, though, can be fully confident that Jesus will rule as "KING OF KINGS, AND LORD OF LORDS" (Rev. 19:16). This confident faith should impact our lives, causing believers to live with spiritual boldness and courage.

2. Isaiah's prophecy (Isa. 9:6-7). Isaiah's magnificent prophecy was resplendent with a personal and eternal emphasis. It is overwhelmingly conceded that the "child" mentioned in verse 6 is a reference to Jesus, the Messiah. The Son of David's future reign will be characterized by peace, justice, and righteousness. God's passionate love will assure that His promise will be fulfilled.

Followers of Jesus Christ live in a culture characterized by arrogance, greed, and injustice. In the midst of this godless world, God still calls His people to lives of spiritual impact and illumination (cf. Matt. 5:13-14). Obeying this holy calling is made easier by the knowledge that God is passionate about establishing His Son as King and that His children will rule and reign with Him.

3. Jesus' birth (Matt. 1:18-22). King David probably thought that God's promise of a future son would be fulfilled in Solomon. God, though, had someone else in mind. Matthew revealed that Jesus would be born to a virgin named Mary who was engaged to Joseph, a descendant of King David.

The conception and engagement process was difficult for Joseph to endure. He was fully prepared to end the relationship in a quiet manner so that Mary would not be disgraced. But God protected His perfect plan. He appeared to Joseph in a dream and assured him that Jesus' birth would fulfill that "which was spoken of the Lord by the prophet" (Matt. 1:22).

Christians should be thoughtful and discerning people, especially when the Lord sovereignly allows difficult and demanding times to impact their lives. Instead of making rash decisions—or even thoughtful decisions that are not sensitive to the leading of the Holy Spirit—followers of Jesus Christ should include the spiritual disciplines of prayer and Bible reading in their decision-making process. This will enable them to know God's good and perfect will.

—*Thomas R. Chmura.*

World Missions

Every Jewish person raised in an observant home knew about the Messiah who was to come. It was part of his upbringing. One could not be a good Jew and be without that knowledge. It was something as sacred as male circumcision and even keeping the Sabbath. Simply put, it is Jewish to the very core. The Jews were also told that this Messiah was the Son of David. Jesus was a Jew, and when He spoke to the Jewish people, He knew their vocabulary. He told them about Himself.

Here is what we need to know about carrying this thought into the world of missionary activity and evangelization. Since there is a Messiah and a lot of people are looking forward to meeting Him, it is important to verify this Messiah's credentials. After all, there have been many false messiahs in the past. Was this one going to be any different? It is our task as believers in this Messiah to let the whole world know of this Messiah. His name is Jesus.

The Bible reminds us that this Messiah Jesus came for this primary purpose: to "save his people from their sins" (Matt. 1:21). Everywhere one travels around the world, we see signs of desperate people trying to earn their forgiveness through various acts of devotion and penance. Some use prayer wheels. Others worship before idols or climb high mountains to worship a deity situated in the heights in an effort to reach a state of inner peace and forgiveness.

In our lesson text this week, we are reminded that this Son of David whom God has prepared for our salvation and for our peace has already been given to us. He gave up His throne in heaven and paid for our sins on the cross so that we might have this peace. And while we do not understand all of it, it is the only answer we have that really works. This Son of David, chosen before the beginning of time, is the only answer we need. The Bible charges us to tell the world this exceptionally good news.

We dare not forget that Jesus came to save us from our sins. The name Jesus makes the devil tremble, for he knows that he is a defeated enemy. We need to give this quiet assurance to the hurting world around us. Jesus' Great Commission charges us with this great message that we are to take to the world. We are to do this by every means possible. But we cannot do this if we have not experienced it ourselves. If that is the case, we bring discredit on the message we carry.

One who has known God's forgiveness in Jesus is the greatest testimony to the saving power of our loving Lord. Augustine was once a wayward lad, wasting his life away in the world. Then the power of our Lord Jesus gripped him. This was an answer to the relentless and unyielding prayers of his mother, Monica. His writings and his life have brought many to Jesus. That is what the promised Messiah, the Son of David, can do for anyone who is willing to turn to Him. He came to die. The Cross is worth it.

We dare not forget why this Son of David came into this world. He came to save us. This is a need in our world that will never go away. There will always be someone here who needs a Saviour. Evangelism will need to go on until everyone in the world has had an opportunity to hear the good news about this Davidic covenant Messiah. We therefore must share this good news with the world.

—A. Koshy Muthalaly.

The Jewish Aspect

Ninety-two missionaries to the Jews met recently in a western city. Bible exposition dealt with a variety of themes. The most gripping study was given to the all-important question "In light of the murder of six million Jews in the Nazi concentration camps, how do you inform the Jews that Jesus is their long-sought Messiah?"

Many of those we must reach are, frankly, angry with God. "Where was God when the six million were murdered simply because they were Jews?" That is a very difficult question to answer. Of course, God was not unaware or insensitive to that slaughter. How it must have wrenched His righteous soul!

The conference studied a number of reports of the Holocaust—the name usually given to the attempted extermination of the Jewish people. Christian Jews in the concentration camps did all they could to pass on the message of the Messiah.

One Jewish missionary to his own people managed to continue to preach the gospel during those dark days of the 1940s. Rachmiel Frydland, a Polish Jewish Christian, entered the walled-up Jewish ghetto of Warsaw in 1944 and encouraged suffering believers. He led more to faith in Christ. He left the ghetto shortly before it was destroyed. He survived the war, married a French Jewish survivor, and took up ministry to Jesus in this country.

Judaism today teaches an appreciation of Jesus as a Jew but denies His right to David's throne. The rabbis are firmly committed to concealing the truth about Jesus from their people. This opposition takes many forms. For example, one of the few very martial hymns in the synagogue service is from half of Zechariah 14:9. The half verse reads, "In that day shall there be one Lord, and his name one." The first half of the verse, which is never sung, is "And the Lord shall be king over all the earth." Is it possible the rabbis know that the King is the Lord Jesus?

Judaism goes to great lengths to shield the people from the truth of the Lord's sacrifice for sin. In Zechariah 12:10 we have a prophecy of how the Jews will mourn when they realize anew the calamity of their rejection of Jesus. The text says, "They shall look upon me whom they have pierced." It was a Roman spear that pierced the side of our Saviour (John 19:34), but it was partly due to a conspiracy of the Jewish rulers that Jesus suffered and died.

Piercing was not a Jewish form of execution. The Jews have denied any complicity in the matter. In one text, they changed one Hebrew letter to radically change the word "pierced" to some meaningless word.

Much of Judaism denies there is a Messiah, denies Jesus as that Messiah, and effectively has no doctrine of a heaven or hell. In one city's synagogue, the rabbi said that 20 percent of his congregation is atheist. Atheism is a perfectly acceptable position for a member to hold. Another 20 percent claim to be agnostic.

The rabbi concluded by saying that about 8 percent of his congregation attends synagogue services because they fear that God might take vengeance on them. Only about 12 percent attend and actually enjoy the services.

In spite of this lamentable record of Jewish unbelief, the Apostle Paul assures us that "God hath not cast away his people which he foreknew" (Rom. 11:2). One day they will turn to David's Son, and that will herald the dawn of a new day for Israel.

—Lyle P. Murphy.

Guiding the Superintendent

Jesus is called "Son of David" sixteen times in the New Testament. As a man, Jesus was in the family line of David through Joseph and Mary, and was therefore an eventual heir to David's throne. More significantly, Jesus was the Son of God and thereby King of kings and Lord of lords. God raised Him from the dead to be King of the Jews and to have lordship over everyone. His servants are those who have faith in Christ alone.

DEVOTIONAL OUTLINE

1. Christ as David's everlasting Seed (Ps. 89:35-37). Numbers 23:19 says, "God is not a man, that he should lie; neither the son of man, that he should repent: hath he said, and shall he not do it? or hath he spoken, and shall he not make it good?" In a society where truth seems elusive, how encouraging it is to know that believers can stand on the incorruptible Word of our holy God! "For all the promises of God in him are yea, and in him Amen" (II Cor. 1:20).

Everyone who has established a personal relationship with Christ becomes part of God's irrefutable promise to David that his kingdom would not cease but rather increase. We are that seed of great promise and the faithful witnesses kept by the power of God. We are established for all generations to come, just as the sun and moon continue in the presence of God.

2. Christ is our everlasting hope (Isa. 9:6-7). How often have we been comforted by the hope that this passage inspires? Isaiah, God's distinguished prophet, spoke of the majestic Christ—His wisdom, power, and peace—in the present tense, although Jesus would not appear until some seven hundred years later. Isaiah's declaration that an heir of David would always rule God's kingdom was a direct link to the Davidic covenant and the human advent of Christ as Saviour of the world. Christ, God's grace, would fulfill the old law and rule in justice and righteousness. The kingdom would expand to include whoever will confess Christ as King and place undaunted trust in Him before His return.

How long will Christ's justice and peace prevail? "From henceforth even for ever" (Isa. 9:7). Our God Himself will see to it, for He is a jealous God and will not allow the affection of His chosen people to be captured by false gods.

3. Christ as our promised Saviour (Matt. 1:18-22a). This passage could be considered a lesson in faith. It took faith for young Mary to trust the Angel Gabriel, who said that she would be the mother of our Lord. It took faith for Joseph to accept that his dream was, in fact, from God and that he was unwittingly a part of God's greater plan for the accomplishment of His pledge made to David long ago. It takes that same faith for the sinner seeking salvation to believe in the virgin birth—that it was a step toward our redemption so "that we might receive the adoption of sons" (Gal. 4:5).

AGE-GROUP EMPHASES

Children: Assure them that God's Word is true and that they can trust Him to keep His promises.

Youths: They may become discouraged in their efforts to understand Scripture. Help them understand that prayer and faith are the keys to appreciating God's Word.

Adults: Encourage them to strive to become steadfast witnesses of the trustworthiness of our loving and faithful God.

—*Jane E. Campbell.*

Scripture Lesson Text

PS. 110:1 The LORD said unto my Lord, Sit thou at my right hand, until I make thine enemies thy footstool.

2 The LORD shall send the rod of thy strength out of Zi'on: rule thou in the midst of thine enemies.

3 Thy people *shall be* willing in the day of thy power, in the beauties of holiness from the womb of the morning: thou hast the dew of thy youth.

4 The LORD hath sworn, and will not repent, Thou *art* a priest for ever after the order of Mel-chiz'e-dek.

ACTS 2:22 Ye men of Is'ra-el, hear these words; Je'sus of Naz'a-reth, a man approved of God among you by miracles and wonders and signs, which God did by him in the midst of you, as ye yourselves also know:

23 Him, being delivered by the determinate counsel and fore-knowledge of God, ye have taken, and by wicked hands have crucified and slain:

24 Whom God hath raised up, having loosed the pains of death: because it was not possible that he should be holden of it.

29 Men *and* brethren, let me freely speak unto you of the patriarch Da'vid, that he is both dead and buried, and his sepulchre is with us unto this day.

30 Therefore being a prophet, and knowing that God had sworn with an oath to him, that of the fruit of his loins, according to the flesh, he would raise up Christ to sit on his throne;

31 He seeing this before spake of the resurrection of Christ, that his soul was not left in hell, neither his flesh did see corruption.

32 This Je'sus hath God raised up, whereof we all are witnesses.

NOTES

32

An Everlasting King

Lesson: Psalm 110:1-4; Acts 2:22-24, 29-32

Read: Psalm 110:1-7; Acts 2:22-36

TIMES: approximately 1004 B.C.; A.D. 30   PLACES: Jerusalem; Jerusalem

---

GOLDEN TEXT—"The Lord said unto my Lord, Sit thou at my right hand, until I make thine enemies thy footstool" (Psalm 110:1).

Introduction

Over the centuries, rulers have made outlandish claims about their power and gone to astonishing extremes to perpetuate it. Hitler's claim that his Third Reich would last a thousand years now seems laughable, but its spirit is hardly new. Qin Shi Huang (or Shih Huang-Ti), the first emperor of a unified China, only ruled eleven years, but he boasted that his influence would last ten thousand generations. He had over seven thousand terra cotta soldiers placed in his mausoleum to accompany him in death.

Many empires have had cults surrounding their rulers that have demanded worship. Egyptian pharaohs claimed to be incarnations of the god Horus. Beginning with Augustus, Roman emperors received worship from their subjects. Japanese emperors and their families claimed descent from the sun goddess.

There has been one major problem in this. They all died. But there is one exception. The Messiah, the Son of David, will reign forever. This week's lesson examines two Scriptures that bear this out.

LESSON OUTLINE

I. A PROPHETIC VIEW OF THE KING—Ps. 110:1-4

II. AN APOSTOLIC WITNESS OF THE KING—Acts 2:22-24, 29-32

Exposition: Verse by Verse

A PROPHETIC VIEW OF THE KING

PS. 110:1 The LORD said unto my Lord, Sit thou at my right hand, until I make thine enemies thy footstool.

2 The LORD shall send the rod of thy strength out of Zion: rule thou in the midst of thine enemies.

3 Thy people shall be willing in the day of thy power, in the beauties of holiness from the womb of the morning: thou hast the dew of thy youth.

4 The LORD hath sworn, and will not repent, Thou art a priest for ever after the order of Melchizedek.

The God-King's exaltation (Ps. 110:1-2). This psalm is a messianic prophecy given by David. He recorded a divine utterance from the throne room of heaven: "The Lord (Yahweh) said unto my Lord (Adonai), Sit thou at my right hand." Jesus' later use of this Scripture (Matt. 22:44; Mark 12:36; Luke 20:42) reveals that David wrote it, that it was inspired by the Holy Spirit, and that it refers to the Messiah.

According to Psalm 110:1, Yahweh spoke to One called "Adonai" (Lord, Master) and welcomed Him to sit at His right side, the place of honor and authority. He was to occupy this position "until I make thine enemies thy footstool." The analogy of a footstool arose from ancient conquerors' practice of placing their feet on the necks of the conquered (cf. Josh. 10:24; I Kings 5:3; Isa. 51:23).

This utterance clearly refers to the Messiah and His coming victory over the nations. But it posed a conundrum for the Jews, for they held the Messiah to be the Son of David. Yet, as Jesus pointed out to them, David called Him "Lord" (Matt. 22:44). How could He be both David's son and David's Lord? The answer is that this One must also be the Son of God—a divine-human combination (cf. Ps. 2:1-12; Dan. 7:13-14). Only Jesus Himself fulfilled this requirement (Matt. 26:63-65).

The New Testament church believed without question that Jesus fulfilled this prophecy, both in ascending to the Father's right hand and in ultimately subduing all His enemies (cf. Acts 2:34-35; Heb. 1:3, 13). Paul went even further and anticipated the day when He would turn over His kingdom to His Father (I Cor. 15:24-28).

Psalm 110:2 speaks more specifically of the Messiah's rule: "The Lord shall send the rod of thy strength out of Zion." Many translate "rod" as "scepter," which is the insignia of authority used by rulers. But the usual word for "scepter" is a different Hebrew word. It seems more likely that "rod" here refers to a rod of judgment against one's enemies (cf. Isa. 9:4; 11:4; Rev. 2:27; 19:15). The Messiah is seen subduing all foes and ruling over them.

The rod of His strength is extended "out of Zion" (Ps. 110:2). His royal throne will be in Jerusalem, David's city, which will be elevated in glory (Ps. 2:6; Isa. 2:3; Zech. 2:10-12). From there His authority will extend to the ends of the earth (Ps. 2:8-9; Isa. 2:4; Zech. 8:22; 9:10). "In the midst of thine enemies" (Ps. 110:2) means that all His former enemies will be forced to submit to Him (132:18).

The Priest-King's dominion (Ps. 110:3-4). The King has not only enemies to subdue but also willing soldiers to fight for Him. "Thy people shall be willing in the day of thy power" pictures His followers as freewill offerings who give themselves willingly. "The day of thy power" can be translated "the day of Your army." It refers to the day when the Messiah will muster His army for battle.

This is no ordinary army. They will go forth "in the beauties of holiness" (Ps. 110:3). This poetic phrase refers to holy garments, such as those of the high priest on the Day of Atonement (Lev. 16:4) or of the Levitical singers preceding Israel's army (II Chron. 20:21). Such garments signify purity (Rev. 3:4-5; 19:8, 14), and this is essential for those who do battle for the Holy One.

"From the womb of the morning" (Ps. 110:3) should be taken with the following phrase, "thou hast the dew of thy youth." The sense of the statement is probably this: "Your young men are to You as dew from the womb of the morning." The morning is pictured as bringing forth dew, which in turn illustrates the nature of the young warriors who fight for the Messiah. In addition to being willing and holy, they will be as dewdrops—fresh, vigorous, and of great numbers (cf. II Sam. 17:12).

It is not surprising that the Messiah's warriors will be purified, for He is not only a King but also a Priest. A priest stands before God on behalf of man. In Old Testament times, the offices of king and priest were carefully separated, and a king usurping priestly duties was severely punished (cf. I Sam. 13:8-14; II Chron. 26:16-21). The priests all came from the family of Aaron in the tribe of Levi (cf. Num. 3:10). The Davidic kings, on the other hand, came from the tribe of Judah. So the two offices were mutually exclusive.

But the Messiah will be a priest "after the order of Melchizedek," not Aaron (Ps. 110:4). Melchizedek was a king of Salem (identified with Jerusalem) in the days of Abraham and at the same time "the priest of the most high God" (Gen. 14:18). Nothing is known of him except that he blessed Abraham and took tithes from him (vss. 19-20). Here the Lord swears that the coming Messiah will fulfill the pattern of priesthood set forth in Melchizedek, joining the functions of priest and king.

The prophecy of a coming Priest-King is repeated in Zechariah 6:9-15 with the symbolic crowning of Joshua, the high priest. It is said that One called "The BRANCH" will be "a priest upon his throne."

God sealed this commitment with a solemn oath: "The Lord hath sworn, and will not repent" (Ps. 110:4). Accompanying His oath with the declaration that He would never change His mind is the strongest statement He could have made that His word would stand firm.

The Lord swore that His Messiah would be a Priest forever after Melchizedek's order. This could not have been possible for David or any of his earthly descendants, for they all died. But the Messiah, being God, is eternal and can therefore rule forever.

The writer of Hebrews, arguing that Christ's priesthood is superior to that of Aaron, made much of this prophecy (Heb. 5:1-10; 6:20). He pointed out that Melchizedek was an apt picture of Jesus, being without a recorded lineage and superior to Abraham (and his Levitical descendants), from whom he received tithes (7:1-10). He foreshadowed the One who, unlike the Aaronic priests, would never have His priesthood interrupted by death (vss. 23-28).

AN APOSTOLIC WITNESS OF THE KING

ACTS 2:22 Ye men of Israel, hear these words; Jesus of Nazareth, a man approved of God among you by miracles and wonders and signs, which God did by him in the midst of you, as ye yourselves also know:

23 Him, being delivered by the determinate counsel and foreknowledge of God, ye have taken, and by wicked hands have crucified and slain:

24 Whom God hath raised up, having loosed the pains of death: because it was not possible that he should be holden of it.

29 Men and brethren, let me freely speak unto you of the patriarch David, that he is both dead and buried, and his sepulchre is with us unto this day.

30 Therefore being a prophet, and knowing that God had sworn with an oath to him, that of the fruit of his loins, according to the flesh, he would raise up Christ to sit on his throne;

31 He seeing this before spake of the resurrection of Christ, that his soul was not left in hell, neither his flesh did see corruption.

32 This Jesus hath God raised up, whereof we all are witnesses.

Jesus' mighty deeds (Acts 2:22). The second segment of our lesson reveals how the promised King had begun to fulfill prophecy. Our text is taken from Peter's sermon on the Day of Pentecost, when the Holy Spirit was given in a special way to Jesus' early disciples. Peter stepped forward to explain the meaning of the Spirit's manifestations.

After explaining that the Spirit's coming was the fulfillment of prophecy (Acts 2:14-21), Peter quickly focused on Jesus. He addressed the crowd as "ye men of Israel" (vs. 22), which included both Palestinian Jews and those who had come from abroad to the feast. He reminded them of facts they already knew about "Jesus of Nazareth," whose reputation had spread across the entire land.

Peter made the point that Jesus was "approved of God" (Acts 2:22). The proof of this lay in the marvelous works He had done. "Miracles" emphasizes the power behind His deeds. "Wonders" stresses the fact that people marveled at them. "Signs" looks to the divine significance to which they pointed. Peter reminded the crowd that they had seen all of these accrediting deeds firsthand, placing on them the responsibility of making correct judgments about Jesus.

Jesus' death and resurrection (Acts 2:23-24). In spite of the evidences of His deity, the people had rejected Jesus and put Him to death. To be sure, this was "by the determinate counsel and foreknowledge of God." It was in His plan. Yet those standing before Peter were guilty, for it was they who had put Him on the cross, using the "wicked hands" of the Romans to do it. God superintends all that occurs, but He holds responsible those who do evil and have evil motives.

But God did not allow evil to triumph. He raised Jesus from the dead. It was important to emphasize this, for in the eyes of Peter's listeners, Jesus was executed as a criminal. God delivered Him from death because it was not possible for Him to be held in its grip. Death's inability to hold Him was due to His deity (cf. John 1:14) and to the reliability of the prophetic Scripture that follows. So by rejecting Jesus, Peter's generation had made themselves enemies of God.

David's prophetic words (Acts 2:29-30). Peter now quoted David's words in Psalm 16:8-11 to show that the resurrection of Christ was foreseen even by him. The passage, given here in Acts 2:25-28, speaks of joy at the Lord's right hand because He would not permit His Holy One to see corruption (undergo decay).

But Peter then pointed out that these words could not have referred to David (Acts 2:29). He made an earnest appeal: "Men and brethren, let me freely speak unto you of the patriarch David." David was a "patriarch" in the sense that he founded the royal line, just as the twelve sons of Jacob were patriarchs of Israel's tribes (7:8).

Peter called attention to the fact that David was dead and buried and remained so. They knew this because his tomb was there in Jerusalem (cf. I Kings 2:10).

David thus must have been speaking as a prophet when he spoke of One who would not see corruption (Acts 2:30). David, indeed, was aware that the Holy Spirit at times spoke through him (cf. II Sam. 23:1-2). Thus, Psalm 16 was a messianic psalm, corresponding to his prior knowledge of what God would do. He knew "God had sworn with an oath to him, that of the fruit of his loins, according to the flesh, he would raise up Christ to sit on his throne" (Acts 2:30).

Some Greek manuscripts do not include the reference to Christ's resurrection in Acts 2:30. They merely state that God had sworn to seat one of David's descendants on his throne. This would then be a reference to the Davidic covenant, with its promise that his throne would be established forever (II Sam. 7:12-16). Nevertheless, as the next verse points out, David was indeed prophesying of the resurrection of Christ.

Jesus' fulfillment of the prophecy (Acts 2:31-32). Peter now applied David's words to the present scene. As a prophet, David had looked ahead and spoken of the resurrection of Christ (the Messiah). He specifically foretold that "his soul was not left in hell, neither his flesh did see corruption." The Greek word for "hell" here is "hades," corresponding to the Hebrew "Sheol" in the original psalm. This is simply the place of the dead, or the grave. It does not imply that Jesus went to a place of torment.

Nor did Jesus' body "see corruption" (Acts 2:31). It did not decay, and He was raised bodily from the grave. Though His resurrection body was glorified and not subject to the usual physical limitations (cf. Luke 24:31; John 20:19, 26), it was a real body that could be touched (Luke 24:37-43). In this body He ascended to heaven, and in the same body He will return (Acts 1:9-11).

Peter now made his point: "This Jesus hath God raised up" (Acts 2:32). Jesus is the Messiah of whom David spoke, and God raised Him up in accordance with David's prophecy. But He did more; He received Jesus into heaven itself to be seated at the Father's right hand, and the ascended Lord has sent forth the Holy Spirit to bear witness of Him through His followers (vs. 33). To support this, Peter quoted from Psalm 110:1 (cf. Acts 2:34-35), which we have already studied in this lesson.

Thus, Peter took two psalms that are difficult to understand and showed how they made sense when seen fulfilled in Jesus Christ. But to these he also added the apostles' personal testimony: "whereof we all are witnesses" (Acts 2:32). They, who had previously not believed He would rise again, had seen Him and were compelled to believe. They also had seen Him ascend to heaven and heard the angel's promise of His return.

What were the implications of this for Peter's Jewish audience? He concluded, "Therefore let all the house of Israel know assuredly, that God hath made that same Jesus, whom ye have crucified, both Lord and Christ (Messiah)" (Acts 2:36). By crucifying Jesus, they had set themselves against God Himself. They could now do nothing but repent and claim His grace (vss. 37-40). Only then could they claim the spiritual blessings made possible by their Messiah.

—Robert E. Wenger.

QUESTIONS

1. Whose utterance did David record in Psalm 110? To whom did He speak?
2. How can we explain the fact that David called two persons "Lord"?
3. From where will the Messiah rule? How far will His rule extend?
4. Through what kind of army will the Messiah conquer His enemies?
5. Who was Melchizedek? How did he prefigure Christ's priesthood?
6. What was the occasion for Peter's sermon in Acts 2?
7. What was God's role in Jesus' death, and what was the role of the Jews and the Romans?
8. Why could the words of Psalm 16:8-11 not refer to David?
9. Of what event was David prophesying, according to Peter?
10. What were the dire implications of Jesus' resurrection for Peter's audience?

—Robert E. Wenger.

Preparing to Teach the Lesson

In this week's lesson we will examine the prophecies in Psalm 110 from the perspective of the Day of Pentecost.

TODAY'S AIM

Facts: to show that the prophecies of the coming King were fulfilled in Jesus' death, resurrection, and ascension.

Principle: to show that before Christ could reign as King, He had to fulfill His ministry on the cross.

Application: to show that we should not be discouraged if events seem to deny the promises of God.

INTRODUCING THE LESSON

Show your class a photograph of a new car. Explain that the finished product is made up of various parts. In a similar way, several events had to occur before the promised King could be introduced.

DEVELOPING THE LESSON

1. The King's eternal priesthood (Ps. 110:1-4). As you begin class, ask a student to dramatically read out loud Psalm 110:1-4. Ask your class to make some observations about verse 1. Who is speaking? To whom is he speaking? What is David doing? Help your students see that David was recording a conversation between two people—the Lord and a person David called "my Lord."

The first use of "LORD" is all capitalized. In the Bible, this is a common way to translate "Yahweh," the covenantal name of God in the Old Testament. The speaker is therefore God the Father—Yahweh. The person He is speaking to is identified by David as "my Lord." As king, David would not refer to any other person on earth as his lord. God was speaking to the future King who would sit on David's throne, the Messiah. The New Testament identifies Him as Jesus.

The LORD instructed the Lord to sit at His right hand. No mere human being is qualified to sit at the right hand of God in heaven. However, the Son of God *is* qualified. God told Him to occupy this position until He has subdued His enemies.

Point out to your class the images within the first three verses that depict a king. First, His enemies will become His footstool. This implies He will be on a throne.

The late Hebrew scholar William Gesenius defined the word "rod" (*mateh*) in the phrase the "rod of thy strength" as a king's scepter (*Gesenius' Hebrew and Chaldee Lexicon to the Old Testament,* Baker).

The Lord was to "rule" (Ps. 110:2) in "the day of [His] power" (vs. 3). From the perspective of the Old Testament, David was referring to the future King who would sit on his throne forever, in keeping with God's covenant.

Centuries later, Jesus asked the Pharisees what they thought of Christ (the Greek word for "Messiah") (Matt. 22:41-45). "Whose son is he?" Jesus asked. They replied that the Messiah would be "The son of David." Jesus then used Psalm 110 to confound them and bring them to realize the meaning of Scripture. The point Jesus made from the psalm was that David, being the father, would not call his own son his Lord; nor would he submit to him as his lord. The reverse was true. The son would submit to the father. Further, if God was speaking to David's son, instructing him to sit at His own right hand and share His throne, then this son was more than human. David's son must himself be deity in order to sit at the right hand of God. Upon hearing this explanation, the Pharisees had no response.

The Lord added a further dimension to this coming King: He would also have an eternal priesthood. Just as Melchizedek was a priest and king over Salem (early Jerusalem), so the messianic King would serve in a dual capacity. This priesthood would be outside the Levitical and Aaronic priesthood familiar to Israel. The author of Hebrews explained this in greater detail (4:14—5:11; 7:1—8:6).

2. The crucified King (Acts 2:22-24). On the Day of Pentecost, Peter stood before the multitude of people in Jerusalem and proclaimed that the person proved by God to be the Messiah of Israel had been crucified and resurrected. In a combination of God's determined purpose and foreknowledge and the lawless actions of the leaders and people of Israel, the King had been put to death.

Help your students understand that since Jesus was the promised King and Priest who was to reign forever and because He was, as prophesied, God in the flesh and innocent of any sin, it was impossible for Him to remain in the grave.

Remind the class of the prophecies of Isaiah studied in the previous lesson. Note that in Acts 2:25-28, Peter quoted David's words in Psalm 16:8-11 regarding the resurrection.

3. The resurrected King (Acts 2:29-32). It is important to note how the Davidic covenant provides the backdrop to the events of the crucifixion, burial, and the resurrection of Christ as well as to the events of Pentecost, when the church was born. The various issues surrounding the covenant and David's writings concerning the promised King provide evidence of the need for the resurrection in addition to foretelling its occurrence.

Peter used the Davidic covenant, David's role as a prophet, and David's words to show that his descendant would sit on the throne. David prophesied that the Messiah-King's body would not experience the decay of the grave. This implies that He would die but that He then would be resurrected.

Peter also used David's nearby tomb as evidence that David was not speaking about himself. David had been buried for hundreds of years, and his tomb's location in Jerusalem was common knowledge.

The final evidence was the personal testimony of the eyewitnesses to the resurrected Christ and the empty tomb. At the moment Peter was speaking, Christ was fulfilling the role of sitting at the right hand of God, as David had foretold.

ILLUSTRATING THE LESSON

Before there could be a crown, there had to be a cross. Because of Jesus' obedience to death, God raised Him and exalted Him (Phil. 2:5-11).

CONCLUDING THE LESSON

As you conclude the lesson, point out that God will always keep His promises, even though events in between may seem to say otherwise.

ANTICIPATING THE NEXT LESSON

In the next lesson we will catch a glimpse of Christ in heaven, surrounded by His worshippers.

—Carter Corbrey.

PRACTICAL POINTS

1. Living a godly life in an ungodly world glorifies God (Ps. 110:1-3).
2. When God promises us something, we can be sure He will never change His mind (vs. 4).
3. God demonstrates His power and presence in our lives not necessarily by dramatic miracles but by His consistent and unfailing provision (Acts 2:22).
4. The Lord always delivers His children in the right way and at the right time (vss. 23-24).
5. Just as the Father has fulfilled His promises to David, so will He fulfill His promises to us (vss. 29-31).
6. Jesus' resurrection illustrates God's power to raise us too (vs. 32).

—Anne Adams.

RESEARCH AND DISCUSSION

1. Is it reassuring to read God's promises for His people? What specific promises has He fulfilled for you? Can you describe what happened? Did this enable you to serve Him better? How?
2. Pretend you were in Peter's audience. What part of his message might affect you the most? Would you have scoffed at what Peter said? Why?
3. What would Christ's relationship to David mean for Peter's audience? What does it mean for you? What does the relationship say about God's promises to David? Does this encourage your faith?

—Anne Adams.

ILLUSTRATED HIGH POINTS

We all are witnesses

A professional sports team in my city drafted a young superstar. Upon his arrival, the team printed T-shirts with the phrase "we are all witnesses" to display our pride in having this exceptional player on our team.

The player's tenure was a mere seven years, but it left thousands of fans with an assortment of paraphernalia bearing the once-popular logo.

Peter used the phrase "we all are witnesses," but he did not use it to describe the fleeting excitement delivered by a gifted athlete. He referred to the Lord and Christ, the Son of God, who would rise from the dead and live forever.

Make thine enemies thy footstool

In 1939, a fifteen-year-old African-American young man hid in a train's freight car. His parents had prompted him to leave his hometown of Danville, Virginia, because he had offended a prominent citizen there.

His arrival "up north" was anything but liberating for the lad. Discrimination appeared to be as prevalent in the north as it was in the south. He scraped along, taking odd fix-it jobs and domestic work until World War II began.

In 1941, chasing the dream of equality, this young man joined the navy. Even there the shadow of prejudice stalked him. Segregated, he again faced the destructive foe of racism.

This man served his country, raised a family, and lived to see his fourth generation. Most important, he knew Jesus Christ as his Saviour. As he closed his eyes in death in 2009, he awoke to a place without hatred, injustice, or pain.

Every enemy will become Jesus' footstool. In every conflict we face, Jesus will guide us to victory.

—Beverly Jones.

Golden Text Illuminated

"The Lord said unto my Lord, Sit thou at my right hand, until I make thine enemies thy footstool" (Psalm 110:1).

Psalm 110:1 is one of the verses most frequently quoted in the New Testament. It is cited in Acts 2:34-35 and Hebrews 1:13. Jesus also quoted it as He debated with the Pharisees during the week before His crucifixion (Matt. 22:44; Mark 12:36; Luke 20:42-43). In fact, Jesus applied this psalm of David directly to Himself.

David's psalm begins, "The Lord said unto my Lord." The two Hebrew words translated "Lord" in this verse are different. The first word is *Yahweh*, which is the personal name of God and emphasizes His eternal self-existence. The second word is *Adonai*, a word that stresses supremacy. Both terms are used for God; yet David distinguished between the two here. David said that God spoke to David's ("my") Lord. The question, then, is, Who is David's "Lord"?

Jesus clearly identified Himself as David's Lord, the Messiah, or Christ (cf. Matt. 22:42-43). So while the Christ was David's descendant—the "son of David," as the Pharisees recognized—He was also David's superior, his "Lord." Jesus' opponents considered "son of David" too lofty a title to be applied to Jesus, but Jesus was pointing out that it really gave Him too little honor. He was not only David's son but also David's Lord.

This is evident from the following words of Yahweh that David recorded. God the Father ("The Lord") told the Messiah ("my Lord") to sit at the right hand of God until God made the Messiah's enemies His footstool. The "right hand" is the place of authority equal to that of God Himself. When Jesus was on trial before the Jewish Sanhedrin, He told the high priest, "Hereafter shall ye see the Son of man sitting on the right hand of power" (Matt. 26:64).

God the Father also promised to make the Messiah's enemies His "footstool." This vivid picture speaks of when God would bring all people into subjection to David's Lord. The New Testament reiterates this promise to Christ (cf. I Cor. 15:24-28; Phil. 2:9-11).

Jesus' argument at least implied that as Son of David, Messiah, and Lord, He is deity. He is God in the flesh, the One whom David described as "Lord," the One who will sovereignly reign over all. God was "promising the [Christ] such pre-eminence, power, authority, and majesty as would be proper only for One who, as to his person, from all eternity was, is now, and forever will be God" (Hendriksen, *Exposition of the Gospel According to Matthew*, Baker).

David wrote of Jesus, and Jesus is the Messiah and Lord. Jesus was saying to the Pharisees that to reject Him was to reject David's Lord. Yet reject Him they did.

It is interesting to note how Jesus upheld the inspiration of Scripture in quoting Psalm 110:1. His argument hinged upon Adonai being David's superior. *Adonai* alone could not convey this idea, since it can also be applied to mere men. Rather, the idea of superiority is communicated by the word "my," which in Hebrew is a one-letter suffix. Thus, much of Jesus' argument ultimately rested on a single letter in God's written Word.

—*Jarl K. Waggoner.*

Heart of the Lesson

"Did you know that the United States once had a king? Actually, he wasn't a king—he was an emperor. During the gold-rush days of the 1800s in San Francisco, a man named Joshua A. Norton lost everything he had in market speculation. When that happened, something happened to his mind. He declared himself Norton I, Emperor of These United States.

"Joshua A. Norton lived and died confused and wrong because people recognized him as emperor when he wasn't. Over 2000 years ago, people recognized Jesus as King when He entered into Jerusalem on the back of a donkey colt. But unlike Joshua A. Norton, Jesus really was King" (www.sermoncentral.com).

In this week's lesson, we learn about the eternal authority of the risen Lord Jesus Christ. When He assumes His future throne, His rule will never end.

1. A song of royalty (Ps. 110:1-4). Writing as a prophet and a poet, David reported a serious and sincere prophetic statement of God concerning the Messiah who would share God's power and position. David wrote that a time would come when God will grant to His Son the right to utterly subdue His foes. There will be a host of volunteers who will gladly join in following Jesus as their King.

Psalm 110:4 carries on, describing the serious and sincere character of God's statement. The Messiah's dominion is described as that of a priest like Melchizedek. He would be a King-Priest, combining two offices. His reign would be without beginning and without end, just like Melchizedek's.

The rule and reign of the everlasting King Jesus will be eternal and attractive. Without a hint of strong-armed compulsion, an innumerable host of holy disciples will join their King in His reign. It will be their distinct privilege to freely give of their time and talents to accompany the strong rule of King Jesus from Jerusalem.

2. A sermon of resurrection (Acts 2:22-24, 29-32). The Apostle Peter had witnessed not only the resurrected Saviour but also His ascension into the heavens (cf. 1:3, 9). As a result, Peter felt empowered to courageously address an assembled throng of people who had just witnessed the power of the Holy Spirit with amazement and confusion.

Peter recounted not only Jesus' crucifixion and death at the hands of godless men but also His resurrection from the power of death. Peter then boldly stated that the patriarch and prophet David, although dead and buried, knew that God had promised that one of his descendants would rule from his throne. That descendant is the resurrected Lord Jesus Christ.

The everlasting King demands nothing less from His followers than their bold and courageous proclamation that He has overcome the power of death and lives at the Father's right hand.

Christians live in a culture that is dominated by irony. On one hand, the culture calls for inclusive diversity of opinion and belief. On the other hand, when Christians take advantage of opportunities to share their faith in the public square, that same diverse culture either stifles their expressions or blatantly forbids them to voice their beliefs.

Christians must embrace the delicate balance of demonstrating an others-centered mercy with courage to affirm the absolute truths of God's Word. A lost and dying world does not need dialogue; it needs to be redeemed through faith in Jesus Christ.

—*Thomas R. Chmura.*

World Missions

A king implies the existence of a kingdom. In our lesson this week, we learn about the everlasting King. No earthly king has an everlasting kingdom, so obviously this lesson is not talking about the kings we normally think of. The focus of our lesson is on the royal nature of Jesus the Messiah, the King. He was promised to us a very long time ago as part of the covenant that God made with His people. King David talked about the reality of this everlasting King many years before Jesus was born.

It must be pointed out here that the Old Testament and its prophecies looked into the future to this coming King. The Hebrew name for Jesus is Yeshua, which means "God delivers." We must see the everlasting King as our Deliverer. This is the concept that the world outside our churches does not yet fully understand! God has already provided a Deliverer in the form of the everlasting King Jesus. In the storms of our lives, we need a Deliverer, and we already have a King who will give us His peace.

There is something else that the world needs to know: this King is powerful and provides us with victory over those things that trouble us. The wiles of the evil one are no match for the love of Jesus for us. The everlasting King is able to put down every enemy that comes into our path to destroy us. This is the good news of the gospel of our Lord Jesus. We have a King who takes care of His people and is able to protect us from every catastrophe that faces us. Good kings protect their people, and our God does that.

Our God is the Mighty One. He has the power to meet every need of His people. Since He is in charge of the heavenly kingdom and we are part of it, He is our Ruler and our Provider. There is a lot of poverty in the world and also a lot of chaos. This King tells us that He will meet every need and give us peace. He will put down our enemies. All this is very good news for any who will turn to this covenant-keeping King. We are to let the world know about Him.

It is very sad that there are still people in our day of instantaneous communication who have not yet heard of this Messiah-King. He has promised to return to the earth and set up His reign on earth in peace and prosperity. It is imperative that we help prepare the world for this coming King. There is still room in His kingdom for anyone who is willing to come in and be part of it. Our King wants us to come into the kingdom, and He wants us to share in all His glory.

We cannot overlook the most important fact. When this King appears to receive us, it will be to an everlasting kingdom. This means it has no end. It is a simple truth but one that is easy to overlook. The world needs to know that there is a permanent and everlasting solution to every need. The answer is found in Jesus, the everlasting King, alone. What a sad state of affairs it is that multitudes are confused and despairing because they have not heard of this permanent solution!

As Christian believers, we are called to be missionaries of the gospel, carrying this good news of the Saviour to the ends of all the earth. Like Paul, we are to be constrained by the love of Christ as we do our part to let others know about this King.

—A. Koshy Muthalaly.

The Jewish Aspect

The man who answered the door was Jewish, middle-aged, and immaculately groomed. I launched into my usual presentation, explaining that I was a Christian interested in pointing out to the Jewish people that their Bible says clearly that Jesus is the Messiah of Israel.

"Do not bother," he said, "for I am fully persuaded that Jesus was the Messiah." I was stunned. I knew there were a few around who were persuaded of the Lord's throne rights to David's kingdom, but this was my first encounter with a convinced messianist.

I quickly recovered. Through the discussion that followed, I determined that the conviction was in the past tense. The man at the door was not able to move from the concept of a historic Messiah to knowing Jesus as his Messiah. Jesus was not his Saviour and Lord.

How sad it is that someone who studied the Messiah so carefully and forfeited former convictions had missed the most crucial part of the story! It is another expression of the consuming unbelief of the Pharisees and Sadducees of Jesus' day and the Judaism of our time.

Our lesson title is "An Everlasting King." That is what the Jewish people need—the bright hope set before the children of Israel in the promised kingdom of David! The very first verse in the New Testament speaks of "Jesus Christ, the son of David, the son of Abraham" (Matt. 1:1). He was ordained to His throne. Believers will be with Him in that great thousand-year reign.

How did the Jews lose their way on this important truth? Satanic opposition is a primary source of responsibility. Satan can no longer slay the Lord Jesus, so he must confuse the natural seed of Abraham, the Jews. He must also viciously attack born-again believers, who have been recipients of God's grace and have been vessels for God, releasing many people from Satan's prison of sin.

Judaism, as you can see, has no lasting King in the manner portrayed in Scripture. In the sixteenth century, a small group of kabbalistic Jews taught of a God who limited himself, for he had to evolve like a mere man. Kabbalism has strains that go back to first-century Judaism. A wide variety of esoteric teachings come from this movement. Some modern celebrities have found it fashionable to study this material.

There is no goal for life in Judaism. The thought of a kingdom where Jews would have preeminence is not something understood, as I found in an interview with a young Jew. They speak of an end-time project called "tikkun." "Tikkun" means "repair of the world." It is more of a good-works project than the crowning of the King-Messiah.

In spite of all these negatives, it is important to note that more Jews have come to know the Messiah Jesus in the last forty years than at any other time in history. Out of these newly saved Jews, surprising numbers step forward to reach out to their own Jewish people. In the United States, Jews have been afforded a measure of security they have not known in any other part of the world. In that relative security, many find it easier to explore the incompleteness of their faith in a thoughtful way.

I like to suggest that Jews begin with a study of messianic prophecy. This has been a totally neglected teaching in Judaism for reasons that will suggest themselves. They know of no suffering Messiah, so the concept of a Messiah dying on a Roman cross is new truth that must be proved by Scripture.

—Lyle P. Murphy.

Guiding the Superintendent

This week's lesson presents evidence of the certainty of God's determination to convince His people of His infallible oath to raise up Jesus, the eternal power and authority of God, to rule the kingdom of heaven and earth. The Old Testament repeatedly declares it, and the New Testament confirms it.

DEVOTIONAL OUTLINE

1. God's purpose is determined from eternity (Ps. 110:1-4). The Gospel of Matthew records that David was in the Spirit when he recorded God's conversation with His Son, Jesus (22:43-44), whom He has raised from the dead. God told Him to rest from His labor and suffering at the hand of sinful man. In the meantime, God will set things in order for Christ's final and ultimate rule of the kingdom of God. Christ—the Lion of the tribe of Judah—will govern a people willing to subject themselves to His kingly priesthood even in the face of His enemies.

This should be seen today in the earnest worship of modern, Spirit-filled Christians. These believers have set their hearts to begin each day with Jesus on their minds and have purposed in their spirits to submit to the leading of the Holy Spirit, guided by the knowledge that (from His resurrection and ascension through all eternity) Christ is King.

2. God's purpose prevails over death and the grave (Acts 2:22-24). The Apostle Peter finished clarifying the events of Pentecost to the Jews. He then gave them a depth of understanding about the man Jesus of Nazareth, of whom Nathaniel asked the question "Can there any good thing come out of Nazareth?" (John 1:46). Peter's goal was to affirm that the abundant, wondrous works performed by God through Christ, which the disciples themselves had witnessed, were God's testimony demonstrating to the Jews regarding the authenticity of Jesus' priesthood.

It was God who had foreordained that "the Son of man must be delivered into the hands of sinful men, and be crucified" (Luke 24:7). But Christ would rise again, as there was no power on earth that could withstand God's execution of His word and works.

3. God's purpose is to exalt Jesus Christ as Lord (Acts 2:29-32). Peter knew and respected the fact that the Jews revered David as prophet and king. Nevertheless, he proceeded to assert that neither David's death nor Christ's crucifixion constituted the death of David's dynasty or of God's divine oath of perpetual kingship. Peter reminded them of the prophetic words of their favorite son verifying that the resurrection of Christ was preordained in accordance with God's commission of Christ as the everlasting King (cf. Ps. 132:11).

Christ had died, but He did not stay in the grave. He had, indeed, risen and was seen by "above five hundred" (I Cor. 15:6).

AGE-GROUP EMPHASES

Children: Even small children understand that nothing lasts forever. But teach them that God's Word never changes; His promises are everlasting.

Youths: Remind them of God's special love for and favor toward David, and assure them that they can have a similar relationship with God if they love and revere Him.

Adults: In Isaiah 55:9, God said, "So are my ways higher than your ways." Even in those times when we do not understand God's ways, we can always trust His Word.

—*Jane E. Campbell.*

Scripture Lesson Text

REV. 5:6 And I beheld, and, lo, in the midst of the throne and of the four beasts, and in the midst of the elders, stood a Lamb as it had been slain, having seven horns and seven eyes, which are the seven Spir'its of God sent forth into all the earth.

7 And he came and took the book out of the right hand of him that sat upon the throne.

8 And when he had taken the book, the four beasts and four *and* twenty elders fell down before the Lamb, having every one of them harps, and golden vials full of odours, which are the prayers of saints.

9 And they sung a new song, saying, Thou art worthy to take the book, and to open the seals thereof: for thou wast slain, and hast redeemed us to God by thy blood out of every kindred, and tongue, and people, and nation;

10 And hast made us unto our God kings and priests: and we shall reign on the earth.

11 And I beheld, and I heard the voice of many angels round about the throne and the beasts and the elders: and the number of them was ten thousand times ten thousand, and thousands of thousands;

12 Saying with a loud voice, Worthy is the Lamb that was slain to receive power, and riches, and wisdom, and strength, and honour, and glory, and blessing.

13 And every creature which is in heaven, and on the earth, and under the earth, and such as are in the sea, and all that are in them, heard I saying, Blessing, and honour, and glory, and power, *be* unto him that sitteth upon the throne, and unto the Lamb for ever and ever.

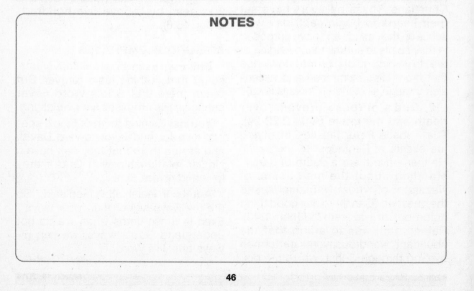

NOTES

Worthy Is the Lamb

Lesson: Revelation 5:6-13

Read: Revelation 3:7; 5:5-13; 6:12—7:17; 22:16

TIME: about A.D. 96   PLACE: from Patmos

GOLDEN TEXT—"Worthy is the Lamb that was slain to receive power, and riches, and wisdom, and strength, and honour, and glory, and blessing" (Revelation 5:12).

Introduction

What did Jesus look like when He walked the earth? We tend to have a stereotyped picture of His appearance because of artists' portrayals, but the Bible is silent concerning His appearance. This silence is for our benefit, because God wants us to focus on Jesus' spotless character rather than on His physical appearance.

Scripture uses various terms to depict His character and accomplishments. Jesus Himself used some of these. He referred to Himself as the Son of Man, the Bridegroom, the Good Shepherd, the Door, and the Light of the World. He is the Resurrection and the Life, the Bread of Life, the True Vine.

Another title, first used by John the Baptist, is the Lamb of God, who has carried away our sins. As the Lamb, He appears again in Revelation—this time in a different capacity, as this week's lesson will show.

LESSON OUTLINE

I. THE MANIFESTATION OF THE LAMB—Rev. 5:6-7

II. THE RESPONSE OF THE BEASTS AND ELDERS—Rev. 5:8-10

III. THE RESPONSE OF THE ANGELS—Rev. 5:11-12

IV. THE RESPONSE OF ALL CREATURES—Rev. 5:13

Exposition: Verse by Verse

THE MANIFESTATION OF THE LAMB

REV. 5:6 And I beheld, and, lo, in the midst of the throne and of the four beasts, and in the midst of the elders, stood a Lamb as it had been slain, having seven horns and seven eyes, which are the seven Spirits of God sent forth into all the earth.

7 And he came and took the book out of the right hand of him that sat upon the throne.

The Apostle John, a prisoner on the island of Patmos because of his faith, was given a series of revelations concerning both present and future. While he was "in the Spirit" (Rev. 1:10), he saw a vision of the glorified Christ (vss. 10-20), who gave him messages for the seven churches of Asia Minor. These messages were for their present spiritual welfare (chaps. 2—3).

But after this, John was spiritually transported to heaven to receive visions of what the future held (Rev. 4:1). There he saw the throne of God and beings who gave Him continuous worship (vss. 2-11). These included four beasts and twenty-four elders.

The right hand of the One on the throne held a "book" (Rev. 5:1), or scroll, which was sealed with seven seals. An angel asked who was worthy to open the scroll, but none in the whole universe was found worthy (vss. 2-3). To John this was a great tragedy, and he "wept much" (vs. 4). But one of the twenty-four elders comforted him and revealed that "the Lion of the tribe of Juda, the Root of David" (vs. 5) had "prevailed," or won the victory, and could therefore open the scroll.

His appearance (Rev. 5:6). John no doubt expected to see a mighty lion to represent the conquering Messiah. But to his amazement, standing in the center of the throne, surrounded by the four beasts and the elders, was a lamb. One cannot imagine a greater contrast, especially since the word for "lamb" means a young lamb. Yet Jesus combines both characteristics. At His first coming, He took the role of a lamb (cf. John 1:29); at His second, He will conquer and rule as a lion (cf. Rev. 19:11-16).

The Lamb John saw looked as if it had been slain (Rev. 5:6). This no doubt means it had on it the marks of the wounds that had caused its death. Since the Lamb stood there no longer dead, it obviously represents the resurrected Christ (cf. 1:18). But it is the scars that, ironically, show how He has prevailed and

overcome. The shameful death of the cross was for Him the means of victory over the powers of evil (cf. John 12:31-33; Col. 2:14-15).

Along with the scars of death, this Lamb had "seven horns" (Rev. 5:6). Horns usually signify aggressive strength and authority (cf. Deut. 33:17; I Kings 22:11). In Scripture horns at times refer to the powers or rulers of Gentile kingdoms (cf. Dan. 7:24; Zech. 1:18-21; Rev. 12:3; 13:1). But the Lamb has superior might to overcome them, for the presence of seven horns signifies the perfection of strength in Him.

He also had "seven eyes, which are the seven Spirits of God sent forth into all the earth" (Rev. 5:6). This describes the Holy Spirit in His fullness (cf. 1:4; 4:5). "Eyes" symbolize His observation of all that occurs on the earth, to which He has been sent (cf. Zech. 3:9; 4:10). This agrees with Jesus' teaching that the Spirit would be sent forth to exalt Him, increase spiritual understanding, and convict the world (John 14:26; 16:7-15).

His role (Rev. 5:7). As John watched the Lamb, "he came and took the book out of the right hand of him that sat upon the throne" and prepared to open the seals one by one. We learn from later chapters that the opening of these seals, followed by the sounding of seven trumpets and the emptying of seven vials, brought divine judgments on the wicked of the earth. Thus, the scroll's message was not salvation but judgment on those who had rejected salvation.

The slain Lamb is the only one qualified to release this judgment. Through His death and resurrection He has "prevailed" (Rev. 5:5) and now has the authority to mete out retribution on those who have refused His offer of reconciliation. His judgments will eventually purge the earth and prepare for His eternal kingdom.

THE RESPONSE OF THE BEASTS AND ELDERS

8 And when he had taken the book, the four beasts and four and twenty elders fell down before the Lamb, having every one of them harps, and golden vials full of odours, which are the prayers of saints.

9 And they sung a new song, saying, Thou art worthy to take the book, and to open the seals thereof: for thou wast slain, and hast redeemed us to God by thy blood out of every kindred, and tongue, and people, and nation;

10 And hast made us unto our God kings and priests: and we shall reign on the earth.

Their worship (Rev. 5:8). In chapter 4 the four beasts and twenty-four elders worshipped the God who sat on the throne (vss. 8-11). Now they "fell down before the Lamb" (5:8), giving Him worship as well. Each of them had a harp, or lyre, one of only two instruments mentioned in Revelation (the other being the trumpet). Each also had a golden vial, or bowl, filled with "odours," or incense.

These bowls of incense are said to symbolize the prayers of the saints. "Saints" is a term used in the New Testament of all Christians (cf. I Cor. 1:2; Phil. 1:1; Col. 1:2). Their prayers are as incense, rising to God and giving Him pleasure (cf. Ps. 141:2; Rev. 8:3-4). The Greek word for "prayers" here is a general one, but it usually denotes petition, not praise. The saints may well be asking God to vindicate all those who have suffered, complete His judgments, and bring in His kingdom (cf. Rev. 6:10; 8:3-5).

Their song (Rev. 5:9-10). The beasts and elders sang "a new song" that had never been sung in heaven before. It was a song of praise to the Lamb, corresponding to their earlier praise for the One on the throne (4:8, 11). "Thou art worthy," they sang, "to take the book, and to open the seals thereof" (5:9).

The reason He was worthy was that He had been slain and had redeemed sinners to God through His blood. The Greek tense used here indicates that this was an event that occurred at a specific time. So it must refer to the crucifixion of Jesus at Calvary. His shed blood was the price of redemption for all who trust Him. To be redeemed means "bought out of the market." It is the word Paul used in telling the Corinthians, "Ye are bought with a price" (I Cor. 6:20; 7:23).

The phrase "hast redeemed us to God" (Rev. 5:9) implies that those who once were the property of sin have, through Jesus' redemption, now become the property of God. They are His to use as He sees fit to glorify Himself. There is a question about the wording here. Some manuscripts omit "us," and thus some translations substitute "men" and make the reference to human saints in general.

While this small variation may not be important in itself, it could make a difference in who is singing the song. If "us" is the proper translation in Revelation 5:9, those who are singing (the twenty-four elders) must be glorified saints who themselves have been redeemed. If "men" is correct, the elders could be angelic beings, though they also could be human. Since angels join in the praise only later (vs. 11), perhaps it is better to see the elders as human.

In any case, the redeemed include people from every tribe and language and ethnic group and nation. The impact of Jesus' death has crossed all lines— tribal, linguistic, ethnic, and political. Therefore, the Cross is central to all that is found in the sealed scroll. It is the basis not only of redemption but also of the judgments about to fall on those who have rejected Christ.

The song continues: "And hast made us unto our God kings and priests" (Rev. 5:10). God originally made Israel His "kingdom of priests" (Exod. 19:6). He later designated the Christian church "a royal priesthood" (I Pet. 2:9) and "kings and priests unto God" (Rev. 1:6). As priests, we are to witness to His salvation, bringing His gospel to sinful humanity and them to Him. We also bring Him sacrifices of praise and good deeds in our worship (Heb. 13:15-16).

But the elders' song indicates that saints are kings as well as priests (Rev. 5:10). As such, we will reign on the earth. We are not presently reigning, so this must refer to the future kingdom of Christ. When He establishes His millennial reign, we will reign with Him (20:4-6). Our priesthood will also continue through that time (vs. 6), though it is not mentioned as part of the new heaven and earth that follow. When sin and death have been erased, a priesthood is no longer necessary.

THE RESPONSE OF THE ANGELS

11 And I beheld, and I heard the voice of many angels round about the throne and the beasts and the elders: and the number of them was ten thousand times ten thousand, and thousands of thousands;

12 Saying with a loud voice, Worthy is the Lamb that was slain to receive power, and riches, and wisdom, and strength, and honour, and glory, and blessing.

Their number (Rev. 5:11). Joining the four beasts and twenty-four elders in praise were "many angels round about the throne." They formed, as it were, an outer circle around those few who had sung of human redemption. Angels are God's messengers, assigned to responsibilities throughout His creation. They were created individually by God, since they do not procreate (cf. Matt. 22:30). Though they are superior to humans and can be striking in appearance, they are not divine (cf. Heb. 1:4-8, 13-14).

Angels are so numerous that they seem beyond human calculation. Here the number John saw was "ten thousand times ten thousand, and thousands of thousands" (Rev. 5:11). In this context, the numbers should not be taken literally but might read "myriads upon myriads, and thousands upon thousands." John was straining the use of numbers to communicate that they were innumerable. This confirms Daniel's earlier vision, when he saw angels ministering to the Ancient of Days (Dan. 7:9-10).

When arrested, Jesus declared that it would have been a small matter for His Father to dispatch twelve legions of angels (72,000) to rescue Him (Matt. 26:53). It is possible that each child of God is assigned an angel, since Jesus declared of His "little ones" that "their angels" (Matt. 18:10; cf. Heb. 1:14) always have access to God. Similarly, the writer of Hebrews declared that the "heavenly Jerusalem" to which believers have come has "an innumerable company of angels" (12:22).

Their worship (Rev. 5:12). The multitude of angels John saw devoted themselves to adoring the Lamb. Angels do not experience salvation as humans can, but they are fascinated observers of it (Eph. 3:10; I Pet. 1:12). They were intimately involved in all key aspects of Jesus' earthly life—His birth, temptation, agony in Gethsemane, resurrection, and ascension (cf. I Tim. 3:16).

Now, in the heavenly throne room, the angels have the opportunity to praise the victorious Lamb, at whose accomplishments they can only marvel. They are not specifically said to sing, but they do voice their praise in an awesomely loud refrain. They proclaim Jesus worthy of a sevenfold recognition.

First, He is worthy to receive "power" (Rev. 5:12). This word signifies ability or strength to perform. Though Christ intrinsically possesses divine power, the angels here express His worthiness to exercise it fully. He is also worthy to receive riches. This does not refer to what He possesses, for all things already belong to Him. Rather, it is a recognition of His worthiness to have this wealth, proved through His finished work.

Wisdom is not only vast knowledge but also the skill and discernment to use it well. Christ has all treasures of wisdom in Himself (Col. 2:3), and He has manifested it in His work of redemption (I Cor. 1:23-24). The angels extol Him for this, as well as for His strength, which speaks of raw might or force as lodged, for example, in one's arm, which is the basis for all His mighty deeds.

The angels also proclaim Christ's right to receive "honour" (Rev. 5:12). This word, derived from the idea of value or price, speaks of the esteem He deserves for His Person and work (cf. Phil. 2:9-10). Closely tied to this is the glory He deserves. Glory, which sometimes includes splendor and radiance, also speaks of majesty and renown. Christ is worthy of all these. Finally, He is worthy of blessing, of being lauded and extolled. To bless Christ is to speak well of Him, giving Him the praise He deserves.

THE RESPONSE OF ALL CREATURES

13 And every creature which is in heaven, and on the earth, and under the earth, and such as are in the sea, and all that are in them, heard I saying, Blessing, and honour, and glory, and power, be unto him that sitteth upon the throne, and unto the Lamb for ever and ever.

The chorus of praise to the Lamb that began with twenty-eight beings (Rev. 5:8-10) and spread to innumerable angels (vss. 11-12) now was taken up by "every creature" (vs. 13). It swelled from every corner of the universe—the heavens, the earth, the realms under the earth, and the sea. All creation acknowl-edged His worth (cf. Ps. 103:22; Phil. 2:10).

The fourfold doxology of "blessing, and honour, and glory, and power" (Rev. 5:13) was directed to both "him that sitteth upon the throne, and unto the Lamb." The worship originally directed to the Father (4:8-11) was now extended to His crucified and risen Son as well. And the praise voiced by all creatures went on forever and ever.

This glorious scene reminds us that our God—Father, Son, and Holy Spirit—deserves praise from all His creatures, including us. This involves the praise of both consecrated lips and consecrated lives.

—*Robert E. Wenger.*

QUESTIONS

1. In the Apostle John's vision, where had he been taken?
2. What contrasting images of Christ are given in Revelation 5?
3. What was the significance of the seven horns and seven eyes on the Lamb in John's vision?
4. Why is the slain Lamb alone qualified to open the seals on the book?
5. Who were the first to bow down and worship the Lamb?
6. What does it mean to be redeemed? How was our redemption obtained?
7. In what sense are Christians both kings and priests?
8. How are angels related to the earthly life of Jesus as well as to Christian believers?
9. What seven qualities did the angels ascribe to the Lamb?
10. What lesson does the whole creation's worship leave for us?

—*Robert E. Wenger.*

Preparing to Teach the Lesson

This week's lesson takes us to the future moment just before the judgments of the tribulation begin. The seven-sealed scroll that contains the judgments cannot be opened until Christ, the Lamb, comes forward. At His appearance, heaven explodes in worship.

TODAY'S AIM

Facts: to show that as the Lamb who gave Himself to pay for man's sin, Jesus is worthy to open the scroll and unleash the judgments of the tribulation upon the world that rejects Him.

Principle: to show that as the Lamb who was sacrificed to redeem sinful mankind, Jesus is qualified to also be our Judge if we reject Him.

Application: to show that whether we accept or reject Christ, we will one day acknowledge His worthiness as Redeemer and Judge.

INTRODUCING THE LESSON

This week's lesson is set in the context of Jesus' revelation to the Apostle John. Become familiar with the first three chapters of Revelation, where John saw Jesus in His present relationship to the church. In chapter 4, John was transported to heaven, where he saw the throne of God surrounded by the elders and the four living creatures as they worshipped Him. John was overcome with grief when he saw a scroll that could not be opened because no one was found worthy to do so.

DEVELOPING THE LESSON

Begin the class by asking students to describe what Jesus looks like. They will probably respond by describing the images they have seen in paintings. Remind them that the only descriptions of Him in the Bible come from the book of Revelation.

1. The Lamb takes the scroll (Rev. 5:6-7). As John gazed upon the incredible scene of the throne and the surrounding worshippers, he saw a Lamb that had the appearance of having been slain. The Lamb is a reference to Christ, who had been crucified as the substitute for man. The fact that the Lamb is now alive is an allusion to His resurrection.

It would be helpful to remind your students that Jesus was pictured as a lamb by Isaiah (Isa. 53:7), by John the Baptist (John 1:29), and by His fulfillment of the Old Testament sacrifices, including Passover. In each of these cases, what was in view was His death for man's sin.

In Revelation 1, John saw Jesus with a completely different appearance. The emphasis in chapter 5 is on the fact that the Lamb's death at the hands of and for the sake of humanity qualified Him to open the scrolls that will unleash God's judgment upon the world that rejected Him.

John's description also speaks of the Holy Spirit's awareness of all the earth. This pictures God's omniscient knowledge of mankind and the fact that the time was ripe for judgment.

2. The creatures and elders worship the Lamb (Rev. 5:8-10). As the Lamb took the scroll, He began to be worshipped. The four living creatures were first introduced in 4:6. Compare John's description with the seraphim described in Isaiah 6 and the cherubim in Ezekiel 10. The creatures appear to be angelic beings. With your class, compare the seraphim's worship of God in Isaiah 6:3 with the creatures' worship of the Father in Revelation 4:8 and of Christ in chapter 5.

The identity of the twenty-four elders is not clearly stated. Perhaps they represent the church that is in heaven at that time.

The song to the Lamb (Rev. 5:9-10) may provide a clue. In this song, the elders spoke of their redemption by the Lamb's blood; of their having come from every tribe, tongue, people, and nation; and of the fact that Jesus had made them kings and priests. These were redeemed people from around the world.

Their white garments suggest purity and point to the completed wedding of the Bridegroom and bride (Rev. 19:7-8). Their gold crowns suggest that they have already been judged at the judgment seat of Christ and have received their rewards. Laying their crowns before God shows acknowledgment of yieldedness.

Direct your students' attention to the song that the elders sang. It declared the Lamb's worthiness based on His redemption of the great diversity of people who will then reign with Christ on the earth. It appears that only the elders sang the song. Since angels cannot be redeemed and will never rule, the song of redemption belongs only to redeemed people.

3. The angels worship the Lamb (Rev. 5:11-12). It would be helpful to draw a rough layout of the worship scene on the board. In the center stand the throne of God and the Lamb. On four sides are the living creatures. In a wider circle surrounding God and the Lamb are the twenty-four elders. Beyond and encircling them all is a vast sea of angels.

In their praise, the angels were referring to the Lamb in the third person. The angels were therefore addressing others about the worthiness of the Lamb. They declared that He was worthy to receive worship. They acknowledged seven attributes He possesses.

4. Every creature worships the Lamb (Rev. 5:13). Next John heard the universal worship of all creation. He did not see them all, but he heard their voices coming from every direction. Every creature of heaven, the earth, under the earth, and in the sea voiced its praise. This would include lost humanity and fallen angels.

Stress to your students that this scene seems to show that even those who opposed Christ and are forever separated from Him will one day admit that His judgments on them were justified.

Even though the Lamb's opening of the scroll will unleash the tribulation judgments, all of creation will worship Him. Had this universal worship taken place before He opened the scroll, there would be no need for its judgments. John apparently saw the worship scene before and the ultimate scene after the Lamb opened the scroll. Even those judged will admit that the Lamb is justified in His judgments.

ILLUSTRATING THE LESSON

The Lamb is worthy to be praised.

JESUS DESERVES OUR PRAISE

WORTHY IS THE LAMB

CONCLUDING THE LESSON

John witnessed the magnificent scene of the Lamb being worshipped by all creation. Soon after this, the Lamb unleashed the judgments that the world deserved for rejecting His gift of salvation.

ANTICIPATING THE NEXT LESSON

The triumphal entry of Christ into Jerusalem will be our next study.

—*Carter Corbrey.*

PRACTICAL POINTS

1. Just as Christ, as the Lamb, was in the midst of the elders, so He should always be the center of our lives (Rev. 5:6).
2. In eternity, as on earth, Christ takes charge of providing for our salvation (vs. 7).
3. A believer's prayer is never unheard and will be answered in God's time and in His way (vs. 8).
4. All things become new for a sinner whom Christ redeems (vss. 9-10).
5. As we love and serve Christ, our appreciation of His worthy sacrifice grows (vss. 11-12).
6. Knowing of Christ's ultimate adoration lets us remain focused on Him while others reject Him (vs. 13).
—Anne Adams.

RESEARCH AND DISCUSSION

1. The book of Revelation uses many symbolic images. Does this make the passage confusing or more inspiring? Why do you think God used this type of wording?
2. What do "the prayers of saints" (5:8) include? Do you believe God answers all prayers? Have you ever felt He did not answer yours?
3. What does it mean to say that the Lamb is worthy? You could also say He is praiseworthy, admirable, or credible. Which of these words best describes Christ?
4. The depiction of Christ as a Lamb would have been familiar to a Jewish reader. Discuss what this means. Is there a more modern way to say this?
—Anne Adams.

ILLUSTRATED HIGH POINTS

And we shall reign on the earth

In A.D. 871, King Alfred of England was at war with the fierce Danes from across the North Sea. A legend says he disguised himself and found a job on a humble farm to avoid capture. One day the farmer's wife asked him to watch her cakes in the oven while she worked outside. King Alfred, his mind burdened by the war, forgot about the cakes, which burned to a crisp. The woman was furious with him and even slapped his face. At that moment, royal servants rushed in, fell on their knees, and greeted the laborer as their king.

"Forgive me!" cried the woman. "I didn't think of your being a king."

"Forgive me," said Alfred kindly. "I didn't think of your cakes being burnt."

Royalty, at times, is disguised and placed in ordinary settings. All who belong to Jesus will reign on earth with Him. Like King Alfred, we may be in humble circumstances. Even so, we must concentrate on our kingly charge—to live for Christ now so we can reign with Him later.

Worthy is the Lamb that was slain

Arlington National Cemetery in Washington, D.C., gives a breathtaking view of thousands of headstones, aligned in perfect rows, marking the graves of U.S. statesmen and veterans. Prominent is the Tomb of the Unknowns, memorializing unknown servicemen who gave their lives in battle. This poignant scene speaks of courage in the face of death. They gave all for our freedom, and we should remember and honor their sacrifice.

Jesus sacrificed His life not to subdue a nation but to free us from our sins. "Worthy is the Lamb that was slain" (Rev. 5:12). This should be the motto of our hearts.
—Beverly Jones.

Golden Text Illuminated

"Worthy is the Lamb that was slain to receive power, and riches, and wisdom, and strength, and honour, and glory, and blessing" (Revelation 5:12).

The fifth chapter of Revelation presents a heavenly vision of worship around the throne of God. The vision actually begins in chapter 4, when the Apostle John was invited to "come up" to heaven to see "things which must be hereafter" (vs. 1). From this point forward, the focus is on future events, as John is shown what will take place in the time immediately preceding the second coming of Christ, which is described in 19:11-21.

In his vision, John was transported to heaven to witness events there during that time of trouble on earth just prior to Christ's return. This time of trouble is often referred to as the tribulation.

There in heaven, John witnessed a dramatic scene before the throne of God: the Lamb stepped forward as the only one worthy to take a book from the hand of God and open its seals (Rev. 5:1-7). The Lamb is an obvious reference to the exalted Lord Jesus Christ. The "book" or scroll, contains the prophetic judgments that are to come upon the earth. The opening of this book unleashes the judgments of the tribulation period upon the earth (chap. 6). Jesus alone is qualified to release these judgments.

The Lamb's taking of this book ignites a period of worship in heaven, as various creatures fall down before Him in praise. The angels, as well as the beasts and twenty-four elders, worship the Lamb. The elders here probably represent the church, all those who have been translated into heaven prior to the tribulation. However, the worship that is described here is soon expanded to include every created being (Rev. 5:13).

The focus of this heavenly worship is the "Lamb that was slain." Though the resurrected, glorified Saviour is now in heaven, it is His work on earth that is remembered. It is His substitutionary death, taking the punishment for our sins, that makes Him especially worthy of heaven's praise. The heavenly worshippers declare Him "worthy . . . to receive power, and riches, and wisdom, and strength, and honour, and glory, and blessing."

Power, riches, wisdom, and strength actually are divine attributes that are here ascribed to God the Son, Jesus Christ, and He is praised for them. He is all-powerful (Rev. 1:8) and all-wise (I Cor. 1:24, 30), and He is rich in grace (Eph. 1:7; 2:7; 3:8, 16).

"Honour," "glory," and "blessing" express the worship due Him from His creation. To honor, glorify, and bless Christ is to exalt Him above all others. As the "Lamb that was slain" for our sins, He is indeed worthy of all our honor and worship.

While the symbolism we find in this chapter of Revelation can be difficult for us, the message of our golden text is crystal clear. Christ, the Lamb, will receive eternal worship, and He is worthy of it all. As believers, our eternal destiny is one of continual worship before the throne of God and the Lamb. Likewise, our lives today should be marked by continual worship of the Lamb who was slain.

—*Jarl K. Waggoner.*

Heart of the Lesson

In his book titled *The Satan Syndrome* (Zondervan), Nigel Wright wrote, "There is a fundamental sense in which evil is not something that can be made sense of. The essence of evil is that it is something which is absurd, bizarre, and irrational. It is the nature of evil to be inexplicable, an enigma and a stupidity."

Even though the essential nature of evil is absurd and inexplicable, the reality is that evil exists and dramatically damages humanity. In the midst of this unfathomable damage, the world is left wandering in unbelief, wondering whether anyone or anything is able to eradicate or even mitigate the evil that overwhelms it.

As humans desperately search for the answer to life's problem of evil, the Bible reveals the eternal answer in the Person who is worthy above all others—Jesus Christ, the Lamb of God.

1. The Lamb described (Rev. 5:6-10). John had previously shed tears of sorrow because no one could be found to open the seven-sealed scroll (vs. 4). One of the elders then comforted John by telling him that the Lion of the tribe of Judah was capable of opening the book and its seals (vs. 5). With renewed hope, John looked for the Lion; instead, he found the Lamb who appeared to have been slain.

The Lamb that John described with multiple images then took the seven-sealed scroll from His Father's hand. This symbolic action of ownership and authority prompted a worshipful response from the four living creatures and the twenty-four elders.

Many honorable earthly rulers have tried to exert just authority and overcome injustice and evil. Their best efforts are always inadequate. There will come a time, though, when a spiritual Ruler of worth will assume His inherited throne and destroy evil with His righteous reign. In preparation for the Lamb's eternal consummation of God's promise to David, Jesus' followers must vocalize their admiration to the One who alone deserves to receive their praise.

2. The Lamb exalted (Rev. 5:11-13). God's mandate to Adam and Eve to have dominion over the earth was corrupted by sin (cf. Gen. 1:28; 3:1-7). Jesus Christ, the Lamb of God, the God-Man who represents redeemed humanity, will restore God's mandate. When the Lamb took the seven-sealed scroll from His Father's hand, innumerable angels, along with the living creatures and elders and accompanied by all creation, sounded forth their praise of exclusive and matchless worth.

As I consider this quarter's final lesson in the first unit of study, several lessons of application come to mind. First, when believers contemplate the future, it is comforting and reassuring to know that God has revealed His well-defined plan, which encourages His people to subdue evil through thoughtful, devoted lives.

Second, a unique and eternal Person of immeasurable worth will fulfill God's well-defined plan. At best, life on earth can be characterized by disappointment. The Lamb of God, though, will provide His children in their future kingdom with true satisfaction.

Finally, God's people have the opportunity to express their satisfaction through praise. Today, believers express their worship of the Saviour through songs of praise and adoration. In the future, God's people will join the hosts of heaven in a glorious song of worthiness to the Lamb of God.

—*Thomas R. Chmura.*

World Missions

In many parts of the world, people think they have devised ways to take care of their sins. In some cases they bathe in "holy" rivers that are believed to wash away their sin. In other situations they kill animals to appease the wrath of the deities that could destroy them. In many such cases, an animal has to die in order for their sins to be taken away. In the Bible, we read of our Lord Jesus, who died for us so that our sins might be fully forgiven.

The Scripture tells us that Jesus "was foreordained before the foundation of the world" (I Pet. 1:20) for this sole purpose. It was in the mind of God our Father even before the world was created. It is truly good news that our loving God thinks of us long before we are even conceived in our mothers' wombs. This is simply amazing!

This week we look at the Lamb who was slain on our behalf. The Lamb of God had to give up His life for us so that we might have life.

The simple truth of Scripture is this: there was no one else who was worthy to bear the sins of mankind as Jesus did. Jesus also reminds us that He will not return until every person in the world has had some opportunity to be exposed to the saving power of the good news of His ability to save us. It is mind-boggling to think that God Almighty would leave heaven to come to earth because He loved you and me so much. Before Creation, Jesus chose to take care of our salvation (I Pet. 1:20). He died thinking of you and me.

We must not forget that gods who come down in the form of man are common to many other religions. These are sometimes known as avatars, or manifestations. But our Lord Jesus is not like these manifestations. He is God in the flesh, and He is powerful. He is the worthy Lamb of God, who did not just walk among us but came to take our place of punishment. This is very good news for the world! It means that our Lord Jesus is the only one who is worthy to save the world from sin.

We have to ask ourselves whether we truly believe this wonderful message of salvation. If we do, we should hardly be able to wait to tell someone else about this wonderful news. It is good news for the whole world. There is now a solution to the sin problem. The cure for sin has been found. The eternal sacrifice has been identified in our Lord Jesus, and He truly, utterly, and completely saves people of every tribe, tongue, and nation from the clutches of depravity and sin.

There is another dimension that we have not yet considered here. This pure "Lamb of God, which taketh away the sin of the world" (John 1:29), by virtue of His sacrifice, is now worthy to be worshipped. He is worthy to receive all honor and glory and blessing. He is the embodiment of all riches, wisdom, and strength. In a world where people are searching desperately for an answer to their need for salvation, Jesus emerges as the One who is worthy of the worship of every human being.

If we truly believe that Jesus is worthy of all worship, then we should obey Him and take this message to the ends of the earth. People in remote villages and people in urban jungles will find their deepest needs met when they encounter Jesus, the Lamb of God.

—A. Koshy Muthalaly.

The Jewish Aspect

Missionaries to the Jews make full use of the Passover Feast, or seder, to demonstrate to the Jewish people that Jesus is, indeed, "the Lamb of God, which taketh away the sin of the world" (John 1:29). But Christians attending their first Jewish seder are shocked to find that the annual Passover Feast contains almost nothing of importance from the central text on the celebration in Exodus 12. It renders the feast a dead letter.

The lamb is missing in the seder of Judaism. How could this be? Well, there is a concerted and contrived effort to remove the possibility that the Jewish layman will understand that there is a Lamb and that His sacrifice is the sole means of deliverance from sin. Consider this—there is no mention in the seder of the instruction to select the very best and healthiest lamb on the tenth day of Nisan (Exod. 12:3-5).

Next, the blood of the lamb was to be placed on the outer surfaces of the door of the home (Exod. 12:7, 21-23). How the Egyptians must have howled in derision at such an unaccustomed display! Within hours, those who had laughed uproariously mourned bitterly the loss of the firstborn in homes without the scarlet mark!

No, there is no mention of the marking of the homes in the Jewish seder. The Lord foresaw this rejection of the truth when He told Moses that the memorial of the blood on the doorposts was to be a permanent part of the Passover Feast (Exod. 12:22-24).

Surely the Jews could not fail to mention the lamb in their service! Indeed, they do. The lamb is represented by the roasted shank bone of a lamb that is on a central plate with several other items used in the service. It is called Zaroah, and it is said to represent the lamb offered not in Egypt but at the temple! This shank bone has no place in the service and is not mentioned.

The Christian Passover seder, offered in praise of the Lamb, is based on the truth of our text for today: "For thou wast slain, and hast redeemed us to God by thy blood out of every kindred, and tongue, and people, and nation" (Rev. 5:9). This is the message Jews need to hear today.

A cultural anthropologist had been raised in an Orthodox Jewish home in London, England. After completing his university education, he went to the Philippines to do anthropological studies of primitive tribes. He happened to visit a tribe that had been reached by Christian missionaries. The young scholar ridiculed Christians as forces who changed tribal customs and ceremonies. The tribal leader told the young man, "If missionaries had not come to our people, your head would be rolling in the bush right now!"

The chief then asked, "Where is your Lamb?" The young Jew had a lifetime of seder memories but knew nothing of the Lamb. It preyed on his mind until he was saved.

Satan understands well the importance of the Lamb. In Revelation 13:11 we have a description of a beast who represents the satanic empire. This beast will have two horns "like a lamb." Dr. Henry M. Morris said of this beast, "He will originally counterfeit the gentle character of Christ, . . . but his 'inspired' words will be those of Satan, the old dragon" (*The Revelation Record,* Tyndale).

"Where is your Lamb?" If Jesus is yours, share the Lord's story with someone this very day. Otherwise, there may be no tomorrow for him.

—Lyle P. Murphy.

Guiding the Superintendent

One of the ways the world measures individual status or success is by titles or degrees. Most of the marks of high achievement require the seeker to meet certain qualifications, put forth unusual effort, or pay an initial fee to obtain special honor or recognition. The most prestigious earthly attainment, however, can in no way compare to the title "Lamb of God." Any amount of hard work pales in the face of the horrendous suffering and injustice that Jesus endured to earn it.

DEVOTIONAL OUTLINE

1. Acknowledging the Lamb (Rev. 5:6-10). John had perhaps wiped away his tears after hearing from one of the elders that "the Lion of the tribe of Juda, the Root of David, hath prevailed to open the book, and to loose the seven seals thereof" (vs. 5). John must have been amazed to have looked around and seen not a Lion but a Lamb that had been slain as a result of bearing the sins of the world. Yet the Lamb lived and stood among the elders and the four beasts with perfect and absolute sovereignty, wisdom, and power in heaven and in earth.

In taking the book, Jesus authenticates Himself as God the Son, the only one the Father can trust with the daunting task of executing godly judgment on the world.

In acknowledgment of the Lamb as the ransom He so freely became in exchange for wretched sinners, it is entirely proper to bow in worship and sing sacred songs of high praise. He is the one by whose blood all of humankind has been redeemed and with whom the multitude of overcomers shall reign.

2. Praiseworthy is the sacrificial Lamb (Rev. 5:11-13). Only the body of John was exiled to the isle of Patmos; John's spirit was free. When we keep our minds on God regardless of our circumstances, He will reveal Himself to us in astonishing ways. Our God is a God of comfort, and He reassured John that his sufferings for the advancement of God's church were not in vain. God showed him the glory that the faithful saints will experience in the end.

Every believer shall join this innumerable cloud of angels around the throne of God—along with the twenty-four elders, the four beasts, and the extended universe. We shall rejoice as we honor and praise our God and our Lord and Saviour, Jesus Christ, ascribing to Him our best, though imperfect, worship. The praise of the One who sits on the throne and of the crucified Lamb will be ongoing. Can we praise and thank God enough for all that He has done for us?

AGE-GROUP EMPHASES

Children: Children seek affirmation and are often jealous when their peers receive special recognition. Teach them that Jesus is the worthy Lamb because He serves both God and man and that they too should learn to love and serve others.

Youths: Discuss some of the many facets of Jesus. He is the Son of God, the Son of Man, the Lion of the tribe of Judah, and the Lamb of God. Remind the students that no human can fully comprehend God and that being a Christian means accepting God's truths by faith.

Adults: Assure them that although they may be experiencing a difficult test or trial, they are not without hope. God will reveal His purpose and plan for this period of suffering. Encourage them to worship and praise Him in spite of their adversity.

—*Jane E. Campbell.*

Scripture Lesson Text

ZECH. 9:9 Rejoice greatly, O daughter of Zi'on; shout, O daughter of Je-ru'sa-lem: behold, thy King cometh unto thee: he *is* just, and having salvation; lowly, and riding upon an ass, and upon a colt the foal of an ass.

MATT. 21:1 And when they drew nigh unto Je-ru'sa-lem, and were come to Beth'pha-ge, unto the mount of Ol'ives, then sent Je'sus two disciples,

2 Saying unto them, Go into the village over against you, and straightway ye shall find an ass tied, and a colt with her: loose *them,* and bring *them* unto me.

3 And if any *man* say ought unto you, ye shall say, The Lord hath need of them; and straightway he will send them.

4 All this was done, that it might be fulfilled which was spoken by the prophet, saying,

5 Tell ye the daughter of Si'on, Behold, thy King cometh unto thee, meek, and sitting upon an ass, and a colt the foal of an ass.

6 And the disciples went, and did as Je'sus commanded them,

7 And brought the ass, and the colt, and put on them their clothes, and they set *him* thereon.

8 And a very great multitude spread their garments in the way; others cut down branches from the trees, and strawed *them* in the way.

9 And the multitudes that went before, and that followed, cried, saying, Ho-san'na to the son of Da'vid: Blessed *is* he that cometh in the name of the Lord; Ho-san'na in the highest.

10 And when he was come into Je-ru'sa-lem, all the city was moved, saying, Who is this?

11 And the multitude said, This is Je'sus the prophet of Naz'a-reth of Gal'i-lee.

NOTES

The Entrance of the King

Lesson: Zechariah 9:9; Matthew 21:1-11

Read: Zechariah 9:9-10; Matthew 21:1-11

TIMES: about 475 B.C.; A.D. 30   PLACES: Jerusalem; Bethphage

---

GOLDEN TEXT—"The multitudes that went before, and that followed, cried, saying, Hosanna to the son of David: Blessed is he that cometh in the name of the Lord; Hosanna in the highest" (Matthew 21:9).

Introduction

Old Testament prophecies foretold specific events in Jesus' earthly life—including the triumphal entry.

The honor paid to heroes and celebrities is familiar to us. Motorcades and parades enable us to pay tribute to presidents, soldiers, and championship teams.

Ancient societies had similar ways to recognize their heroes. The Romans sponsored processions called triumphs to honor victorious generals and emperors. Accompanied by politicians, musicians, sacrificial animals, spoils of war, and chained captives, the victor rode in a chariot with a slave holding a crown over his head. People lined the garland-decorated streets to shout their tributes.

Jesus' royal entrance into Jerusalem had some similarities to this—but many significant differences as well. This lesson explores how this event fulfilled Zechariah's prophecy.

LESSON OUTLINE

I. THE KING'S ARRIVAL FORE-TOLD—Zech. 9:9

II. THE KING'S ARRIVAL PLANNED—Matt. 21:1-5

III. THE KING'S ARRIVAL FUL-FILLED—Matt. 21:6-11

Exposition: Verse by Verse

THE KING'S ARRIVAL FORETOLD

ZECH. 9:9 Rejoice greatly, O daughter of Zion; shout, O daughter of Jerusalem: behold, thy King cometh unto thee: he is just, and having salvation; lowly, and riding upon an ass, and upon a colt the foal of an ass.

An exhortation to rejoice (Zech. 9:9a). The first eight verses of Zechariah 9 probably portray the coming invasion of Near Eastern lands by Alexander the Great, the Macedonian conqueror. His conquests of Syria, Phoenicia, and the Philistine cities are detailed. It is also accurately foretold (vs. 8) that Israel would emerge un-scathed from his campaigns.

But in Zechariah 9:9, there is an abrupt change. From the conquering Alexander on his warhorse we are introduced to a King of a different sort. The prophet called upon the "daughter of Zion" and the "daughter of Jerusalem" to rejoice and shout at the entrance of their Messiah. "Daughter" poetically personifies Zion, the original fortress David conquered, and Jerusalem, the larger city.

A description of the King (Zech. 9:9b). The prophet then gave the reason for rejoicing: Israel's King manifests a marvelous combination of attributes. First, "he is just." He has a righteous character and therefore will rule justly (cf. Isa. 11:4-5). He also has salvation. He has salvation in Himself and can therefore bestow it upon others. As the Righteous One, He died for the unrighteous so that they might be saved (cf. I Pet. 3:18).

Third, this King is "lowly, and riding upon an ass, and upon a colt the foal of an ass" (Zech. 9:9). This approach suggests both peace and humility. Unlike the prancing warhorse of Alexander, the donkey is an animal of peaceful pursuits (cf. Gen. 49:11). Although it is true that persons of distinction rode on donkeys in early times (cf. Judg. 10:4; 12:14), this did not last beyond Solomon's day, when horses were imported and used widely. Thereafter, donkeys were only menial beasts of burden.

The addition of the words "and upon a colt the foal of an ass" (Zech. 9:9) gives a further explanation of the animal to be used. "And" should be taken as "even." The Messiah would ride a young donkey—indeed, one that had never been ridden before (cf. Luke 19:30).

THE KING'S ARRIVAL PLANNED

MATT. 21:1 And when they drew nigh unto Jerusalem, and were come to Bethphage, unto the mount of Olives, then sent Jesus two disciples,

2 Saying unto them, Go into the village over against you, and straightway ye shall find an ass tied, and a colt with her: loose them, and bring them unto me.

3 And if any man say ought unto you, ye shall say, The Lord hath need of them; and straightway he will send them.

4 All this was done, that it might be fulfilled which was spoken by the prophet, saying,

5 Tell ye the daughter of Sion, Behold, thy King cometh unto thee, meek, and sitting upon an ass, and a colt the foal of an ass.

The place (Matt 21:1a). After about three years of public ministry, Jesus was traveling to Jerusalem for the last time. He had been at Jericho and was approaching Jerusalem from the southeast. The road passed through Bethany and Bethphage on the southeastern slope of the Mount of Olives before crossing that hill and descending into the Kidron Valley, just east of the city. It was at Bethphage that the drama of Jesus' triumphal entry began to unfold.

The instructions (Matt. 21:1b-3). Jesus was keenly aware of the prophecy He was about to fulfill, so He prepared for it carefully. He dispatched two unnamed disciples to "the village over against you," presumably Bethphage. He said, "[There] ye shall find an ass tied, and a colt with her: loose them, and bring them unto me."

Matthew is the only writer who mentioned the use of two animals, a mother and her colt. Some have attributed this to Matthew's misunderstanding of Zechariah's prophecy, but this was not the case. It was merely Matthew's way of stressing what Mark 11:2 and Luke 19:30 state overtly—that the colt had never been ridden before. It was therefore wise to bring the mother to walk alongside the colt to keep it calm amid the crowd while Jesus rode.

Jesus also instructed the disciples how to answer "if any man say ought unto you" (Matt. 21:3). He recognized that an owner or caretaker might question two men unknown to him untying his animals (cf. Mark 11:3; Luke 19:31). If this happened, they were to answer, simply, "The Lord hath need of them" (Matt. 21:3). This would satisfy the questioner.

Although Jesus' exact knowledge of the donkeys' location can be explained by His supernatural insight, it is more likely that He had set up a prior arrangement with the owners. And while they might not know the disciples, they would honor the pre-arranged response. They most likely were believers in Jesus as Messiah.

The significance (Matt. 21:4-5). Matthew, who wrote his Gospel with Israel especially in mind, pointed out many aspects of Jesus' earthly life as fulfillments of prophecy. Thus, he called attention here to the foretelling of this event in Zechariah 9:9. He probably omitted the words "just, and having salvation," because he wished to emphasize something else—Jesus' humble and peaceable approach to His people.

This approach was typical of His first advent as a whole. He became human, shedding the divine privileges to which He was entitled (Phil. 2:6-8). While He could have demanded that others wait upon Him, He came "to minister, and to give his life a ransom for many" (Mark 10:45). While He could have wielded the axe of judgment against sinners, He died instead so that they might escape judgment (John 3:17). He even prayed for those who put Him on the cross (Luke 23:34).

But it will not always be so. The One who rode into Jerusalem on a donkey's colt will return as a Judge, riding a white horse (Rev. 19:11-16) and sweeping away all His enemies. He came the first time as the Lowly One to reconcile men to God (II Cor. 5:18-19).

But He will return as the Mighty One, punishing those who refuse to be reconciled (Jude 1:14-15).

THE KING'S ARRIVAL FULFILLED

6 And the disciples went, and did as Jesus commanded them,

7 And brought the ass, and the colt, and put on them their clothes, and they set him thereon.

8 And a very great multitude spread their garments in the way; others cut down branches from the trees, and strawed them in the way.

9 And the multitudes that went before, and that followed, cried, saying, Hosanna to the son of David: Blessed is he that cometh in the name of the Lord; Hosanna in the highest.

10 And when he was come into Jerusalem, all the city was moved, saying, Who is this?

11 And the multitude said, This is Jesus the prophet of Nazareth of Galilee.

Jesus' procedure (Matt. 21:6-7). The two disciples "went, and did as Jesus commanded them." Matthew does not say where the animals were tied, but Mark reveals that they were near the entrance to the village where two roads came together (11:2, 4). On this occasion, as on others, the disciples saw that Jesus' words were completely reliable. They found the animals at the very place He had described.

Matthew does not record the reaction of the keepers of the animals. But both Mark and Luke reveal that the disciples were indeed asked why they were untying them. Mark calls the questioners "certain of them that stood there" (11:5), while Luke identifies them as the owners (19:33). The disciples answered as Jesus had instructed, and they were permitted to take the animals to Jesus. This reinforces the idea that Jesus had made prior arrangements with the owners.

The two disciples brought both the donkey and its colt to Jesus. Then, joined by the other ten disciples, they began to prepare for the entrance into the city. They laid their cloaks on the animals, making saddles on which Jesus could sit. They may have saddled both because they were unsure of which one Jesus would ride.

"And they set him thereon" (Matt. 21:7) reads literally, "He sat on them." "Them" does not mean that Jesus somehow straddled both donkeys; that would be absurd. Rather, it refers to the garments the disciples had placed on the colt. Thus, Jesus rode the colt, with the mother walking alongside to keep the unbroken animal steady in the crowds.

Thus, Jesus began His royal approach to Jerusalem. After giving His credentials to them for three years, this was His official presentation to Israel as their Messiah. Typically, He did not demand their loyalty; He *offered* Himself for their acceptance. But, knowing that they would reject His offer, He would on this day weep over Jerusalem (Luke 19:41-44). He would foretell its destruction, for its people did not recognize the time of God's visitation to them.

The crowd's response (Matt. 21:8-9). As Jesus and the Twelve approached the city, "a very great multitude" joined them. To understand why the crowds were so large, we must remember that this was Passover season. Jewish pilgrims from all over the Roman world were pouring into Jerusalem. Many were already approaching on this road across the Mount of Olives. At this time of year, Jerusalem's population swelled to many times its normal size.

This crowd of pilgrims was joined by another crowd coming out from the city. This second group knew of Jesus' recent miracle of raising Lazarus from the dead. When they heard that Jesus was approaching, they went out to welcome Him (John 12:17-18). So these two crowds merged and accompanied Jesus as He rode into Jerusalem. He found Himself in the midst of crowds that both preceded and followed Him (Matt. 21:9). Some knew Him well; others were encountering Him for the first time.

This multitude "spread their garments in the way" (Matt. 21:8) as a carpet for Jesus to ride on. This was a recognition of His kingship (cf. II Kings 9:13). Some also cut down tree branches and spread them out in the roadway. This should not be confused with the practice of using substantial branches to make booths for the Feast of Tabernacles. These were smaller branches over which the donkeys could walk. John specifically mentions palm branches (12:13).

Both crowds accompanying Jesus shouted praises to God: "Hosanna to the son of David: Blessed is he that cometh in the name of the Lord; Hosanna in the highest" (Matt. 21:9). These words come primarily from the messianic Psalm 118. "Hosanna" means, literally, "save now," but by Jesus' day it was also used as an acclamation, meaning something like "Hallelujah!" or "Glory to God!" In this context, it may have signified both a recognition of Jesus' eminence and a plea for His deliverance.

By referring to Jesus as "the son of David" (Matt. 21:9), the people were acknowledging His kingship. In fact, as John reports it, they cried, "Blessed is the King of Israel" (12:13). Closely connected with this was the cry "Blessed is he that cometh in the name of the Lord" (Matt. 21:9). While this in itself was not a messianic exclamation, its meaning here is clear. Mark reports it as "Blessed be the kingdom of our father David, that cometh in the name of the Lord" (11:10).

Many, of course, did not understand the spiritual aspect of His kingdom. Israel had groaned under foreign rule for hundreds of years. An interlude of independence had been cut short by the Romans, and national aspirations had been dashed. No wonder they longed for their Messiah! But many saw Him only as a political leader who could restore Israel's fortunes. Even Jesus' disciples failed to grasp the need for His suffering (cf. Matt. 16:13-28).

"Hosanna in the highest" (Matt. 21:9) could be taken two ways. As an acclamation, it would be equivalent to "Glory to God in the highest" (Luke 2:14). But as an appeal, it would mean "Save now, You who dwell in the highest heaven." In either case, the people had correctly identified Jesus with messianic deliverance. But their limited view of His kingdom left them vulnerable and confused when He later yielded to His enemies without resistance.

The city's reaction (Matt. 21:10-11). Jesus' entrance caused as much of a stir in Jerusalem as had the announcement of His birth by the wise men (cf. 2:3). "All the city was moved, saying, Who is this?" (21:10). Perhaps because Jesus had spent so little time in Judea, He was not well-known in Jerusalem. But it was also possible that "Who is this?" was a question not about His identity but about His national significance. "Who is this man who can cause this much excitement in Jerusalem?"

We know that the religious leaders were greatly disturbed by the messianic accolades He received. They asked Him to rebuke His disciples for their words (Matt. 21:16; Luke 19:39) and fumed that "the world is gone after him" (John 12:19). All Jerusalem was moved, but many were not happy about Jesus' arrival.

In response to the question of who Jesus was, those in the crowd answered, "This is Jesus the prophet of Nazareth of Galilee" (Matt. 21:11). This accurately describes His historical setting, though "prophet" seems inadequate. But the people had no other frame of reference,

and much of His Galilean ministry was prophetic in nature. Besides, Moses had foretold the coming of a great Prophet (Deut. 18:15-18), and Jesus was recognized as the fulfillment (cf. John 7:40; Acts 3:22-23; 7:37).

Of course, the reference to Nazareth and Galilee could have been a stumbling block to many, for that area had a bad reputation (John 1:46). But Galileans coming to Jerusalem wore Jesus' connection with them as a badge of honor. The pity was that even most of them failed to comprehend the true nature of His kingdom. So its consummation still awaits His second coming.

—*Robert E. Wenger.*

QUESTIONS

1. Why did Zechariah call upon Zion and Jerusalem to rejoice?
2. How does Zechariah's portrayal of Israel's King differ from his portrayal of Alexander the Great?
3. From what point did Jesus begin His royal entry into Jerusalem?
4. What roles did the two animals in Matthew's account have?
5. How will Jesus' demeanor at His second coming differ from what He displayed at the triumphal entry?
6. Why did Jesus weep over Jerusalem on this day?
7. What two crowds joined together to welcome Jesus?
8. What did the garments and branches on the road signify?
9. How do we know from the people's words that they were acclaiming Jesus as King?
10. What was the reaction in Jerusalem when Jesus arrived?

—*Robert E. Wenger.*

Preparing to Teach the Lesson

Every Old Testament prophecy that has already been fulfilled was fulfilled literally. This week we will examine one such prophecy from the book of Zechariah, as well as its fulfillment in Jesus' triumphal entry.

TODAY'S AIM

Facts: to show that Jesus fulfilled the prophecy of Zechariah 9:9.

Principle: to show that Old Testament prophecies have been fulfilled in the coming of Christ.

Application: to show that Jesus fulfilled the prophecies about the Messiah, proving He is the Messiah.

INTRODUCING THE LESSON

Since the promised coming of the Messiah is central to the purpose of the Bible, it was crucial that specific details of His coming be provided in order to identify Him correctly when He came. Zechariah provided some of those details, and Jesus clearly fulfilled them.

DEVELOPING THE LESSON

1. The King will come (Zech. 9:9). As you begin the lesson, briefly explain the nature of Bible prophecy. It will also be helpful to explain the following overview of Zechariah.

The prophecies in Zechariah 9 through 11 focus primarily on the first coming of Israel's Messiah, while chapters 12 through 14 foretell the Second Coming. The passage preceding our lesson text, 9:1-8, is usually regarded as a prophecy of the campaign of Alexander the Great through Israel in 332 B.C. While the surrounding countries were overtaken, Alexander spared Jerusalem, merely visiting the city. (For an interesting account of this, read Josephus, *Antiquities of the Jews,* 11.8.)

In great contrast to Alexander's im-posing military presence and character, Zechariah presented the Messiah entering Jerusalem as a humble King. Zechariah encouraged Jerusalem to look forward with joy to the arrival of its true King.

Stress to your students that the character of the future King would be in great contrast to that of many of the kings in Israel's past who were corrupt and unfaithful to the Lord.

Zechariah wrote that it was Israel's King who was coming. At the time of his writing, Israel had no king. When Jesus appeared on the scene, Israel's kings were of the Herodian dynasty, a line of leaders chosen or approved by Rome. Herod the Great was from Edom and was viewed by the Jews as not being qualified to be king.

The coming King would be the Righteous One (cf. Ps. 45:6-7; Isa. 11:3-5; Jer. 23:5). This future King would also bring salvation. The Hebrew word Zechariah used for salvation is *yasha,* from which the name *Yeshua* comes. This is the Hebrew name for Jesus.

Zechariah foretold that this just King would be lowly. The word "lowly" can mean "humble," as well as "afflicted" or "weak."

How would Israel be able to recognize this King when He arrived? Emphasize that God provided a physical action that would signal the Messiah-King's arrival in an unmistakable way, particularly in conjunction with all the other related prophecies (cf. Dan. 9:24-27). The coming King would arrive on a donkey.

Compare God's presentation of His King with David's presentation of Solomon as his successor (I Kings 1:28-40).

2. Hosanna to the Son of David (Matt. 21:1-11). Zechariah's prophecy was fulfilled literally when Jesus presented Himself to Jerusalem in His triumphal entry. Daniel had also prophesied of this event (Dan. 9:24-27). From the breakdown and calculations of Daniel's seventy weeks, there are those who feel that he accurately foretold, under the inspiration of the Holy Spirit, the exact day when Jesus entered Jerusalem in fulfillment of Zechariah's prophecy. While Daniel's prophecy is too complex to use in class for this lesson, it would be helpful to become familiar with it.

The parallel passages of Mark 11:1-11, Luke 19:29-44, and John 12:12-19 also describe the presentation of Jesus to Jerusalem as the King, although only Matthew recorded that the colt was tied next to its mother.

At this point it would be helpful to have a map of first-century Jerusalem and the Mount of Olives in order to show your class how Jesus' entry took place.

Bethphage was on the Mount of Olives east of Jerusalem, separated from the city by the steep Kidron Valley. One can look down upon the city from the top of the mount.

Compare the Gospel accounts, and point out how Jesus fulfilled Zechariah's prophecy. It is especially important to note that for the first time in His ministry, Jesus prepared to officially present Himself to Israel as its King.

As was his pattern, Matthew explained how Jesus fulfilled the prophecies of both Zechariah 9:9 and Isaiah 62:11. Matthew combined elements of both prophecies into one.

Once the colt was brought to Jesus, He began His journey down the Kidron Valley toward Jerusalem. The multitude of people in Jerusalem for the Passover heard that Jesus was on His way (John 12:12-13). They gathered palm branches and went to meet Him, spreading their garments and the branches on the path in front of Him (Matt. 21:8). Jesus was surrounded by the multitudes.

The word "hosanna" is Hebrew for "save now." The phrase is found in Psalm 118:25, in which the author asked God to save him. Psalm 118 was one of the Hallel Psalms (113–118), which were traditionally sung as the people ascended to Jerusalem for the Feast of Passover.

Note that the multitudes addressed Jesus as "the son of David" (Matt. 21:9). This phrase had become a term for the Messiah, as had the statement "Blessed is he that cometh in the name of the Lord." The overall picture shows that Jerusalem was welcoming its messianic King. Sadly, the brief celebration was only superficial and would not last through the week.

ILLUSTRATING THE LESSON

Jesus rode a donkey into Jerusalem, just as Zechariah prophesied.

JESUS IS KING

TRUST HIM TODAY!

CONCLUDING THE LESSON

Jesus presented Himself to Israel as its King in fulfillment of Old Testament prophecies. God's promises are true.

ANTICIPATING THE NEXT LESSON

Next week we will look at Jesus' second cleansing of the temple, which took place the day after He presented Himself as Israel's King.

—Carter Corbrey.

PRACTICAL POINTS

1. God approaches us with grace and love, not with vindictive judgment (Zech. 9:9).
2. We often experience God's plan for us in unanticipated and unexpected ways (Matt. 21:1-3).
3. Fulfilled prophecy helps us see God's presence in history as well as in our lives (vss. 4-5).
4. No task done to glorify Christ is ever small or unimportant (vss. 6-7).
5. Serving Christ is not difficult in good times; we truly show our love for Him when we do His will even in hard times (vss. 8-9).
6. When we consistently serve Christ, it enables others to recognize Him as Saviour and Lord (vss. 10-11).
—*Anne Adams.*

RESEARCH AND DISCUSSION

1. Did Christ make prior arrangements for the donkey He rode? If not, how did He know it would be available?
2. What would it have meant if Jesus had walked into Jerusalem? Have you ever felt that God intervened in any of your plans? What happened? What did you learn?
3. Do you think many in the Jerusalem crowd genuinely believed in Christ as He rode by? Which do you think is more effective for a gospel presentation—preaching to a crowd or personal witnessing?
4. Jesus was a celebrity as He entered the city. Does being famous today help a Christian serve God better? Why or why not? Discuss.
—*Anne Adams.*

ILLUSTRATED HIGH POINTS

Behold, thy King cometh

On February 16, 1861, at about 4:30 P.M., President-elect Abraham Lincoln, his wife, their two young sons, and the presidential entourage pulled into the train depot in Buffalo, New York, a stop on his inaugural tour. The visit had been advertised from Springfield, Illinois, to Washington, D.C., for weeks, and Buffalo was buzzing with anticipation. The crowds were enthusiastically cheering as the train pulled in. "Lincoln fever" had overtaken the city with an excitement that continued far into the night. Lincoln left at 5:45 the morning of February 18 after spending Sunday in Buffalo. Though Lincoln's visit would be a little over thirty-six hours long, the spectacle surrounding his arrival electrified the city.

Jesus' entrance into Jerusalem took top billing in the city. People stopped their activities to witness the King moving among His people. The King will come again—this time not riding humbly on a donkey but in triumph and power. Our anticipation of His coming should keep us excited and watchful. The King is coming—this time as the victorious King of kings.

Hosanna in the highest

A preschool teacher asked her students to name their favorite television shows. The first hand to go up was that of a precocious four-year-old. The child proceeded to name her favorite show, then her other favorite show, and finally her "best favorite" show. This little lady was not indecisive about her choices, nor was she confused about the meaning of the word "favorite." She simply found it necessary to rank her preferences in ascending order.

Jesus wants to be our "best favorite," the highest pursuit we have.
—*Beverly Jones.*

Golden Text Illuminated

"The multitudes that went before, and that followed, cried, saying, Hosanna to the son of David: Blessed is he that cometh in the name of the Lord; Hosanna in the highest" (Matthew 21:9).

At the time, Jesus' triumphal entry into Jerusalem must have seemed like the high point of His ministry on earth. He was enthusiastically welcomed like a king by multitudes of people who were there to celebrate Passover.

Traditionally, Psalms 113 to 118, known as the Hallel, were sung at Passover. So the cries of "Hosanna" and "Blessed is he that cometh in the name of the Lord," which come from Psalm 118:25-26, normally would not have been unusual. Yet the crowd specifically applied this psalm to Jesus, aware that it is "distinctly Messianic" (Hendriksen, *Exposition of the Gospel According to Matthew,* Baker). "Hosanna" means "save now," which was especially significant in light of Jesus' earthly mission (cf. Luke 19:10).

The crowd addressed Jesus by a messianic title, "the son of David," and combined this with their quotation of Psalm 118:26: "Blessed be he that cometh in the name of the Lord." The meaning cannot be missed.

Many in the crowd had come from Galilee, where they had witnessed firsthand Jesus' teaching and works. They longed for the Messiah's coming and national deliverance. When they saw Jesus mounted on a donkey and riding toward Jerusalem, their thoughts must have turned to the prophecy of Zechariah 9:9, which Matthew himself tells us was fulfilled in Jesus' actions (Matt. 21:4-5). This must have confirmed for them that Jesus was in fact the prophesied Messiah, and they rushed to publicly declare the Messiah's arrival.

The people spread garments and palm branches before Him, thus honoring Him as the King they believed Him to be. Others, coming out of the city (John 12:12-13), joined in welcoming the King of the Jews. "Hosanna in the highest" indicates that "Messiah was regarded as a gift from God, the One who dwells in the highest heaven and is worthy of the prayers and the praises of all" (Hendriksen).

There is no doubt the people were declaring Jesus as the Messiah, who had come to deliver God's people. Just a few days later, however, the crowds in Jerusalem were no longer crying "Hosanna" but rather "crucify him" (John 19:15). While we cannot know how many of those who had declared Him Messiah were also among the crowd calling for His crucifixion, it is clear that those who welcomed Him as their King had completely abandoned Him within days, for no one came to His defense.

It seems that those who cried "Hosanna," or "Save now," were looking only for salvation from political oppression and never grasped the fact that the Messiah had come to save them from their sins. While they quoted Psalm 118:25-26 in welcoming the Messiah, they failed to understand the preceding verses in that psalm: "I will praise thee: for thou hast heard me, and art become my salvation. The stone which the builders refused is become the head stone of the corner" (Ps. 118:21-22; cf. Matt. 21:42). Political freedom would mean nothing without spiritual freedom, and spiritual salvation could come only through the death of the rejected Messiah.

—*Jarl K. Waggoner.*

Heart of the Lesson

"What is my greatest spiritual desire?" For followers of Jesus Christ, this is a powerful question to ask and consider. In many instances, the question of desire will include the spiritual discipline of anticipation.

Anticipation should be a familiar concept for believers. Jesus told His followers that they should "watch" and be "ready" for His return (Matt. 24:42, 44). Peter exhorted Christians to anticipate Jesus' return (I Pet. 1:13). Jude told Christians to stay anchored in God's love as they eagerly awaited Jesus' return (Jude 1:20-21).

In this week's lesson text, we learn about anticipation fulfilled. When Jesus entered Jerusalem on a donkey, the people were confronted with royalty. Sadly, only a few committed themselves to following God's promised King.

1. Zechariah's prophecy of Israel's coming King (Zech. 9:9). Zechariah prophesied about the coming of a future Messiah-King whose character would be unique and worthy of praise. The prophetic words were directed specifically to God's people, who were commanded to rejoice and shout as victorious conquerors.

The Messiah-King would be different from all earthly rulers. First, He would come for His people and not for Himself. Second, His character would be just and humble, empowered for the purpose of gracious deliverance. Finally, His entrance would be characterized by gentle meekness instead of pomp and circumstance.

Zechariah's prophecy contained provocative power and urgency. He incited God's people to enthusiastic anticipation of their coming Messiah-King. Today, God's people should anticipate the ultimate fulfillment of Zechariah's prophecy with passionate fervor. God's creation has never been in greater need of an unselfish and others-centered King. Let us echo John's desire: "Even so, come, Lord Jesus" (Rev. 22:20).

2. Matthew's record of Jesus' triumphal entry (Matt. 21:1-11). In anticipation of His royal entrance into Jerusalem, Jesus gave His disciples specific instructions, and they immediately obeyed. With admiring multitudes preparing the entry path with outer garments and tree branches and with multitudes invoking God's blessings and shouting prayers of deliverance, Jesus entered the city.

When Jesus' royal entrance was completed, the multitudes became agitated and somewhat fearful because there was no consensus as to the identity of this Person who had just entered the city. The majority of people stated, "This is Jesus the prophet of Nazareth of Galilee" (Matt. 21:11).

This week's lesson text presents challenges to followers of Jesus Christ and to people who are struggling with spiritual realities. Jesus' triumphal entrance into Jerusalem challenges believers to lives of obedience. Jesus' command concerning a specific beast of burden may have seemed awkward, but His disciples followed through. A. W. Tozer said, "The man that believes will obey; failure to obey is convincing proof that there is not true faith present" (*Man: The Dwelling Place of God,* Wingspread Publishers).

Many people still struggle with the true identity of Jesus Christ. Some are indifferent. However, some still have hearts that are open to the truth. God's people should fervently pray that the unsaved would remain receptive to the gospel and trust Jesus as their Lord and Saviour by faith.

—*Thomas R. Chmura.*

World Missions

The visit from a king or queen or other important personality always brings a sense of excitement into any community of people. Our lesson this week talks about the coming of a King. But this King was different. The people looked forward to His coming. Every good Jew knew that a Messiah-King was coming soon. The prophets of old had talked about Him, and this message had been handed down through the generations. Every Jewish child got to hear about this King who would come.

That the King was coming was good news for the community. That the King was the Son of David whom the prophets talked about was even better news. He was sent by God Himself. In fact, the Bible tells us that He was coming "in the name of the Lord" (Matt. 21:9). This means that this King was coming as God Himself and had the characteristics of the One who sent Him. What would you do if you knew a king was coming your way? It certainly calls for preparation. It is time to get ready for royalty.

The prophets have also told us that this King is coming again. On His first visit, the common people recognized Jesus as the coming King whom the prophets had talked about, but the religious leaders brushed Him aside as yet another charlatan. The truth was that He was, indeed, the King of kings the prophetic voices had so unmistakably talked about through the ages. And these same prophets have given us warning that Jesus the King is coming to rule on His second and final visit.

Jesus is indeed the Son of David the sages talked about in the Bible. This time the King is coming as the One who will rule. The King is coming to take care of His kingdom. We have been warned of His coming, and therefore we are to be prepared to receive Him. There are still many in this world who have not yet heard about this King. We have been called to share the good news with the world around us. The entrance of this King means deliverance and salvation for His people.

The coming of King Jesus also means that there will be a just judgment. He is coming this time as the Judge of all mankind. This is unlike His first coming. The first time He came in all humility. This time He is coming in all power and glory. The Bible tells us that He will rend the skies and that the trumpets will proclaim His arrival as King of kings and Lord of lords. The news about this sudden coming of Jesus must be told to all the world so that all can be ready.

The world also needs to be told that this King will come in glory. The first time He came, the only crown that adorned His head was a crown of thorns. This time it will be a crown of gold, and all the universe will bow before Him. It will be the culmination of all of history as we know it. The same Son of David proclaimed by the prophets is the Jesus who is returning, and He is coming quickly. We need to help the world prepare for this King.

The Old Testament prophets have reminded us that we must help all people know that this King is coming again and that when He comes we all need to be ready to receive Him. He is, indeed, the promised Son of David, and He will be here again soon to receive those who have put their trust in Him.

—A. Koshy Muthalaly.

The Jewish Aspect

Our theme for today, "The Entrance of the King," takes us to that day when Jesus rode into Jerusalem for the closing episodes of His earthly ministry. The story then draws us back to the record of the foundation of the nation of Israel in the meal that marked the end of the captivity in Egypt. Both stories feature the Jews but are critically important to Christians.

The instructions for that last meal are found in Exodus 12, beginning at verse 3. God told Moses that on the tenth day of the month of Nisan, they were to "take to them every man a lamb, according to the house of their fathers, a lamb for an house." The instructions go on to say, "And ye shall keep it up until the fourteenth day of the same month: and the whole assembly of the congregation of Israel shall kill it in the evening" (vs. 6).

This lamb was to be the very best in the flock. The custom was to place this choice animal in a separate pen in order to ensure its flawless condition for the offering on the fourteenth of Nisan.

Are you thoroughly puzzled about what the story of the Passover lamb has to do with the entrance of King Jesus in the city of Jerusalem? We will clear up the mystery very shortly.

In Matthew 21:1-3 we learn that as He "drew nigh unto Jerusalem," Jesus sent two of His disciples into a village where they would find a donkey tied up with her colt. The disciples were to make a request on His behalf so that He could ride into the city. Our text does not tell us the time of day that the entry took place, but we know from Jewish custom that a day begins and ends at sunset. The entry fell on a day that included the start of the tenth day of Nisan, which is the very day that the lamb was traditionally selected for Passover.

Jesus was presented to the Israelites as "the Lamb of God, which taketh away the sin of the world" (John 1:29). He was the Lamb without spot or blemish. With no taint of sin, He was God's perfect sacrifice.

Luke tells us the donkey Jesus rode on was in exact fulfillment of Zechariah 9:9: "The whole multitude of the disciples began to rejoice and praise God with a loud voice for all the mighty works that they had seen; saying, Blessed be the King that cometh in the name of the Lord" (Luke 19:37-38). People of faith appeared to recognize the King-Messiah and praised Him with the words of Psalm 118, the traditional hymn of Passover.

There is no accounting for unbelief, for some Pharisees insisted that Jesus rebuke His disciples for the belief that Jesus was the Messiah. Jesus said that if the disciples held their peace, the very stones of the street would cry out (Luke 19:39-40).

Israel rejected the offer of the kingdom in the Person of Jesus. As He went into Jerusalem, Jesus "wept over it" (Luke 19:41). Dr. Alva J. McClain commented, "He knew that the acclamation of the fickle multitude would within a few hours be turned into a savage demand for his death" (*The Greatness of the Kingdom*, BMH Books). Sure enough, they would soon cry out, "Crucify him, crucify him" (Luke 23:21); that day was Nisan 14, when the Passover lamb removed from the pen of security had to be slain!

Nothing bespeaks the tragic Lamb story as does the fact that no lamb has a place in the Jewish Passover Feast today. Oh, the lamb is there in the shank bone, but it has no place in the ceremony. There is no lamb whose blood spared the firstborn.

—Lyle P. Murphy.

Guiding the Superintendent

Human beings are naturally amazed when a prediction comes true, but it is spiritually uplifting when the Bible leads us from the origin of a prophecy to its fulfillment. This week's lesson illustrates how Holy Spirit-inspired New Testament writers, writing about what they had seen and heard, validated many of the Old Testament prophecies.

DEVOTIONAL OUTLINE

1. Jesus' royal entry foretold (Zech. 9:9). The nation of Israel suffered many years of violent attacks from their enemies. In addition to the ravages of war, internal conflict divided Israel, for not all their leaders were men of God. Despite this, Zechariah's message to Israel was to rejoice and to rejoice exceedingly that their Messiah would soon come to save His people from total destruction.

2. Jesus' royal entry fulfilled (Matt. 21:1-5). The Gospel of Matthew to the Jews presents Jesus as Israel's messianic King. In this account, we see the omniscient Jesus setting the stage for His triumphant arrival in Jerusalem. All things had been made ready from the foundation of the world. Jesus assigned two disciples to fetch the beast of burden on which He would ride gloriously into the city. The disciples needed only to follow Christ's instructions.

Anyone who desires a personal relationship with Christ must prepare his heart. In his sermon on Pentecost, Peter said, "Repent, and be baptized every one of you in the name of Jesus Christ for the remission of sins, and ye shall receive the gift of the Holy Ghost" (Acts 2:38). Every believer who trusts Jesus as his Saviour can be useful to the kingdom. We have but to hear, receive, and obey God's Word. Let every heart that awaits the return of our Lord and Saviour rejoice.

3. Jesus' royal entry facilitated (Matt. 21:6-8). When we do not understand Christ's ways, we must simply follow His commands, just as the disciples did. Upon returning with the colt, the disciples positioned Jesus on it as royalty. A great number accompanied Him with palm branches—the sign of victory, peace, and joy. He did not come as the avenging king who Israel had hoped would come to set up a kingdom to overthrow Roman domination. Yet they ascribed to Him the honor and adoration due a sovereign King.

4. Jesus the Deliverer (Matt. 21:9-11). Cries for deliverance were heard as the crowd moved with Jesus into Jerusalem. Israel touted Him as the fulfillment of the Davidic covenant, having all authority, and as Ruler of God's people forever.

The name Jesus had long been noised about; yet there were those who did not know Him. For centuries God's church has been proclaiming the good news about Jesus, who was born in Bethlehem and raised in Nazareth of Galilee. Yet some still ask the question "Who is this?" (Matt. 21:10).

AGE-GROUP EMPHASES

Children: Teach them the importance of obeying God's Word even if they do not fully know all that His Word commands.

Youths: Happiness matters to young people. Explain that true joy can be theirs if they trust Christ as their Saviour and Lord.

Adults: Some adults in your Sunday school may be unsaved. Try to identify them and lead them to Christ.

—*Jane E. Campbell.*

Scripture Lesson Text

ISA. 56:6 Also the sons of the stranger, that join themselves to the LORD, to serve him, and to love the name of the LORD, to be his servants, every one that keepeth the sabbath from polluting it, and taketh hold of my covenant;

7 Even them will I bring to my holy mountain, and make them joyful in my house of prayer: their burnt offerings and their sacrifices *shall be* **accepted upon mine altar; for mine house shall be called an house of prayer for all people.**

JER. 7:9 Will ye steal, murder, and commit adultery, and swear falsely, and burn incense unto Ba'al, and walk after other gods whom ye know not;

10 And come and stand before me in this house, which is called by my name, and say, We are delivered to do all these abominations?

11 Is this house, which is called by my name, become a den of robbers in your eyes? Behold, even I have seen *it,* saith the LORD.

MARK 11:15 And they come to Je-ru'sa-lem: and Je'sus went into the temple, and began to cast out them that sold and bought in the temple, and overthrew the tables of the moneychangers, and the seats of them that sold doves;

16 And would not suffer that any man should carry *any* vessel through the temple.

17 And he taught, saying unto them, Is it not written, My house shall be called of all nations the house of prayer? but ye have made it a den of thieves.

18 And the scribes and chief priests heard *it,* and sought how they might destroy him: for they feared him, because all the people was astonished at his doctrine.

19 And when even was come, he went out of the city.

NOTES

The Cleansing of the Temple

Lesson: Isaiah 56:6-7; Jeremiah 7:9-11; Mark 11:15-19

Read: Isaiah 56:6-8; Jeremiah 7:8-15; Mark 11:15-19

TIMES: between 701 and 681 B.C.; probably 609 B.C.; A.D. 30

PLACES: Jerusalem; Jerusalem; Jerusalem

GOLDEN TEXT—"Is this house, which is called by my name, become a den of robbers in your eyes? Behold, even I have seen it, saith the Lord" (Jeremiah 7:11).

Introduction

After Greek city-states had defeated the Persians in 478 B.C., they formed the Delian League, a confederation for defense against possible further Persian attacks. But before long, Athens began to dominate the League and soon converted it into its own empire of several hundred satellite states.

How quickly worthy projects can be corrupted to achieve unworthy goals! A charter school is established to provide quality education, but after a few years its principal is arrested for stealing its funds. A children's playground becomes a hangout for neighborhood drug dealers.

A biblical example of this tendency is the temple in Jerusalem. Both Solomon's temple and the postexilic temple were built for God's worship. But they became prostituted to purposes that disgraced His name. That is what necessitated Jesus' bold action in this week's lesson.

LESSON OUTLINE

I. THE HOUSE OF PRAYER PROVIDED—Isa. 56:6-7

II. THE HOUSE OF PRAYER POLLUTED—Jer. 7:9-11

III. THE HOUSE OF PRAYER PURGED—Mark 11:15-19

Exposition: Verse by Verse

THE HOUSE OF PRAYER PROVIDED

ISA. 56:6 Also the sons of the stranger, that join themselves to the LORD, to serve him, and to love the name of the LORD, to be his servants, every one that keepeth the sabbath from polluting it, and taketh hold of my covenant;

7 Even them will I bring to my holy mountain, and make them joyful in my house of prayer: their burnt offerings and their sacrifices shall be accepted upon mine altar; for mine house shall be called an house of prayer for all people.

The nature of the worshippers (Isa. 56:6).

This passage is part of a nine-chapter division of Isaiah (chaps. 49—57) that stresses the ministry of the Messiah, seen as the Suffering Servant. In the immediate context (chaps. 54—57), He is seen bringing salvation to both Jews and Gentiles. Chapter 56 focuses on the extension of His spiritual blessings to those previously excluded from Israel's covenant community. To some extent, this is being fulfilled today, though Isaiah's vision carries him forward to the millennium.

At the outset, the Lord announced that His salvation is "near to come" (Isa. 56:1) and that it will be available to those previously left out, eunuchs (vss. 3-5) and foreign proselytes (vss. 6-8). According to the law, eunuchs and certain foreigners were forbidden to worship in the assembly of Israel (Deut. 23:1-8). That will be changed so that all peoples have equal access to the Lord.

Our immediate text deals with "the sons of the stranger" (Isa. 56:6). These are people who have joined themselves to the Lord "to serve him." This expression is used of the service of priests and Levites, and here it signifies that these foreigners will minister to Him as fully as the regularly appointed servants. They also "love the name of the Lord," having taken Him as their own personal God (cf. 2:2-3).

These strangers are also seen as keeping the Sabbath and taking hold of God's covenant (Isa. 56:6). Sabbath keeping is seen in this passage as an evidence of respect for God's covenant in general (cf. vss. 2, 4). From Israel's beginning, the Sabbath was a key sign of their covenant with God (cf. Exod. 31:12-17; Ezek. 20:12-20). Here again it is taken as evidence that foreigners fully identify themselves with Him.

The fullness of their worship (Isa. 56:7).

The Lord takes the initiative and promises, "Them will I bring to my holy mountain." "Them" refers to the non-Israelite worshippers of verse 6. These will be in addition to the "outcasts of Israel" (vs. 8), whom He will regather. To some extent, this is being fulfilled now (cf. Rom. 10:12-13; Eph. 2:13-18); but by referring to "my holy mountain" (Isa. 56:7), Isaiah also foresaw worship in the millennial temple in Jerusalem (cf. Isa. 2:2; 11:9; 65:25; Jer. 3:17).

Having brought peoples of all nations to Himself, the Lord will "make them joyful in [His] house of prayer" (Isa. 56:7), for it will be "an house of prayer for all people." This was not originally true of Solomon's temple, though he prayed that Israel's testimony might draw foreigners to Jerusalem to "pray toward this house" (I Kings 8:42). Nor did the second temple welcome strangers unconditionally, though it included the Court of the Gentiles.

But Christ's death has demolished national barriers, and all believers worship God on an equal footing (cf. Gal. 3:28; Col. 3:11). So too, in the future kingdom the worship of all true believers will be equally acceptable. Scholars differ on whether "burnt offerings" and "sacrifices" on an "altar" (Isa. 56:7) should be taken literally. Some believe animal sacrifices will be restored in the millennium; others prefer to take these terms as symbols of worship in general. In either case, all will have equal access to God.

THE HOUSE OF PRAYER POLLUTED

JER. 7:9 Will ye steal, murder, and commit adultery, and swear falsely, and burn incense unto Baal, and walk after other gods whom ye know not;

10 And come and stand before me in this house, which is called by my name, and say, We are delivered to do all these abominations?

11 Is this house, which is called

by my name, become a den of robbers in your eyes? Behold, even I have seen it, saith the LORD.

The hypocrisy of the worshippers (Jer. 7:9-10). Our second text comes from a section of Jeremiah (chaps. 7—10) commonly called his "temple address." God commanded him to stand before the temple and proclaim coming judgment because of Judah's false religion (7:1-2). It should probably be identified with the opposition to Jeremiah recorded in chapter 26. If so, this address was given at the outset of the ungodly reign of Jehoiakim (II Chron. 36:5, 8).

Jeremiah especially denounced the delusion that the presence of the temple would keep Judah from harm (Jer. 7:4). False prophets were using the temple as a kind of talisman, or object of faith, saying that because of its very presence in Jerusalem, Judah could repel any attack. Jeremiah told the people frankly that godly deeds, not ceremonial observances in a sanctuary, would please God and preserve them (vss. 3-7).

As it was, the people's conduct fell far short of their profession. Their personal behavior included stealing, murder, adultery, and falsehood—all violations of the Decalogue (Jer. 7:9). In addition, said Jeremiah, they burned incense to Baal and followed other gods, ones they had never known. They may have kept up the appearance of worshipping Yahweh, but their hearts were with the false deities they had imported.

What compounded their guilt was the fact that they practiced all these sins while practicing outward worship at the temple (Jer. 7:10). The temple was their "lucky charm." They could go there and claim immunity from attack, claiming, "We are delivered to do all these abominations." Their sacrifices were unrelated to the lives they lived.

Too often, professing Christians follow the same pattern. Going to their house of worship once a week is an exercise totally divorced from their daily behavior. They go because they believe it will gain them God's favor and ward off disasters. They then return home to cheat, lie, lust, lose their temper, steal, and speak evil. God owes them nothing for their church attendance, for their hearts are far from Him.

The defilement of the temple (Jer. 7:11). Israel's temple was no ordinary building. The Lord could say it was "called by my name" (7:10, 14, 30; 32:34). This was Solomon's intent when he built it (cf. I Kings 8:12-21). While he knew the Lord could not be contained in a house (vs. 27), he saw it as His dwelling among His people to which they could direct their prayers (vss. 29-30).

But the temple had been prostituted to unspeakable corruption. Its misuse by Athaliah's sons had necessitated extensive repairs by Joash (II Chron. 24:7). Ahaz later replaced the altar of sacrifice with one of Assyrian design (II Kings 16:10-14) and had the temple doors closed (II Chron. 28:24). After Hezekiah reopened them and restored proper worship (29:17-19), Manasseh desecrated the house with altars to false deities (33:4-5). Josiah once again cleansed it (34:3-4), but now it was polluted again (Jer. 7:30).

But it was not so much the physical pollution of the premises but the improper motives of the worshippers that the Lord now denounced. It had become to them like "a den of robbers" (Jer. 7:11). Robbers sought temporary refuge in mountain caves until they had planned their next raid. So too these hypocrites treated this holy place as an asylum from God's judgment before they headed back into their sinful lives.

The Lord declared, however, that He had seen it all. He sees actions, reads motives, and judges what He sees. He hinted at this judgment in the next verse, where He urged the people to remember what He did to Shiloh, Israel's first-century place of worship.

There Israel revered the ark of the covenant as Jeremiah's generation revered the temple, even expecting it to bring victory in battle. But its wicked priests were killed, and the ark was taken away (I Sam. 4).

THE HOUSE OF PRAYER PURGED

MARK 11:15 And they come to Jerusalem: and Jesus went into the temple, and began to cast out them that sold and bought in the temple, and overthrew the tables of the moneychangers, and the seats of them that sold doves;

16 And would not suffer that any man should carry any vessel through the temple.

17 And he taught, saying unto them, Is it not written, My house shall be called of all nations the house of prayer? but ye have made it a den of thieves.

18 And the scribes and chief priests heard it, and sought how they might destroy him: for they feared him, because all the people was astonished at his doctrine.

19 And when even was come, he went out of the city.

Jesus' action (Mark 11:15-16). The cleansing of the temple was Jesus' first act after He entered Jerusalem in apparent triumph. Upon arriving, He went into the temple to look around; but since it was late, He retired to Bethany for the night (vs. 11). When He came back the next morning, He acted decisively to purge the corruption He found there (vs. 15). This is the second time He cleansed the temple; the first time, at the beginning of His ministry, is recorded in John 2:13-22.

Jesus "began to cast out them that sold and bought in the temple, and overthrew the tables of the moneychangers, and the seats of them that sold doves" (Mark 11:15). In the large outer Court of the Gentiles, the high priest had authorized a market to sell items needed for temple sacrifices. It was easier for pilgrims coming to festivals from a distance to buy their sacrificial animals there than to bring them with them. Other items, such as oil, salt, and wine, also were sold there.

The money changers were present because the annual temple tax had to be paid in Tyrian currency. Other transactions could be handled more conveniently in this coinage as well. So pilgrims arriving with Greek or normal Roman money had to exchange it. Exorbitant rates were often charged for this service, and the prices for sacrificial items were often inflated as well.

Though these economic activities were essential to worship in the temple, they did not have to be conducted within the temple itself. It was primarily to this practice that Jesus objected. He put a stop to these transactions, overturning the tables and seats of money changers and vendors and ordering them all out of the temple.

In addition, He "would not suffer that any man should carry any vessel through the temple" (Mark 11:16). This refers not to those who came to worship but to those who simply walked through the temple area as a shortcut from one part of the city to another. Such a practice reveals how this holy place had been profaned. It was no longer revered as God's dwelling; it was merely another building with a courtyard to be crossed. Jesus vehemently objected to this attitude.

Jesus' teaching (Mark 11:17). Jesus did not hide the reason for His actions. He applied two Old Testament texts we have already considered to the situation before Him. The first was Isaiah 56:7: "Mine house shall be called an house of prayer for all people." In keeping with the original meaning, it can be translated, "My house shall be called a house of prayer for all nations." Isaiah had foreseen that non-

Jews would be allowed to worship in the temple, and by Jesus' day some were doing so (cf. John 12:20).

But although Gentiles were permitted to worship in the outer court of the temple, it had now been appropriated for commercial use. And even if some space for worship yet remained, the atmosphere was anything but conducive to it. The sounds of haggling and of bleating animals, accompanied by the smells of a livestock market, deterred any attempt at worship. The Jewish religious leaders were effectively barring Gentiles from the worship that Scripture had promised them.

Jesus' second quotation, "But ye have made it a den of thieves" (Mark 11:17), is taken from Jeremiah 7:11. As already noted, in its original context, this meant that people were treating the temple as robbers used their hideout—as a refuge between raids. Here the connotation is somewhat different and probably twofold. First, the vendors and money changers were engaging in fraud and dishonesty in their transactions. Second, they were robbing Gentiles of the opportunity to worship the true God.

The reaction (Mark 11:18-19). In purging the temple, Jesus was asserting His messianic authority (cf. Mal. 3:1-3) and overruling the authority of the priesthood. They would eventually challenge Him on this (Mark 11:27-28), but for now they kept silent and instead "sought how they might destroy him" (vs. 18). Their murderous plotting was born of fear; if He led a popular uprising, their power would be broken permanently.

But they knew they could not arrest Him publicly; that would merely inflame the crowds, who were "astonished at his doctrine" (Mark 11:18). The verb for "astonished" is especially vivid, indicating that they were stricken out of their senses with amazement. They could hardly believe anyone would do what Jesus had just done. And the teaching that supported it made perfect sense.

Thus, the stage was set for the final confrontation. Jesus, with the huge Passover crowd temporarily behind Him, had challenged the religious establishment. It was certain that they would eventually strike back. But for now, they did not lay hands on Jesus. When evening came on, He and His disciples left the city. Most likely He returned to Bethany (cf. Mark 11:11; Luke 21:37).

Jesus' zeal for His Father's house of prayer led Him to purify it for true worshippers. How tragic that those who were religious leaders in Israel did not learn the lesson He intended!
—*Robert E. Wenger.*

QUESTIONS

1. What previously excluded persons did Isaiah foresee participating in temple worship?

2. How did the death of Christ affect the Gentiles' access to God?

3. Why did Jeremiah's countrymen think they could suffer no harm?

4. Did Jeremiah's contemporaries' temple worship affect their behavior? Explain.

5. In what ways had Solomon's temple been defiled?

6. Why had a market been set up in the temple in Jesus' day?

7. What did Jesus do to end this market? Why?

8. How were Gentiles hindered from temple worship in Jesus' day?

9. In what sense had the Jewish leaders of Jesus' time made the temple a "den of thieves" (Mark 11:17)?

10. How did the leaders react to Jesus' purification of the temple?
—*Robert E. Wenger.*

Preparing to Teach the Lesson

In our previous lesson we saw how Jesus fulfilled prophecy by presenting Himself as Israel's King in His triumphal entry.

TODAY'S AIM

Facts: to look at the details of Jesus' cleansing of the temple.

Principle: to show that God disapproves of those who keep others from coming to Him.

Application: to show that God wants to give believing Gentiles access to Himself.

INTRODUCING THE LESSON

God intended the nation of Israel to be a holy people through whom He would reach the world. His desire was for people from outside Israel to come to Him. For this reason, the temple contained a courtyard for the use of believing Gentiles. However, in Jesus' final week of ministry, it was necessary for Him to drive out those who had converted this courtyard into a corrupt marketplace.

DEVELOPING THE LESSON

1. A place for Gentiles (Isa. 56:6-7). God promised to welcome those foreigners who truly trusted in Him. He would give them a place within His house and within His walls. He would also give them a better and an everlasting name, and He promised never to cut them off.

Point out to your students the threefold evidence of a foreigner's allegiance to the Lord.

First, the foreigner would serve the Lord. His service to the Lord would be intentional and enthusiastic.

Second, the believing foreigner would "love the name of the Lord" (Isa. 56:6). He would have a heartfelt desire for God's presence and a genuine inner yearning to be associated with Him.

Third, the foreigner would be available and obedient in serving the Lord.

Such a foreigner would live according to God's righteous standards as He had revealed them. He would also affirm God's eternal covenant with Israel. He would embrace the Lord, understanding that God had made a place for him even though he was a foreigner.

God promised to bring this former stranger into His "holy mountain," or Jerusalem, and would "make [him] joyful in [His] house of prayer" (Isa. 56:7). The believing foreigner would have an acceptable place to worship in the temple.

In his prayer dedicating the first temple, Solomon included the provision for believing Gentiles to come and worship (I Kings 8:41-43).

2. A den of thieves (Jer. 7:9-11). Point out to your class that about one hundred years had passed between Isaiah's message and this one from Jeremiah.

As Babylon was on the verge of destroying Jerusalem, the leaders and people of Judah comforted themselves with the false belief that the temple's presence guaranteed the city's safety. However, as God had revealed to Ezekiel, the temple had become polluted with false worship and idols.

God instructed Jeremiah to stand at the entrance to the temple and warn the people to repent, even though such an attempt was futile (Jer. 7:2-3). Jeremiah asked the people how they could sin so grievously and at the same time come to the temple, thus making God's house an accomplice in their iniquity (vss. 9-10). His list of six sins the people were guilty of actually involved seven of the commandments. The fact that they excused their sin with the presence of the temple demonstrated that they took His name in vain. In essence, they had made the house of God into a den of thieves.

Discuss how a person's true spiritual condition, not the exterior appearances of religion, is what is important.

3. A need for cleansing (Mark 11:15-19). Use a large drawing of the second temple (Herod's) as a visual aid. Show your students the Court of the Gentiles, the large courtyard that surrounded the temple. This was where the merchants had set up their shops. In placing the marketplace in the area designated for Gentiles, the Jewish leaders had effectively edged them out of the opportunity to worship properly.

The high priest was responsible for whatever took place in the temple. He not only had to approve these arrangements, but he also would be putting himself in a position to profit financially. At the time of the second cleansing of the temple, Caiaphas was the high priest; but his father-in-law, Annas, the former high priest, seemed to be the power behind the scenes.

On the previous day, after arriving to the shouts of the welcoming multitudes, Jesus had entered the temple and surveyed the scene. Since it was already late, He left and spent the night in Bethany (Mark 11:11).

Upon His return the next day, Jesus went immediately to the temple and began to chase out the merchants and money changers. On the surface, it would seem that these men were performing a convenient service. Travelers could purchase animals that had been approved by the priests for the sacrifices, and currency could be exchanged for temple money to pay the temple tax. However, there were serious issues of corruption. Among those who profited were the priests and religious leaders, including the high priest.

Upon entering the temple, Jesus drove out the merchants and the money changers, as well as those who were buying. He also put a stop to people using the courtyard as a shortcut.

Once Jesus had driven out the abusers, He stayed in the area and taught about the true purposes of the temple (Mark 11:17), possibly basing His teaching on Isaiah 56 and Jeremiah 7.

Discuss how Jesus established His authority over the temple, the high priest, and the religious leaders. Point out that by staying and teaching, He guarded against the return of the merchants. Discuss the reaction of the religious leaders and the people.

ILLUSTRATING THE LESSON

Sinful people and sinful actions can keep people away from the Lord.

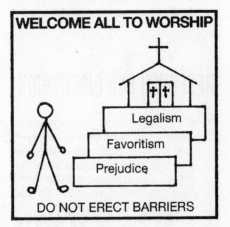

CONCLUDING THE LESSON

Corrupt people in important positions often interfere with the true work of God. There are times when the bold believer must step forward and expose sin and sinful actions in order to correct wrongs.

ANTICIPATING THE NEXT LESSON

In the next lesson we will study how Jesus, the righteous King and Branch of David, faced scourging and shame in the moments before He was led away to be crucified.

—*Carter Corbrey.*

PRACTICAL POINTS

1. God freely and fully accepts everyone who trusts in Him (Isa. 56:6-7).
2. Only the arrogant expect God to overlook their unconfessed sins (Jer. 7:9-11).
3. We should never hesitate to firmly assert our faith (Mark 11:15-16).
4. Focusing on God through worshipping Him helps us realize and appreciate all He does for us (vs. 17).
5. Those who oppose Christ's truth do not accept Him as their Lord (vs. 18).
6. When we serve God, it requires constant attention—even when we think we are not observed (vs. 19).
   —Anne Adams.

RESEARCH AND DISCUSSION

1. Why does God accept non-Jews—"the sons of the stranger" (Isa. 56:6)—when previously He was mostly concerned with the Jews? Do strangers often visit your church? If so, how do you help them feel welcome?
2. Is it right for a church or a ministry to profit as it serves God? Is it greedy or is it permissible to profit? Discuss.
3. Which do you think Jesus found more objectionable—the temple merchants' excessive profits or the chaotic commercial atmosphere they brought to the temple?
4. Why was Jesus so forceful with the temple merchants? Is such an aggressive response ever appropriate today? If so, when? If you know of a current example, discuss it and what it accomplishes.
   —Anne Adams.

ILLUSTRATED HIGH POINTS

Called by my name

When I think about my teenage years, I recall the many times I would leave the house for a date or for an outing with my friends. My father always whispered in my ear: "Remember who you are." I carried his name, and he and Mom had expectations of me to make correct decisions, even when out of their sight.

God, our Heavenly Father, called His temple by His name. He placed His standards on the people who went to worship there. He expected them to remember who they were—worshippers who were to regard the temple as the house of prayer.

We too are called by His name, and we should remember who we are by our lifestyle of prayer and obedience to Him.

Behold, even I have seen it

Most of us have probably heard the expression "He has eyes in the back of his head." This refers to a teacher, a parent, or some other adult who always seems to see what children are doing and catches them in their mischief. Though puzzling to children, adults know that the "eyes" are hindsight, resulting from having once been children and prone to similar behaviors themselves.

Children may think adults are all-knowing, but we know there is only one who knows all—our God, the Creator of the universe. As Jesus saw the wickedness taking place in His Father's temple, He watched not as one who had experienced sin but as the Holy One, who would not tolerate evil. The supposed worshippers were really thieves and robbers. God still sees. He is looking for a people who will wholeheartedly pursue Him in all His perfection.
—Beverly Jones.

Golden Text Illuminated

"Is this house, which is called by my name, become a den of robbers in your eyes? Behold, even I have seen it, saith the Lord" (Jeremiah 7:11).

Jeremiah had a most unenviable task. He was called to prophesy to a sinful and belligerent nation. In fact, even as the Lord called Jeremiah to his ministry, He gave His prophet no hope that his message would be accepted. He would face opposition from every corner of society (Jer. 1:17-19). Even his own village (11:21) and his own family (12:6) would turn against him. Yet through all the persecution and discouragement he faced in approximately fifty years of ministry, Jeremiah remained faithful in calling the nation of Judah to repentance.

The people Jeremiah confronted had turned from the Lord. Many followed false gods of the nations. Others simply went about their lives with no thought of God, pursuing their own pleasures. Most held to their belief in the Lord, but it was little more than a superstition that focused on the glorious temple Solomon had built.

Jeremiah boldly condemned the attitude of the people, who committed every kind of despicable act and yet came to the temple—as if the mere act of acknowledging God was all that was required of them (Jer. 7:9-10). Perhaps because God had miraculously delivered them from the Assyrians some years before (II Kings 19), they believed He would continue to protect them, no matter what they did.

Jeremiah's message from the Lord first reminded the people that "this house," the temple, was "called" by the Lord's name. It was uniquely identified with their God. It was there that God's presence on earth was manifested. The temple was a special place, and the people sensed that. However, it did not alter the way they lived. They wanted the Lord to protect them, not change them. They wanted His blessing, but otherwise they wanted Him to let them do as they pleased.

The hypocrisy of the people was intolerable. The gravity of their sin was highlighted by the fact that they had taken the place that bore the name of the Holy One and turned it into a "den of robbers." This does not suggest that robbery actually took place in the temple. A "den" is a place of refuge, not a place where robbers commit their crimes. But the very fact that those who engaged in various evils came to the temple, not in repentance, but as if nothing were wrong, transformed the temple into a "hangout of criminals" (Jensen, *Jeremiah and Lamentations*, Moody).

Jeremiah assured these people that the Lord saw it all. He was not blind to their evil, and the temple would not protect them from His wrath. Indeed, it did not. Within Jeremiah's lifetime, the temple was destroyed, and the Babylonians devastated Judah and carted the people off into exile.

Jesus quoted this verse when He found the same attitudes present among the people of His day (Matt. 21:13; Mark 11:17; Luke 19:46). Sadly, we find the very same attitudes among many professing Christians today. Let us beware that we do not attend church in the belief that it will provide a "balance" for the sins in our lives and protect us from the consequences of such sins. The Lord sees it all.

—Jarl K. Waggoner.

Heart of the Lesson

"A certain congregation was about to erect a new church edifice. The building committee, in consecutive meetings passed the following resolutions:

1. We shall build a new church building.

2. The new building is to be located on the same site as the old one.

3. The material in the old building is to be used to build the new one.

4. We shall continue to use the old building until the new one is completed" (www.sermonillustrations.com).

This humorous illustration reminds us of how difficult it is for people to let go of things they are sentimental about. In some instances, though, a deep longing for the past can be beneficial. In this week's lesson text, Jesus dramatically reminded people of the essential character of His house—prayer!

1. The Lord's house and strangers (Isa. 56:6-7). Isaiah had revealed God's will about eunuchs who served in the Lord's house (vss. 4-5). He then spoke of non-Jews who determined to worship, minister, and love the Lord with committed servant hearts. They would have access to the temple precincts, where they could freely pray and worship.

God-fearing non-Jews would experience joy in the house of the Lord. When non-Jews worshipped the Lord by offering burnt offerings and sacrifices, God would accept their offerings. In every situation, His house would be a place devoted to prayer.

Today, God dwells in the hearts of His people by His Spirit. But God's people still come to worship Him in buildings. In our so-called progressive society, church buildings should remain consistently devoted to two spiritual principles: prayer and worship.

2. The Lord's house and His people (Jer. 7:9-11). Jeremiah was responsible for declaring God's words to His people. God was indignant about the blatant spiritual hypocrisy that had ensnared His people. God used Jeremiah to tell His people that He was perfectly aware that they were using His house to justify their ungodly lifestyles. In God's sight, this blatant, wicked hypocrisy was tantamount to spiritual thievery that infected the character of His house.

One of the primary excuses nonbelievers give for their unwillingness to believe in Jesus Christ is the hypocrisy of God's people. Although everyone will eventually give an account of their unbelief, the acknowledgment of hypocrisy is sadly correct. God's people must repent and demonstrate by their lives a consistency that will attract enslaved sinners to the eternal freedom of God's salvation by grace through faith.

3. The Lord's house and the money changers (Mark 11:15-19). Jesus Christ traveled to Jerusalem and entered the temple. He discovered people with monetary motives filling the courts of the temple. Following His expulsion of the money changers, the Lord taught about the essence of His house—prayer.

When they heard Jesus teach, His listeners were astonished and amazed. The chief priests and scribes took notice of the listeners' reaction. Their fear compelled them to consider how to bring about Jesus' death.

Many spiritual communities are struggling with finances. In some instances, God's people have resorted to fund-raising events within the confines of the church building. Without being legalistic, we need to be careful not to diminish and compromise the essential character of God's house—prayer!

—Thomas R. Chmura.

World Missions

A tragic reality in the life of the church has been the continual tendency toward segregation according to race or nationality. Some have claimed that Sunday morning worship is the most segregated time of the week! How true and painful that statement is! With few exceptions, this still rings true today despite all the biblical teachings of Christian unity and quality. It also brings home the reality that the missionary task begins at home, in our churches, and where we live.

The power of the gospel message lies in the way it can transform the individual after Jesus Christ has taken residence in his life. It changes the person from within. Our lesson this week focuses on Jesus' cleansing of the temple, the central place for religious activity in His time on earth. The people of God had lost their power because they had lost their focus. They were taking their faith and turning it into something secular and for profit.

The Bible reminds us that the message of the gospel must start with the house of God. As Christians, we will be judged by what we have done with the powerful gospel message that was turned over to us for safekeeping and sharing with others around us. On October 28, 2009, Elesha Coffman reported such a transformation, stating, "Last weekend, white and black Methodist congregations in Philadelphia worshiped together for the first time in more than 200 years." Such a report is music to our Lord's ears.

True transformation within the church, the body of believers, validates the truth of the gospel and shows the power of the gospel message. This is the message that we must take to the ends of the world.

Jesus' death cannot be in vain, and it is the church that must prove to the world that His gospel truly works. If we can show the world that Jesus is worth believing in, then His death will not be in vain. We must carry forth the gospel message that the prophets foretold throughout the ages.

We cannot forget that many people do not believe in the gospel message because we Christians have not been faithful. It is time for the church to clean itself from within. When we begin to show forth the power of transformation that comes from having Jesus residing within, people will sit up and take notice. When Jesus walked this earth, people were astonished at Him and His life. "What manner of man is this, that even the wind and the sea obey him?" (Mark 4:41), they said. "Never man spake like this man" (John 7:46).

Jesus attracted seekers wherever He went, and we have been asked to do the same with the gospel message. People need to know that Jesus can transform them, but those who are entrusted with the gospel must first be clean themselves, for judgment begins at the house of God (I Pet. 4:17). We will be held accountable for what we have done with the message of salvation entrusted to us by God Himself. If we truly believe this gospel, we cannot hoard the message, for it is to be multiplied and shared with others like bread for the hungry.

When we cleanse ourselves, we can then become effective vessels that God can use in His kingdom to bring others to the same saving knowledge that brought us to Jesus. There is something special about the gospel that transforms, but it is carried in earthen vessels (II Cor. 4:7).

—A. Koshy Muthalaly.

The Jewish Aspect

The cleansing of the temple was a very bold act. Dr. Alva J. McClain wrote that Jesus' "initial act was to assert once more his Lordship over the temple" (*The Greatness of the Kingdom,* BMH Books). Jesus "began to cast out them that sold and bought in the temple, and overthrew the tables of the moneychangers, and the seats of them that sold doves." Of all the Gospel accounts of this act, Mark alone adds, "And would not suffer that any man should carry any vessel through the temple" (11:15-16).

Dr. McClain explained, "This cleansing is not to be identified with the earlier cleansing at the beginning of the Lord's ministry, as the great Messianic Prophet (John 2:13-17). The second came at the close of his ministry, and revealed his authority as the Messianic King."

This authority over the temple continued. Matthew tells us in the verse after the description of the cleansing, "And the blind and the lame came to him in the temple; and he healed them" (21:14).

Mark tells us that Jesus walked in the temple the next day. The religious rulers accosted Him, demanding to know by what authority He carried out the temple cleansing and other acts (11:27-28). The following day, Jesus "went out of the temple" (13:1). This was the setting for His sermon on the Mount of Olives. Jesus unquestionably held sway over temple life during those last momentous days of His earthly ministry.

Some may want to point out that the unscriptural merchandising in the temple was the work of a very small number of Jews. Ancient and modern history shows the Jews are by nature openhanded, benevolent people. A conspicuous exception to that manner of life is found in Malachi 3:8-10, where God charged Israel with robbing Him in tithes and offerings. That failure of the Jews took place following the return to the land after the Captivity. In Jesus' day, giving was once more in keeping with the Law of Moses.

The relationship of the Jews to their temple is partly reflected in the history of Zionism, the dream of a national home for the Jewish people. At the close of the 1800s, Europe saw hatred of the Jews expressed in unofficial ways. The Jews did everything they could to fit into life in France, Germany, Austria, and Russia, but they were never accorded genuine acceptance anywhere. A couple of sensational cases of anti-Semitism led to the founding of the Zionist ideal.

A Viennese newspaperman, Theodor Herzl, stationed in Paris, hit upon the idea of trying to find someplace on earth the Jews could call home. Herzl was not involved religiously. He knew little of Jewish life and culture. However, he had felt the sting of anti-Semitism in his professional career.

Herzl was open to any place that would welcome Jews of every background. He became aware that Orthodox Jews in Poland and Russia prayed daily for a return to Israel. For these Jews, no other place on earth was acceptable. Herzl came around to their conviction (Margolis and Marx, *History of the Jewish People,* Atheneum).

The architect of the present State of Israel did not live to see his dream become a reality. His lasting memorial is a blue box in every synagogue for coins for the settlement of the Holy Land. Oddly enough, the first pioneers in the Promised Land were as indifferent to a religious calling as was Herzl himself. They struggled, fought, died, and gave to fulfill Herzl's dream.

—Lyle P. Murphy.

Guiding the Superintendent

This week's lesson focuses on Christ's passion for His church as the place where the Spirit of God resides and where His children may come with an attitude of reverence and honor to pray and to worship Him.

DEVOTIONAL OUTLINE

1. An attitude of holiness (Isa. 56:6-7). There is no need to question God's criterion for spiritual intimacy. One must simply choose holiness and justice and service to the one true God. The covenant of great promise, once restricted to the Jews, is now extended to all mankind. Whoever seeks to worship God in the beauty of holiness in His temple will obey His commandments and honor the day that He blessed and sanctified unto Himself. This approach pleases God. Those who worship Him will come to where God's people gather and rejoice with unspeakable joy.

2. Choosing the way of holiness (Jer. 7:9-11). How foolish it is to provoke God to anger! Corruption and wickedness sever our covenant tie to God, who is a jealous God. He commands, "Thou shalt have no other gods before me" (Exod. 20:3).

God's love and forgiveness are always available to His saints, but He despises blatant disobedience. As God's creation, our bodies belong to Him. How audacious for man to think himself free to be a partaker of the world! Paul asked, "Know ye not that ye are the temple of God, and that the Spirit of God dwelleth in you?" (I Cor. 3:16). The temple of God is holy; it is the seat of God Himself. Will we so freely defile it in the face of God, who sees and will punish our sin?

3. God demands holiness (Mark 11:15-19). As was His custom, Jesus made His way to the temple after entering Jerusalem. This visit was to rid the temple of the corrupt merchandising that was being conducted in the temple court under the guise of providing a necessary service to traveling Jews at the time of the Passover. This event was the second of its kind (cf. John 2:12-16), but the buying and selling continued. Jesus was filled with righteous indignation at the brazen indifference toward His Father's house (even though they were in the Court of the Gentiles), and He again proceeded to cleanse the temple.

Being the Master Teacher, Jesus turned this into a teaching moment. He made the point that from times past it had been established that the temple was where the presence of God dwelled. It was where His children— every believer—could come to pour out their hearts to their Father. Jesus' pursuit of reverence for the temple fueled the Jewish leadership's pursuit of His death, but they were equally apprehensive when they saw how rapt the people were at Christ's words.

Putting man's priorities over God's commands is dangerous. It is far better to be obedient than to risk God's wrath. God *will* have respect for His house and all things that pertain to Him.

AGE-GROUP EMPHASES

Children: Children learn best by example. The teacher's conduct in the church must exemplify holiness and reverence. Be an example your students can follow.

Youths: Respect for the house of God is as much about attitude as behavior. Teach the young people that God expects them to have a holy mindset. Godly behavior will follow.

Adults: Adults need to set the example in showing respect in the place of worship.

—*Jane E. Campbell.*

Scripture Lesson Text

JER. 23:5 Behold, the days come, saith the LORD, that I will raise unto Da'vid a righteous Branch, and a King shall reign and prosper, and shall execute judgment and justice in the earth.

6 In his days Ju'dah shall be saved, and Is'ra-el shall dwell safely: and this *is* his name whereby he shall be called, THE LORD OUR RIGHTEOUSNESS.

ZECH. 6:9 And the word of the LORD came unto me, saying,

10 Take of *them of* the captivity, *even* of Hel'da-i, of To-bi'jah, and of Je-da'iah, which are come from Bab'y-lon, and come thou the same day, and go into the house of Jo-si'ah the son of Zeph-a-ni'ah;

11 Then take silver and gold, and make crowns, and set *them* upon the head of Josh'u-a the son of Jos'e-dech, the high priest;

12 And speak unto him, saying, Thus speaketh the LORD of hosts, saying, Behold the man whose name *is* The BRANCH; and he shall grow up out of his place, and he shall build the temple of the LORD:

13 Even he shall build the temple of the LORD; and he shall bear the glory, and shall sit and rule upon his throne; and he shall be a priest upon his throne: and the counsel of peace shall be between them both.

14 And the crowns shall be to He'lem, and to To-bi'jah, and to Je-da'iah, and to Hen the son of Zeph-a-ni'ah, for a memorial in the temple of the LORD.

15 And they *that are* far off shall come and build in the temple of the LORD, and ye shall know that the LORD of hosts hath sent me unto you. And *this* shall come to pass, if ye will diligently obey the voice of the LORD your God.

JOHN 19:1 Then Pi'late therefore took Je'sus, and scourged *him*.

2 And the soldiers platted a crown of thorns, and put *it* on his head, and they put on him a purple robe,

3 And said, Hail, King of the Jews! and they smote him with their hands.

4 Pi'late therefore went forth again, and saith unto them, Behold, I bring him forth to you, that ye may know that I find no fault in him.

5 Then came Je'sus forth, wearing the crown of thorns, and the purple robe. And *Pi'late* saith unto them, Behold the man!

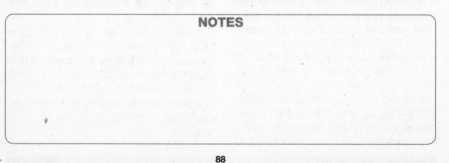

NOTES

The Suffering of the King

Lesson: Jeremiah 23:5-6; Zechariah 6:9-15; John 19:1-5

Read: Jeremiah 23:5-6; Zechariah 6:9-15; John 19:1-5

TIMES: probably between 597 and 586 B.C.; 519 B.C.; A.D. 30

PLACES: Jerusalem; Jerusalem; Jerusalem

GOLDEN TEXT—"The soldiers platted a crown of thorns, and put it on his head, and they put on him a purple robe, and said, Hail, King of the Jews! and they smote him with their hands" (John 19:2-3).

Introduction

Alfred the Great, an Anglo-Saxon king of the late ninth century, is considered one of England's best rulers. At one point, however, he was threatened by the Danes and had to flee. A legend says he took refuge in the hut of a peasant woman. Not knowing him, she assigned him the task of watching the oatcakes she was baking. But, soon lost in thought, he let them burn. She was so angry that she scolded him and hit him with a stick. Many doubt that this ever happened, but it illustrates how a king can be mistreated by a subject when he is not recognized.

The Bible has a parallel to this. Prophets had long foretold the coming of Israel's Messiah. But when "he came unto his own, . . . his own received him not" (John 1:11). In this case, though, they had no excuse.

LESSON OUTLINE

I. THE RIGHTEOUS BRANCH FORETOLD—Jer. 23:5-6

II. THE KING-PRIEST FORESHADOWED—Zech. 6:9-15

III. THE PROMISED KING HUMILIATED—John 19:1-5

Exposition: Verse by Verse

THE RIGHTEOUS BRANCH FORETOLD

JER. 23:5 Behold, the days come, saith the LORD, that I will raise unto David a righteous Branch, and a King shall reign and prosper, and shall execute judgment and justice in the earth.

6 In his days Judah shall be saved, and Israel shall dwell safely: and this is his name whereby he shall be called, THE LORD OUR RIGHTEOUSNESS.

His reign (Jer. 23:5-6a). Jeremiah prophesied in Judah's last days before the Captivity, when corruption was rampant among prophets, priests, and kings. In this chapter he pronounced woe upon the "pastors" (shepherds) who had misused God's "flock" (vss. 1-2) of Judah. These were the unworthy kings of David's line who had led them astray.

But through Jeremiah, the Lord promised to regather the scattered flock and place good shepherds over them (Jer. 23:3-4). The climax to this renewal will be the rule of the Messiah. "The days come" (vs. 5) is a formula used fifteen times in Jeremiah to call attention to noteworthy future events, many of them messianic. Here it refers to the rule of David's "righteous Branch." "Branch" means "sprout" and here speaks of a descendant of David who will fulfill the covenant of II Samuel 7:12-16.

Unlike the rulers of Jeremiah's day, this King will be "righteous" (Jer. 23:5), and His reign will reflect His nature. He will "reign and prosper, and shall execute judgment and justice in the earth." Also, unlike those kings who were mere puppets of foreign empires, He will be a true king, reigning and prospering. "In the earth" makes it clear that He will be an earthly monarch, not just the spiritual Lord of resurrected saints in heaven (cf. 3:17-18).

The earthly nature of His reign is confirmed by the next statement: "In his days Judah shall be saved, and Israel shall dwell safely" (Jer. 23:6). In Jeremiah's day, the kingdom of Israel had long been in captivity, and only Judah remained. But the coming Messiah will rule over a restored and reunified nation (cf. Jer. 33:14-16; Ezek. 37:15-19) and will usher in a time of security.

This security will be both temporal and spiritual. Israel will enjoy safety from former enemies and even the hazards of nature (cf. Isa. 11:6-9; Ezek. 34:25-28). In addition, they will be regenerated and will serve the Lord with pure hearts (cf. Isa. 59:20-21; Jer. 31:31-34; Rom. 11:26-27).

His divine credentials (Jer. 23:6b). The name by which Israel's King will be known is "THE LORD OUR RIGHTEOUSNESS." A name indicates a person's character, and He is here seen as both divine and righteous. "The Lord" is "Yahweh," the covenant name for Israel's God. That He also is the Righteous One goes without saying (Ezra 9:15; Dan. 9:7). He thus imparts righteousness to His rule (Isa. 11:4-5) and to His redeemed subjects (45:24-25). Jesus Christ embodies this role perfectly.

THE KING-PRIEST FORESHADOWED

ZECH. 6:9 And the word of the LORD came unto me, saying,

10 Take of them of the captivity, even of Heldai, of Tobijah, and of Jedaiah, which are come from Babylon, and come thou the same day, and go into the house of Josiah the son of Zephaniah;

11 Then take silver and gold, and make crowns, and set them upon the head of Joshua the son of Josedech, the high priest;

12 And speak unto him, saying, Thus speaketh the LORD of hosts, saying, Behold the man whose name is The BRANCH; and he shall grow up out of his place, and he shall build the temple of the LORD:

13 Even he shall build the temple of the LORD; and he shall bear the glory, and shall sit and rule upon his throne; and he shall be a priest upon his throne: and the counsel of peace shall be between them both.

14 And the crowns shall be to Helem, and to Tobijah, and to Jedaiah, and to Hen the son of Zephaniah, for a memorial in the temple of the LORD.

15 And they that are far off shall

come and build in the temple of the Lord, and ye shall know that the Lord of hosts hath sent me unto you. And this shall come to pass, if ye will diligently obey the voice of the Lord your God.

A symbolic act (Zech. 6:9-11). The book of Zechariah begins with a series of eight visions that Zechariah saw in one night. These visions, intended to encourage the returned Jewish exiles in their reconstruction of the temple, portray aspects of Israel's future glory. Now the visions are concluded with a symbolic act that portrays the Messiah's role in bringing this glory.

"And the word of the Lord came unto me, saying" (Zech. 6:9) takes up the prophetic formula with which the book began (1:1) to authenticate Zechariah's message as from God (cf. 4:8; 7:4; 8:1, 18). This announced not another vision but a literal event in which Zechariah would participate.

The prophet was to go seek out men "of the captivity" (Zech. 6:10)—Heldai, Tobijah, and Jedaiah. They had returned from Babylon bringing treasure to be used in building the temple. All their names are Hebrew and reflect loyalty to the Lord even in their land of exile. The silver and gold they brought probably had been collected from others who still remained in Babylon.

These men were staying at the house of "Josiah the son of Zephaniah" (Zech. 6:10), and to this house the prophet was sent. "The same day" refers to the day on which he had seen the eight night visions (since the day had begun at sunset). The arrival of the delegates from Babylon was providentially arranged to coincide with Zechariah's visions. He was thus to go to them before the visions faded from his memory.

The Lord instructed Zechariah to receive from these men "silver and gold, and make crowns, and set them upon the head of Joshua the son of Josedech, the high priest" (Zech. 6:11). Some of the silver and gold intended for use in the temple was to be used instead to make "crowns." The plural denotes a composite, ornate crown consisting of multiple parts. It was to be placed on the head of the high priest, Joshua.

Such an act was unprecedented in Israel. Levitical high priests wore a miter, or turban, and across the front of it a golden plate (Lev. 8:9; Zech. 3:5) but never an ornate royal crown such as this. The law kept the monarchy and the priesthood separate, so it is clear that this coronation was purely symbolic. This becomes clearer in the following verses.

A prophecy (Zech. 6:12-13). Zechariah was to speak to Joshua as he crowned him, telling him the meaning of the act. "Thus speaketh the Lord of hosts" solemnly declares that the Almighty Lord will accomplish an act to fulfill the symbolism. "Behold the man" brings to mind the later words of Pilate, which we will yet consider (John 19:5).

Here, however, God called attention to "the man whose name is The BRANCH" (Zech. 6:12). This, as we have already seen, is a messianic title that indicates Christ's sprouting forth from the house of David (cf. Isa. 4:2; 11:1; Jer. 33:15; Zech. 3:8). "He shall grow up out of his place" (Zech. 6:12) most likely refers to the humble place of poverty and obscurity in which He would grow up (cf. Isa. 53:2; Mic. 5:2; John 1:46).

This coming Branch would be the one to "build the temple of the Lord" (Zech. 6:12). This statement is repeated for emphasis in verse 13: "Even he shall build the temple of the Lord." He who grows up in these inauspicious conditions will complete this work. This does not refer to the temple then being built, for that would be completed by Zerubbabel (cf. 4:9). Rather, it is the millennial temple alluded to by Isaiah (Isa. 2:2-3; cf. Ezek. 40—43) that He will complete.

Furthermore, He will "bear the glory"

(Zech. 6:13). The Hebrew construction places emphasis on "he," meaning "he himself." Christ alone will bear regal splendor. One aspect of His glory will be to "sit and rule upon his throne." Having suffered for man's redemption and having defeated the forces of wickedness, He will claim the throne He deserves as David's Son (Luke 1:32-33).

In addition, "he shall be a priest upon his throne" (Zech. 6:13). This was the symbolic meaning of the crowning of Joshua. Christ will finally bring together the two offices. His priesthood, prefigured by that of Melchizedek, the king-priest (Gen. 14:18; Heb. 5:6; 6:20), has been validated through the offering of Himself, the perfect Sacrifice (Heb. 7:26-27). He will represent before God those whose sins He has washed away through His blood (vss. 24-25).

"The counsel of peace shall be between them both" (Zech. 6:13) refers to the two offices Christ will occupy—King and Priest. There will never be a conflict between them because they are unified in one Person. His rule can be peaceful and harmonious because its political and spiritual functions will always agree.

A memorial (Zech. 6:14). The composite crown made for this symbolic coronation would not remain Joshua's. It was to be a "memorial"—that is, a reminder—in the temple. It was, first, a reminder of the generosity of the three exiles from Babylon and their Judean host. Their names are repeated here, with variations.

A second reminder given by this crown is of the King-Priest Himself, whose coming it signified. It was intended as a lasting encouragement to the returned exiles. As long as it remained in the temple, it would remind them that their nation could look forward to a glorious future.

An encouragement (Zech. 6:15). Zechariah prophesied further that "they that are far off shall come and build in the temple of the Lord." This prophecy was occasioned by the presence of the three from Babylon who had brought their treasure. They were symbolic of the many from foreign lands who in the millennium will contribute their treasure to offer their worship (cf. Isa. 60:1-10; Zech. 2:11; 8:22-23).

The phrase "and ye shall know that the Lord of hosts hath sent me unto you" (Zech. 6:15) probably refers to the Angel of the Lord, who had revealed the message. This would agree with the use of this wording in the course of the night visions earlier (cf. 2:9-11; 4:9). The final statement, the condition that this prophecy will come to pass if the people obey the Lord does not mean Messiah's reign can be thwarted by disobedience. It means that only the obedient can share in its blessings.

THE PROMISED KING HUMILIATED

JOHN 19:1 Then Pilate therefore took Jesus, and scourged him.

2 And the soldiers platted a crown of thorns, and put it on his head, and they put on him a purple robe,

3 And said, Hail, King of the Jews! and they smote him with their hands.

4 Pilate therefore went forth again, and saith unto them, Behold, I bring him forth to you, that ye may know that I find no fault in him.

5 Then came Jesus forth, wearing the crown of thorns, and the purple robe. And Pilate saith unto them, Behold the man!

The mockery (John 19:1-3). What a contrast to the prophetic portrayals of Messiah's glory do we meet in the trials and death of Jesus! The promised King came, but "his own received him not" (1:11). Hated by those who should have welcomed Him, He was maliciously betrayed and subjected to a series of unjust trials. The Jewish authorities could not inflict capital punishment, so they sent Him to Pontius Pilate, the Roman procurator of Judea, on the pretense that He was a threat to Caesar.

After questioning Jesus, Pilate concluded that He was innocent (John 18:33-38). But, evading his responsibility to release Him, he sent Him to Herod Antipas (Luke 23:6-12), who gave the same verdict (vss. 13-15). Pilate then sought to appease the accusers by crucifying Barabbas instead (John 18:39-40), but they would have none of it. So this pathetic man, motivated by politics, not principle, had Jesus scourged (19:1), though he knew He was innocent.

The worst criminals were scourged before they were crucified. The whip consisted of rawhide strips to which pieces of metal or bone were attached. Some men died from the scourging itself because it was so brutal. Jesus survived it but was then subjected to additional disgrace by the soldiers (John 19:2-3). Mocking His claim to be a king, they pressed a crown of thorns down on His head. They then clothed Him in a purple robe, a mark of royalty, and gave Him a reed for a scepter (Matt. 27:29).

The confession (John 19:4). After this, Pilate presented Jesus to the crowd with the incredible statement "I find no fault in him." If this was so, why had he had Him mistreated? He had probably hoped this lesser punishment would appease the mob, but his tactic failed utterly (cf. vs. 6). He succeeded only in compounding his own guilt in the worst miscarriage of justice the world has ever seen.

The presentation (John 19:5). Jesus was brought forth wearing the crown and the robe, the signs of His mock coronation. He also undoubtedly showed evidences of His beating as well. His face may well have been so disfigured as to make Him unrecognizable (cf. Isa. 52:13-14).

Pilate introduced Him with the words "Behold the man!" (John 19:5). What was the tone of his declaration? It would be tempting to see it as a further mockery of the One who had declared Himself the King over these despised Jews. But more likely it reflected Pilate's inner struggle at this point. We know he was reluctant to execute a man who he knew was innocent and who had made unusual claims (cf. 18:36-37). And here He was, battered yet dignified. A mixture of commiseration and admiration probably permeated Pilate's declaration.

However he meant it, he was unwittingly repeating the words of Zechariah: "Behold the man whose name is The BRANCH" (Zech. 6:12). This One, mocked by common soldiers in a sham coronation, will someday rule in glory as "King of kings, and Lord of lords" (I Tim. 6:15).

—*Robert E. Wenger.*

QUESTIONS

1. How will the rule of the Righteous Branch differ from that of the kings of Jeremiah's day?

2. What kind of security will Messiah bring to Judah and Israel?

3. What was Zechariah to take from the exiles returning from Babylon?

4. What symbolic act was Zechariah to undertake?

5. What work will the coming Branch undertake?

6. What two offices will the Messiah combine in Himself?

7. What was to be done with the crown Zechariah made?

8. Why was Pilate, the Roman procurator, consulted in Jesus' trial?

9. How was Jesus treated by the Roman soldiers?

10. How would you evaluate the actions of Pontius Pilate?

—*Robert E. Wenger.*

Preparing to Teach the Lesson

In the previous lesson we studied Jesus' cleansing of the temple. In this week's lesson we will examine how the Old Testament prophecies about the Messiah as the Branch of David point to Jesus' future role as the King and Priest of Israel.

TODAY'S AIM

Facts: to show that Jesus, as Israel's true King, will reign on the throne as the prophesied Branch of David.

Principle: to show that in fulfilling His role as the Branch, it was necessary for Jesus to first suffer to fulfill His role as both King and Priest.

Application: to show that we cannot understand Jesus as King without understanding His role as our interceding Priest.

INTRODUCING THE LESSON

Find a blossoming branch to bring to class as a visual image for the lesson. Just as the branch shows life in the spring after the deadness of winter, so one day Jesus will occupy the throne of Israel after centuries of its being unoccupied.

DEVELOPING THE LESSON

1. The Branch of David (Jer. 23:5-6). Begin class by putting Jeremiah's passage into its historical context. In the previous chapter, God condemned Jehoiachin and put an end to his reign. He was the next to the last king before Babylon took over Jerusalem. As part of his judgment, God cut off Jehoiachin's descendants from sitting on the throne of David (22:30).

While the reign of David's descendants appeared threatened, the Lord told Jeremiah that He was going to raise up a righteous King, whom He identified as the "Branch" (Jer. 23:5). The Messi-

ah was referred to as a "Branch" in other prophecies as well. Isaiah 4:2 refers to "the branch of the Lord."

There is a clear reference to the Messiah as the Branch of David in Isaiah 11:1-9. In that prophecy, Christ is also pictured as "a rod out of the stem of Jesse."

Jeremiah himself later made an additional reference to Christ as the "Branch of righteousness" (Jer. 33:15) coming from the line of David.

As you lead the study in Jeremiah 23:5-6, point out that Jesus did not totally fulfill Jeremiah's prophecy in His first coming. As Jeremiah foretold, the coming Branch would "reign and prosper." Jesus, however, was mocked as a king and crucified. Jesus' presentation on Palm Sunday was soon counteracted.

Jeremiah foretold that the Branch would "execute judgment and justice in the earth" (Jer. 23:5). In His first coming, Jesus received the judgment of God upon sin at the cross. At His return, He will execute judgment and rule in justice during the millennium (cf. Rev. 19:11).

Jeremiah wrote that "in his days Judah shall be saved" (Jer. 23:6). However, the nation has been temporarily set aside (Rom. 9—11). Israel's salvation is still a future event. Israel will not dwell in safety (Jer. 23:6) until Christ reigns during the millennium.

2. Both King and Priest (Zech. 6:9-15). Point out that while Jeremiah's prophecy was given at the time Jerusalem was being overtaken by the Babylonians, Zechariah wrote after the exiles had returned to Jerusalem and were in the process of rebuilding the temple. Zerubbabel was the governor of Judah (Hag. 1:1), and Joshua was the high priest.

God instructed Zechariah to make a

crown from the gold and silver that had been received as a gift from three returning exiles and to place it on Joshua the high priest's head.

Ask your students why it would be unusual to crown the high priest rather than the governor, Zerubbabel, who was of the line of David. It was important for Joshua to be crowned to show that the coming King would be both King and Priest. The word for "crowns" (Zech. 6:11) is in the plural, which could indicate a form of majesty; it could also suggest a single crown with multiple parts. This may refer to the multiple roles of the future Branch—one to indicate His priesthood and one to indicate His role as King.

Since Joshua did not take the position as king and since the crown was to be placed in the temple as a memorial, it is evident that his crowning was symbolic of the Branch, who would bring people to the Father through the salvation He provides, sit on the throne, and rule over Israel.

Compare the Branch's position as both King and Priest (Zech. 6:13) with the prophecy in Isaiah 9:6-7 and David's prophecy in Psalm 110.

3. The scourged King (John 19:1-5). Read this passage to your class; then ask the students to give their first impressions. Discuss how, even though Jesus was the legitimate and prophesied King of Israel, He was rejected. Note how Jesus was mocked by the Roman soldiers as the King of the Jews. Pilate asked the crowds whether he should release "the King of the Jews" (Mark 15:9) to them. He posted that title on the sign above Jesus' head as the crime for which He was crucified (John 19:19).

Previously, the Jewish leaders accused Jesus of claiming to be the King. Pilate asked Him whether He was that King (Matt. 27:11). Jesus admitted to Pilate that He was the King but that His kingdom was not of this world (John 18:33-37).

As Jesus hung on the cross, the chief priests, scribes, and elders mocked Him, asking why, if He was the King of the Jews, He did not save Himself from the cross at that moment (Matt. 27:41-42).

All of this indicates that while Jesus' reign has begun, it will also take place in the future millennium, in keeping with the Old Testament prophecies.

Discuss with your class how Jesus is both King and Priest after offering Himself as a sacrifice for sins once for all, as explained by Hebrews 7:20-28.

ILLUSTRATING THE LESSON

Jesus, the Branch of David, is both the eternal King and the eternal Priest. Remember that at communion.

JESUS IS KING AND PRIEST

**REMEMBER HIS SACRIFICE
LOOK FORWARD TO HIS RETURN**

CONCLUDING THE LESSON

God's plan for both salvation and the reign of Christ is complex. When the intricate details of history and the fulfillment of prophecy came to their climax, God instituted the reign of Jesus as both King and Priest.

ANTICIPATING THE NEXT LESSON

Next week our study will be focused on the resurrection of Christ and Hosea's reference to the resurrection on the third day.

—*Carter Corbrey.*

PRACTICAL POINTS

1. God's provision for His people through fulfilled prophecy continues today as He provides for our needs (Jer. 23:5-6).
2. A godly ruler is intent on pleasing God, not on acquiring personal power (Zech. 6:9-13).
3. Obeying God and His Word is natural when we seek to please Him (vss. 14-15).
4. Opposition to serving Christ often comes in subtle and unexpected ways (John 19:1-3).
5. Those who reject Christ's message cannot deny His perfect life (vs. 4).
6. Though He is pivotal in history, Christ is as near as a whispered prayer (vs. 5).

—Anne Adams.

RESEARCH AND DISCUSSION

1. What do God's promises to Israel mean for modern Christians? What does this mean for you personally?
2. Do Christians make better national leaders? What if non-Christians were more efficient and experienced? Should Christians support candidates just because they are Christians? Why or why not?
3. Do you think the soldiers were surprised when Jesus did not respond to their taunting? Have you ever been criticized or mocked for your faith? Can you share the event?
4. How do you usually imagine Christ—as a Suffering Saviour or as Resurrected Lord? Explain your answer, and discuss.

—Anne Adams.

ILLUSTRATED HIGH POINTS

I find no fault in him

Four children, ages eleven, ten, five, and four, stood paralyzed in a military-style line-up as their father paced before them, barking, "This is the last time I'm asking. Which one of you pulled all the toilet paper off the roll and left it in that pile on the floor?" The response was a series of "Not me's"; so he decreed a mass punishment of a one-day grounding. The foursome has yet to reveal the truth about the incident, and fifty years later, the culprit has yet to confess. They all recognize, however, that some of them were punished for the deed of another.

Jesus was innocent of any sin; yet He was punished for all mankind. Not demanding justice or retribution, He suffered an agonizing penalty. He did it not because no one else would but because no one else could. Jesus' atoning sacrifice allowed us to stand before our Father and hear Him say, "Not guilty."

Hail, King of the Jews!

"Where you are is not who you are." Ursula often heard these words from her mother as she was growing up on New York's lower east side. Though she lived surrounded by gang and drug violence, Ursula had a burning drive for success. Her mother encouraged her to stay focused and pursue her path to fulfillment. Ursula is now the CEO of a very successful company. She succeeded because she kept her eyes on who she was and did not let her temporary circumstances dictate her destiny.

Jesus stood bleeding in front of a hostile mob. The soldiers mocked Him and sarcastically called Him a king. But Jesus never forgot who He was. How grateful we should be that Jesus, our King of kings, kept His focus on the cross for us!

—Beverly Jones.

Golden Text Illuminated

"The soldiers platted a crown of thorns, and put it on his head, and they put on him a purple robe, and said, Hail, King of the Jews! and they smote him with their hands" (John 19:2-3).

The nation of Israel as a whole rejected Jesus as their Messiah. As the Apostle John wrote, "He came unto his own, and his own received him not" (John 1:11). He was not the kind of Messiah they wanted. He did not call for a national revolt against the Romans but rather for personal repentance and faith in Him, the Son of God.

Jesus offered no comfort to those who touted their obedience to the law; rather, He exposed their religiosity as a sham. Israel's religious leaders had no place for a Messiah who condemned them rather than praised them, and they were determined that He would not be their Messiah and King.

The Jewish leaders were unable, legally, to put Jesus to death; yet they saw no other way of ending His discomforting presence. Thus, when they brought Jesus to Pilate, the Roman governor, they charged Him not with blasphemy, as the Sanhedrin did (Matt. 26:65), but with claiming to be a king and, therefore, a political threat to Rome (Luke 23:2).

Jesus did not deny the charge of being a king. He was indeed the King of the Jews, but He explained to Pilate that His kingdom was not a worldly one like that of the Romans. Jesus' answers and demeanor were enough to convince Pilate that He was no real threat.

Our golden text describes what took place as Pilate was still seeking a way to release Jesus and before he gave in to expedience and the veiled threat that a complaint against him would be brought to Caesar (John 19:12).

Pilate certainly did not see Jesus as a genuine king, and neither did the Romans under his command. After Jesus had been beaten, the soldiers "platted a crown of thorns, and put it on his head." This was an obvious act of mockery. The bloodied body of a simple Jewish man gave no appearance of royalty. Indeed, the very thought of a Jew being king was laughable to the Romans.

The crown, with its thorns, may have been meant to inflict pain on Jesus, but it was also a mocking picture of a pathetic king. The purple robe they put on Jesus was probably a "cloak worn by military officers and men in high position" (Morris, *The Gospel According to John,* Eerdmans). This added to the mockery, which was aimed as much at all the Jews as it was at Jesus, for the thought of the Jews having a king of their own was ludicrous to the Romans.

The soldiers continued to mock Jesus, feigning obeisance to Him and saying, "Hail, King of the Jews!" even as they struck Him with their hands. The irony, of course, is that the One they mocked was in fact King of kings and Lord of lords (Morris).

The actions of the soldiers were reprehensible but at least somewhat understandable in light of their ignorance. But how could the Jewish leaders, who knew Scripture so well, have been so wrong? We must remember that it is not just knowledge of Scripture that is needed but submission to it as well. Those who rejected Jesus did so because of their own pride. They would not humble themselves before God or His Word.

—*Jarl K. Waggoner.*

Heart of the Lesson

"At a reception honoring musician Sir Robert Mayer on his 100th birthday, elderly British socialite Lady Diana Cooper fell into conversation with a friendly woman who seemed to know her well. Lady Diana's failing eyesight prevented her from recognizing her fellow guest until she peered more closely at the magnificent diamonds and realized she was talking to Queen Elizabeth!

"Overcome with embarrassment, Lady Diana curtsied and stammered, 'Ma'am, oh, ma'am, I'm sorry, ma'am. I didn't recognize you without your crown!'" (*Today in the Word,* November 16, 1995).

A crown is a symbol of identity. In most cases, a crown identifies its wearer as a person of royal authority. In this week's lesson, the multitudes' spiritual blindness and a desire to mock Jesus motivated them to place a crown of thorns on the suffering Messiah-King.

1. A peculiar combination of righteous justice (Jer. 23:5-6). The Lord declared through Jeremiah that He would provide a future monarch from the lineage of King David who would rule with wisdom, justice, and righteousness. During His magnificent reign, God's people would experience a season of peace and security. The name of this future Monarch would be "THE LORD OUR RIGHTEOUSNESS."

Our present society is dominated by a sense of perverted justice and acts of unrighteousness. The lives of many people are destroyed and the souls of many people damaged by decisions and events that are motivated by selfish political advancement and wicked disregard for the sanctity of life.

In the midst of this humanist environment, God's people are called to be salt and light (cf. Matt. 5:13-16). Followers of Jesus Christ can accomplish this goal because of the hope they have of the future Monarch who will demonstrate righteous justice.

2. A prophetic expression of peaceful obedience (Zech. 6:9-15). Zechariah was told to secure offerings of silver and gold from people who had returned from the Babylonian Exile, to manufacture at least two crowns, and place them on Joshua. This symbolic gesture was accompanied by Zechariah's prophetic description of a future monarch who would peacefully combine the offices of priest and king.

The crowns would then be placed in the Jewish temple as reminders of a future time when non-Jews would have a relationship with God's house, of the confirmation of Zechariah's prophetic ministry, and of the promised results of conscientious obedience.

It is appropriate at this time to remind God's people that they may receive future crowns that symbolize present spiritual accomplishments (cf. I Cor. 9:25; II Tim. 4:8; Jas. 1:12; I Pet. 5:4). With obedient humility, God's people will cast these crowns at the Saviour's feet.

3. A powerful manifestation of undeserved suffering (John 19:1-5). The Lord Jesus deserved a crown of regal authority. Instead, Pilate tormented Him, and the soldiers adorned Him with a crown of thorns and a purple robe, indicative of His suffering and mankind's mockery of His spiritual authority.

Suffering is often viewed as an unwelcome intruder in the lives of God's people. However, the Bible teaches that suffering is not only inevitable but also incomparable (cf. II Tim. 2:12; 3:12). As a result, suffering can be a catalyst for incomparable ministry and future glory. Let us, therefore, gladly identify with the suffering of our King, Jesus Christ.

—*Thomas R. Chmura.*

World Missions

I come from a land where the pursuit of salvation is visible wherever one goes. It is a land of many religions. The followers of these religions fervently seek their salvation through good works. They go to their temples regularly and place their offerings before the decorated deities. They bow in their religious rituals before them, but they are not truly satisfied. They seek to rid themselves of their sins through ritual washings and through their own sacrificial physical torture and pain.

Worshippers like those described above are not uncommon in this world. Human beings have an innate desire to please someone bigger than we are whom we cannot touch or see. But the message of the simple Christian gospel is that Jesus has already taken our pain. As Christian believers, we have entered into the days leading up to Easter, which helps us remember the intense sufferings of Jesus. But we often forget that He did this so that we do not have to do so all over again.

The biblical emphasis about our Lord Jesus' suffering is that it was "one sacrifice for sins for ever" (Heb. 10:12). This simply means that we never have to do so, because it has already been done for us. The price for our sins has already been paid. Our sins are behind us. This is a glorious message that we have to tell the world around us. God has entrusted us with this wonderful message of peace, and we have to share it with others. How could we dare keep it to ourselves?

If people would only hear this message, listen, and obey it, they would know that they do not have to climb mountains, sit under a tree in all kinds of harsh weather, or even bow before a supposed deity anymore. They can be free from the need to do all such penance. We must admit that many who do such things to atone for their sins are really good people and sincerely mean well. But the sad part is that they have never heard of the Suffering King we have been studying this week. It is up to us to tell the world.

The task of missions is to share what we know of Jesus and what He has done for all of us. The prophets pointed to Him. So we are to go to the ends of the earth with the unparalleled message of a King who came to suffer for us and in so doing give us what we need to save us from the guilt and penalty of our sins. The culmination of Jesus' suffering on earth was the resurrection. The world needs to know that no one ever did what Jesus did. He suffered and rose again.

We as a church must do what we can to support our missionaries around the world. They are going out to the very ends of the earth, just as Jesus commanded us to do. Not all the religions around us are considered missionary religions. Christianity stands out because of the centrality of the message of a Suffering King who gave Himself for the world. If we as Christians took this message seriously enough, our hearts would ache because so many have never heard of our Jesus.

That kind of heartache should spur us on to get involved in the task of missions—to spread to the world the reality of a Suffering King. When we become cold and callous to this message, it hurts the task of missions. We dare not forget His suffering and what it means to us.

—A. Koshy Muthalaly.

The Jewish Aspect

John 19:1-5 presents the touching scene of our Saviour humbled before mere men. Being scourged and mocked by agents of an ungodly Roman government is difficult to contemplate for God come-in-the-flesh.

Jesus experienced intolerable pain and suffering, leading to physical death. An innocent man should not have undergone the anguish He went through. It is essential to look at the sufferings of Jesus, for they were inflicted upon God, the Creator and the Saviour of men.

First of all, "he came unto his own" (John 1:11)—that is, His own things. There was no world for Rome to exploit, no land for Pilate to rule over, but that which Jesus, in the Creation, had made possible (Col. 1:16). "And his own received him not" (John 1:11). What a painful rebuke it was to have His own people revile Him! He seemed to have convinced some of His divine mission, for we read, "As he spake these words, many believed on him" (8:30). A few verses further on, though, we learn that these "believers" were prepared to kill Him, for they were really Satan's children (vss. 37, 43-44).

Mark tells us, "The common people heard him gladly" (12:37). The author of Hebrews noted, "Consider him that endured such contradiction of sinners against himself" (12:3). It is hard to imagine how those under the wrath of God could say anything offensive to the Lord of glory. Officers who failed to arrest Jesus offered as their only excuse, "Never man spake like this man" (John 7:46).

How was it for Jesus to live in a home with His half brothers after the flesh, James and Jude, "for neither did his brethren believe in him" (John 7:5)? Jesus surely looked to the day when both men would be stalwart Christians involved in the production of God's Holy Word.

And what shall we say about the response of the people of Jesus' home district of Galilee? In Luke 10:13-16, Jesus revealed the future for cities that witnessed great miracles. Chorazin is something of a mystery today, but a synagogue there may have heard the call to repent, for the kingdom was at hand. The prophecy concerning its future indicates the inhabitants were apathetic to the Messiah's message.

In the same verse, Bethsaida—the hometown of Peter, Andrew, and Philip and familiar to Jesus—faces a desperate end for failing to accept the teachings of the Lord. Another Bethsaida on the east coast of the Sea of Galilee was the site of the feeding of the five thousand.

Capernaum, perhaps a twin village of Bethsaida, was more the true residence of Jesus than was Nazareth. Matthew came to the Lord there. Simon Peter's wife's mother was healed there, as were a paralytic, a demon-possessed man, and the centurion's servant. Yet the city will be thrust down to hades for its indifference to the message (Luke 10:15).

Luke 19:28-44 describes Jesus' approach to Jerusalem. It was Nisan 10, the day on which a Passover lamb was to be selected for the feast and placed alone in a pen for observation. Jesus is that Lamb (John 1:29). His disciples obtained a colt, the foal of an ass (Luke 19:35), and they placed their clothes on the road (vs. 36).

The people "began to rejoice and praise God with a loud voice . . . saying, Blessed be the King that cometh in the name of the Lord: peace in heaven, and glory in the highest" (Luke 19:37-38). The golden moment was shattered by the rebuke of the Pharisees (vs. 39). The first fully open offer of the kingdom was rejected. On Nisan 14, Jesus was crucified.

—Lyle P. Murphy

Guiding the Superintendent

"Suffering" is a word that some Christians dread and allow to hinder their faith. But suffering connects us with the Saviour and is a necessary component of exalting Him. First Peter 4:13 says, "But rejoice, inasmuch as ye are partakers of Christ's sufferings; that, when his glory shall be revealed, ye may be glad also with exceeding joy." Suffering is not pleasurable, but it is rewarding.

DEVOTIONAL OUTLINE

1. The King is coming (Jer. 23:5-6). In today's unpredictable times of many broken promises, the believer who approaches Scripture from a human perspective may feel some skepticism and doubt. According to a human perspective on time, the promised King was long overdue in Jeremiah's time. But God had His own schedule of events. He declared again that He would indeed raise up an offshoot, a branch of the stump of Jesse, through his son David, whom God had given righteousness, wisdom, and justice for the protection and deliverance of His elect nation.

2. The King declared (Zech. 6:9-15). Christians should be thankful for the instructions God gave Zechariah regarding the symbolic crowning of Joshua as king and priest. This demonstrates God's declaration that His word "shall accomplish that which I please" (Isa. 55:11). God knows the end from the beginning and has a strategy for carrying out His predetermined plan.

It is also informative to note God's use of symbolism. Joshua was not the kingly priest who would save and rule God's people. But he was a type of Christ—the Branch who would come according to the Davidic covenant, suffer, die an ignominious death, and be raised from the dead to sit gloriously on His throne at His Father's right hand. Christ would establish His church. And as the Head of the church, He would mediate peace between God and man, laying a spiritual foundation on which Jews and Gentiles alike could have communion with God.

3. The King suffered (John 19:1-5). Weak-mindedness, a lust for power and position, and a desire to always please others will result in ineffective leadership and poor decision making. As Christians, our faith demands integrity, commitment, and a willingness to stand and, yes, suffer for righteousness and truth. Wavering Christians dishonor Christ and mock Him all over again. These believers tolerate others who disgrace Him, all the while knowing that Jesus is the Christ, the Son of the living God, without any shortcomings, failures, or any such things. The Bible says that Christ freely surrendered to the Cross (cf. 10:18)—an extremely high redemptive price for all who would be saved. For this costly gift we should glory in that Cross and celebrate the One who bore it.

AGE-GROUP EMPHASES

Children: Suffering is not something that children can easily comprehend, but assure them that Christ endured incredible agony because of His unconditional love for them and all humankind.

Youths: Many young people simply live in the moment and feel that life is too complicated. Assure them that God has planned every aspect of their future and that they must stay connected to the Branch.

Adults: Some may be dismayed that God has not yet dealt with or brought resolution to their circumstances. Remind them that God works in His own time for our good.

—Jane E. Campbell.

Scripture Lesson Text

HOS. 6:1 Come, and let us return unto the LORD: for he hath torn, and he will heal us; he hath smitten, and he will bind us up.

2 After two days will he revive us: in the third day he will raise us up, and we shall live in his sight.

3 Then shall we know, *if* we follow on to know the LORD: his going forth is prepared as the morning; and he shall come unto us as the rain, as the latter *and* former rain unto the earth.

LUKE 24:1 Now upon the first *day* **of the week, very early in the morning, they came unto the sepulchre, bringing the spices which they had prepared, and certain** *others* **with them.**

2 And they found the stone rolled away from the sepulchre.

3 And they entered in, and found not the body of the Lord Je'sus.

4 And it came to pass, as they were much perplexed thereabout, behold, two men stood by them in shining garments:

5 And as they were afraid, and bowed down *their* **faces to the** earth, **they said unto them, Why seek ye the living among the dead?**

6 He is not here, but is risen: remember how he spake unto you when he was yet in Gal'i-lee,

7 Saying, The Son of man must be delivered into the hands of sinful men, and be crucified, and the third day rise again.

8 And they remembered his words,

9 And returned from the sepulchre, and told all these things unto the eleven, and to all the rest.

10 It was Ma'ry Mag-da-le'ne, and Jo-an'na, and Ma'ry *the mother* of James, and other *women that were* with them, which told these things unto the apostles.

11 And their words seemed to them as idle tales, and they believed them not.

12 Then arose Pe'ter, and ran unto the sepulchre; and stooping down, he beheld the linen clothes laid by themselves, and departed, wondering in himself at that which was come to pass.

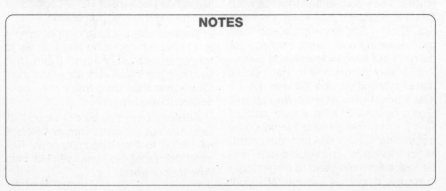

NOTES

The Resurrection of the King

(Easter)

Lesson: Hosea 6:1-3; Luke 24:1-12

Read: Hosea 6:1-3; Luke 24:1-12

TIMES: between 760 and 700 B.C.;
A.D. 30

PLACES: probably Judah;
near Jerusalem

GOLDEN TEXT—"Remember how he spake unto you when he was yet in Galilee, saying, The Son of man must be delivered into the hands of sinful men, and be crucified, and the third day rise again" (Luke 24:6-7).

Introduction

The apostles made it clear that to eliminate Jesus' resurrection is to cut the heart out of Christianity. Paul asserted that without it, our faith would be vain (I Cor. 15:14). It is the ultimate proof of Jesus' messiahship (Acts 2:36) and the Father's acceptance of His atoning work (Heb. 1:3). It guarantees our own resurrection (I Cor. 15:20-23). And it provides the divine power for victory over sin and Satan (Rom. 6:4-6; Phil. 3:10; Col. 3:1). Our risen Advocate pleads our case (I John 2:1).

In Revelation the risen and glorified Christ will return to judge the wicked and rule in glory (19:11-16). His resurrection is thus the focal point of God's cosmic plan and of our faith, life, and hope.

This week's lesson combines two passages. The first calls for the renewal of God's people, and the second records the resurrection on which all such renewal is based.

LESSON OUTLINE

I. THE RENEWAL OF GOD'S PEO-PLE—Hos. 6:1-3

II. THE RESURRECTION OF GOD'S SON—Luke 24:1-12

Exposition: Verse by Verse

THE RENEWAL OF GOD'S PEOPLE

HOS. 6:1 Come, and let us return unto the LORD: for he hath torn, and he will heal us; he hath smitten, and he will bind us up.

2 After two days will he revive us: in the third day he will raise us up, and we shall live in his sight.

3 Then shall we know, if we follow on to know the LORD: his going forth is prepared as the morning; and he shall come unto us as the rain, as the latter and former rain unto the earth.

An exhortation to return to the Lord (Hos. 6:1-2). Hosea prophesied in the eighth century B.C. and directed his message to the kingdom of Israel, the ten northern tribes. He lived in the final days of the kingdom, seeing a decline from a time of economic prosperity and national glory. Jeroboam II had expanded Israel's borders and commerce to an impressive degree. But the spiritual condition of Israel was deplorable. The people continued the calf worship introduced by Jeroboam I and added it to the Canaanite worship of Baal and Asherah. Hosea condemned them for their idolatry, immorality, greed, and injustice (cf. 4:1-2, 11-13).

Signs of God's judgment had begun to appear when the Assyrians invaded the land. Instead of turning to the Lord to deliver them, the Israelites tried to buy off the Assyrian king (Hos. 5:13; cf. II Kings 15:19-20). But doom was inevitable, for the Lord Himself was against them and would tear Israel apart as a lion tears its prey (Hos. 5:14). He would not rescue them until, in their affliction, they again sought Him (vs. 15).

Our lesson text (Hos. 6:1-3) is an exhortation for Israel to return to the Lord. "Come, and let us return unto the Lord" could be the Jews' exhortation to each other or that of Hosea to the nation. Either way, it is a recognition that it was God who had "torn" and "smitten" them. But there is an equal assurance that He will "heal us" and "bind us up" (cf. Deut. 32:39).

We might see the fulfillment of this exhortation in the prayers of godly people of the Exile, such as Daniel, Ezra, and Nehemiah. But Israel as a nation has never yet prayed like this, and the final fulfillment will come at the return of Christ, when the nation is restored to Him (cf. Hos. 14; Zech. 12:9—13:2).

When the restoration comes, it will come speedily: "After two days will he revive us: in the third day he will raise us up, and we shall live in his sight" (Hos. 6:2). The numbers should not be taken literally. Rather, they are a Hebrew idiom in which the second (larger) number is the most that the statement calls for (cf. Job 5:19; Prov. 30:15; Amos 1:3). Since two or three days is a short time, the meaning is that Israel's restoration will be certain and will happen within a short time. It is not a reference to Jesus' resurrection.

The expressions "raise us up" and "live in his sight" (Hos. 6:2), however, do use the figure of resurrection from spiritual death (cf. Eph. 2:1, 5-6). It brings to mind Ezekiel 37:1-14, which pictures the dry bones that represent Israel coming to life and returning to their homeland through the Spirit of God.

An exhortation to know the Lord (Hos. 6:3). "Then shall we know, if we follow on to know the Lord" is really a second exhortation: "So let us know, let us press on to know the Lord." Israel's return to Him involves a growing understanding of the Lord Himself and a heart's desire to know Him better. It was the lack of this experiential knowledge that was destroying them (4:1, 6). But they will desire its increase until all know Him intimately (Jer. 31:34).

As they seek to know the Lord, Israel will find Him just as zealous to extend His blessings to them. His appearance to them is as certain as the dawn of each day (Hos. 6:3). His presence will be as refreshing as "the latter and former rain" is to the earth. Drawing near to Him, they will find Him drawing near to them (cf. Jas. 4:8).

THE RESURRECTION OF GOD'S SON

LUKE 24:1 Now upon the first day of the week, very early in the morning, they came unto the sepulchre, bringing the spices which they had prepared, and certain others with them.

2 And they found the stone rolled away from the sepulchre.

3 And they entered in, and found not the body of the Lord Jesus.

4 And it came to pass, as they were much perplexed thereabout, behold, two men stood by them in shining garments:

5 And as they were afraid, and bowed down their faces to the earth, they said unto them, Why seek ye the living among the dead?

6 He is not here, but is risen: remember how he spake unto you when he was yet in Galilee,

7 Saying, The Son of man must be delivered into the hands of sinful men, and be crucified, and the third day rise again.

8 And they remembered his words,

9 And returned from the sepulchre, and told all these things unto the eleven, and to all the rest.

10 It was Mary Magdalene, and Joanna, and Mary the mother of James, and other women that were with them, which told these things unto the apostles.

11 And their words seemed to them as idle tales, and they believed them not.

12 Then arose Peter, and ran unto the sepulchre; and stooping down, he beheld the linen clothes laid by themselves, and departed, wondering in himself at that which was come to pass.

A morning errand (Luke 24:1). The crucifixion of Jesus, an apparent victory for His enemies, was a devastating blow for His followers. Among these were women from Galilee (cf. 8:2-3) who had ministered to His needs during His ministry. They had stood at a distance at the crucifixion (23:49). Some also had followed those who buried Jesus and observed how His body was interred (vs. 55).

Jesus' body had been placed in a new, rock-hewn tomb belonging to Joseph of Arimathea, a member of the Sanhedrin and a secret disciple of Jesus (Luke 23:50-53). Before leaving the body, he and Nicodemus had wrapped it in linen, along with spices to cover the odor of decomposition (John 19:39-40). A large stone had then been rolled in front of the entrance (Matt. 27:60). The women had prepared spices and perfumes for further anointing after they observed the Sabbath (Luke 23:56).

Thus, "upon the first day of the week, very early in the morning" (Luke 24:1), these women undertook their labor of love. We do not know how many set out, though three of them are named later (vs. 10). The group included those who had prepared the spices "and certain others" (vs. 1). Some had seen the stone rolled before the tomb, and they speculated about how they might remove it (Mark 16:3).

A disappointing discovery (Luke 24:2-3). They need not have worried about the stone, for they found it "rolled away from the sepulchre." Unbeknownst to them, an angel had come earlier and rolled back the stone (Matt. 28:2). At his appearance, the guards posted by Pilate at the Pharisees' request (27:62-66) shook and "became as dead men" (28:4). By the time the women arrived, the guards had left, and they had no way of interpreting the open tomb.

They were further unsettled when "they entered in, and found not the body of the Lord Jesus" (Luke 24:3). Each was left to decide for herself what this might mean. We know that at least one of them, Mary Magdalene, concluded that someone had stolen Jesus' body. She evidently bolted out without hearing an explanation and told this to Peter and John (John 20:1-2). She persisted in believing this until Jesus appeared to her and identified Himself (vss. 11-16).

An encouraging message (Luke 24:4-7). Those who remained at the tomb suddenly saw "two men . . . in shining garments." "Behold" emphasizes their sudden and striking appearance. Matthew and Mark mentioned only one man (Matt. 28:5; Mark 16:5). John, however, wrote of two angels who later spoke to Mary Magdalene (John 20:12). Two were no doubt present, and one acted as spokesman.

The women's first reaction to the angels was fright: "they were afraid, and bowed down their faces to the earth" (Luke 24:5). This was a typical reaction of mortals to heavenly beings (cf. Luke 1:12; Acts 10:3-4). But the angels reassured them: "Why seek ye the living among the dead?" (Luke 24:5). They did not refer to Jesus as risen but as "living." He had life in Himself; death was foreign to His nature (John 1:4; 5:24-26; 14:6). It was therefore incongruous that He should have been in the tomb at all.

The angels continued, "He is not here, but is risen: remember how he spake unto you when he was yet in Galilee" (Luke 24:6). They first clarified why Jesus was not there: He had risen. This removed the perplexity the women had felt (vs. 4). The angels then reminded them that Jesus had actually foretold His resurrection "when he was yet in Galilee" (vs. 6). They implied that the women should have remembered this. These women were from Galilee themselves (23:49), and it was during His Galilean ministry that they had joined Him (8:1-3).

They should have remembered Jesus' statement that "the Son of man must be delivered into the hands of sinful men, and be crucified, and the third day rise again" (Luke 24:7). We have no record of Jesus telling these women these facts, but the Gospel writers recount several occasions when He told the Twelve. We may assume that the Twelve would have told the women what Jesus had said.

The first time Jesus revealed His coming death and resurrection was just after Peter had confessed Him as the Christ (Matt. 16:21; cf. Luke 9:22). So foreign was this prospect from Peter's image of the Messiah that he rebuked Jesus for saying it, drawing a sharp rebuke from Jesus in return (Matt. 16:22-23). The second occasion came just after Jesus had healed a demon-possessed boy. According to Mark 9:31-32, the disciples did not understand His prophecy and were afraid to question Him further (cf. Luke 9:44-45).

Jesus' third prophecy was given as He and the Twelve made their way to Jerusalem for the last time (Mark 10:32-34; Luke 18:31-33). This time He included more detail, indicating that the Jewish officials would turn Him over to the Gentiles. In each prophecy, Jesus mentioned the resurrection on the third day. But His disciples never understood (cf. Mark 9:9-10).

A prompt report (Luke 24:8-10). Once reminded, the women "remembered his words." They had not comprehended them before, but now they made sense. The resurrection had a way of clarifying many things Jesus had said and done (cf. Luke 24:25-27, 44-47; John 2:22; 12:16).

Thus encouraged, the women left the tomb to tell the Eleven what they had learned (Luke 24:9). Along the way, Jesus Himself met them, and they worshipped Him (Matt. 28:8-9). So when they reached the disciples, they could report not only the empty tomb and the angels' message but also the fact that they had seen Jesus Himself. They were firsthand witnesses that the message was true. Jesus had truly risen from the dead!

At this point, Luke named the prominent women in this group (Luke 24:10). First mentioned is Mary Magdalene, named for her hometown of Magdala near the Sea of Galilee. She had become a devoted follower of Jesus after He cast seven demons out of her (Mark 16:9; Luke 8:2). As noted earlier, she probably left the group before she heard the angels' explanation. Her encounter with Jesus is recorded in John 20:1-18.

The second woman mentioned is Joanna (Luke 24:10). She too was a Galilean who assisted in Jesus' ministry. She was the wife of a prominent official, Chuza, who was Herod's steward (8:3). The third is Mary the mother of James (24:10). She, also said to be the mother of Joses, was present at the crucifixion (Matt. 27:56, 61; Mark 15:40, 47). She was the wife of Cleophas (John 19:25). These, along with an unspecified number of other women, broke the news to the apostles (Luke 24:10).

An unbelieving response (Luke 24:11). One would expect the disciples to be overwhelmed with joy at the women's report. Instead, "their words seemed to them as idle tales, and they believed them not." Part of the reason for their skepticism was the cultural bias against women in that day. In both Hebrew and Greco-Roman society, women were thought to be inferior to men, and their witness was therefore held to be untrustworthy.

But besides this bias, the disciples were simply hindered by their lack of faith. As noted earlier, they had been unable to comprehend Jesus' death and resurrection, and even after this He had to rebuke them for "their unbelief and hardness of heart" (Mark 16:14). They would not believe until they had seen Him with their own eyes.

This skepticism, ironically, strengthens the proof for Jesus' resurrection. They were clearly *not* expecting Him to rise, so they would not imagine they had seen Him. Nor would they have stolen His body to make others believe He had risen. They were a defeated, dejected lot, in hiding because they feared what might happen to them next.

A confirming proof (Luke 24:12). Luke includes, however, a glimmer of faith in the experience of Peter. John records how Mary Magdalene told Peter and the other disciple, whom Jesus loved (probably John) (20:2), that someone had stolen Jesus' body. The two of them then ran to the tomb, and Peter went in (vss. 3-7). Luke recorded only Peter's visit, but he, like John, mentioned the "linen clothes laid by themselves" (24:12). This would seem to be evidence that Jesus' body had slipped through them.

Our text does not say this convinced Peter; instead, he went away wondering what had happened. By that evening Jesus would appear to Peter personally (Luke 24:34; I Cor. 15:5). Eventually, all the skeptical apostles saw the risen Christ, and their lives changed forever. And so has the history of the whole world.

—*Robert E. Wenger.*

QUESTIONS

1. To what kingdom was Hosea sent? What conditions existed there?

2. Has Hosea's exhortation to return to God been fulfilled? Explain.

3. To what kind of knowledge of the Lord was Israel exhorted?

4. Why did the women wait until the third day to anoint Jesus' body?

5. What was unsettling to the women when they arrived at the tomb?

6. What does the question "Why seek ye the living among the dead?" (Luke 24:5) tell us about Jesus?

7. What words of Jesus had the women forgotten?

8. Why had the disciples not taken prophecies of Jesus' death and resurrection to heart?

9. How does the disciples' skepticism strengthen proof for the resurrection?

10. What was Peter's reaction after looking into the empty tomb?

—*Robert E. Wenger.*

Preparing to Teach the Lesson

As bleak as any situation might seem to be, there is hope when we trust in the Lord. God warned Israel that He would need to punish them if they turned away from Him. However, He also promised to restore them when they repented and came back to Him with contrite hearts.

When Jesus was crucified and buried, all hope that He was the Messiah seemed gone. However, He had promised He would rise on the third day, and God is always faithful in keeping His promises.

TODAY'S AIM

Facts: to show that God promised to restore Israel when they repented and that He promised to resurrect Christ when He was crucified for man's sin.

Principle: to show that when sin results in judgment, God provides forgiveness and life.

Application: to show that while sin must be punished, God provides forgiveness and the way of salvation when we turn to Him.

INTRODUCING THE LESSON

Disobedience and rebellion cause a child to turn against his father. In order to correct the bad behavior and restore the relationship, the father must bring an appropriate punishment. When Israel turned away from God in sin, He punished the nation as He had promised. God promised to restore them at the appropriate time when they repented and returned to Him.

On a larger scale, mankind's sin had to be punished by a holy God. Jesus took upon Himself the punishment mankind deserved. God accepted Jesus' sacrifice in our place and showed His approval by raising Him from the dead. Since the punishment has been given, we are now invited to come to the Father in the righteousness of Christ.

DEVELOPING THE LESSON

Ask your class to briefly define the role of an Old Testament prophet. Ask what they know about Hosea. Explain that the prophet's role was often very difficult. It was his responsibility to speak for God to the people. He was called into service when the people strayed, and his message was often mixed with judgment and hope. Hosea's experience was especially difficult, for he was given the unique responsibility of marrying an unfaithful and immoral woman to symbolize Israel's unfaithfulness to God.

In his message to Israel, he spoke from the perspective of the book of Deuteronomy, which contained curses for disobedience to God and blessings for obedience. Sadly, Israel had been especially proficient in disobedience, which led to God's judgment.

Hosea 4 through 14 presents a case from God against Israel. In chapter 4 God dealt with Israel's refusal to acknowledge Him. In chapter 5 He dealt with the judgment for this sin.

In Hosea 5:15 God warned that He would turn away from Israel until they genuinely acknowledged their sin and sought Him with their hearts. As we come to our lesson passage, we find a glimpse of hope.

1. Raised up the third day (Hos. 6:1-3). Before we can receive the blessings of God, we must first recognize our sin and guilt. A well-known pastor once said that it is a mistake to tell people they are sinners. However, Scripture shows the opposite to be true. Give your class an opportunity to respond to this.

God revealed that in the future, Israel will realize the truth and will call for a return to the Lord (Hos. 6:1). They will understand and admit that the suffering they have experienced was the proper punishment they deserved from God. At that time they will understand His promise that when they return to Him, He will heal them and bind up the wounds from their discipline.

Have someone from your class read Deuteronomy 30:1-10 aloud. This passage contains an interesting parallel to the resurrection of Christ. In their call to return to the Lord, Israel will anticipate being restored in three days.

Tim LaHaye and Ed Hindson have offered this worthwhile explanation of Hosea 6:1-3. They place the event during the tribulation. The Jewish leaders will call upon the nation to recognize why they have experienced the tribulation and their need to acknowledge Christ.

"In the three days mentioned in Hosea 6:1-3, the confession of Israel's national sin will take place during the first two days. This confession appears in Isaiah 53:1-9 and admits that the nation had looked upon Jesus as nothing more than another man, a criminal who had died for His own sins. However, on this occasion they will recognize that Jesus was no ordinary man, but the perfect Lamb of God, the Messiah Himself. Then on the third of the three days, the people as a nation will be saved, fulfilling the prophecy of Romans 11:25-27" (LaHaye and Hindson, eds., *The Popular Bible Prophecy Commentary*, Harvest House Publishers).

2. Risen on the third day (Luke 24:1-12). Just as Israel will anticipate its own restoration on the third day, so the promise was made by Jesus that He would be resurrected on the third day after His crucifixion.

Focus the attention of the class on Luke 24:7, in which the angel reminded the women of Jesus' own words when He had spoken with them in Galilee.

Have volunteers from the class read the following passages, in which we find Jesus' warnings about His coming crucifixion: Matthew 17:12, 22-23; 20:18-19; 26:2; Mark 8:31; 9:31; and John 3:14; 12:32.

Next, have volunteers read the following passages, focusing on His promise of His resurrection on the third day: Matthew 12:40; 17:22-23; 20:19; Mark 8:31; 9:31; and John 2:19. Note that some of the passages will be repeated.

Often a question will arise about the actual day of the week when the crucifixion took place. It is an interesting study, but it can detract from the main point of the lesson.

ILLUSTRATING THE LESSON

Christ's resurrection frees from sin those who trust in Jesus.

BELIEVERS ARE FREE FROM SIN

JESUS IS RISEN

CONCLUDING THE LESSON

Just as Jesus' disciples should have anticipated His resurrection on the third day after His crucifixion, so Israel can anticipate its restoration when it turns back to God.

ANTICIPATING THE NEXT LESSON

Next week's lesson will examine Jesus' resurrection in light of Old Testament prophecy.

—*Carter Corbrey.*

PRACTICAL POINTS

1. God's enduring promises of renewal are as timeless as He is (Hos. 6:1-3).
2. Jesus is not to be found among the dead figures of history; He is alive (Luke 24:1-3)!
3. God provides answers and guidance when we lack both (vs. 4).
4. We are most aware of God's constant presence when we sense Him working in our lives (vss. 5-8).
5. Sometimes we serve God best not in special circumstances but in our regular routine (vss. 9-10).
6. When we realize that God has helped us in an unforeseen way, it not only strengthens but also encourages our faith (vss. 11-12).

—Anne Adams.

RESEARCH AND DISCUSSION

1. Does assurance of God's forgiveness encourage you? Why or why not? How does this affect your attitude toward new areas of ministry?
2. Jesus often mentioned His resurrection. So why did the women bring spices for the body if they knew He would rise? Discuss.
3. Why do you think the female disciples, not the male disciples, came first to Jesus' tomb? If the male disciples had come first, would they have believed as the women did? Why or why not? Discuss.
4. What do you think puzzled Peter when he looked into the empty tomb? Describe how you might react in that situation.

—Anne Adams.

ILLUSTRATED HIGH POINTS

Let us return unto the Lord

"I'm running away!" Many a child has announced such intentions, usually well before they reach their tenth birthday. Parents respond in a variety of ways, but most accept their offspring's decision to leave home. The child, amazed by the parents' cooperation, usually reneges on the threat or leaves for an abbreviated period of time. Hunger, boredom, lack of dramatic feedback—all may be factors that cause the youngster to relent on the decision to run away. He is normally back home by dinnertime.

Like the insolent child, we at times retreat from our Father. We choose our own desires over His direction. Hopefully we, like the temporary runaway child, return to the Lord before we have caused damage to ourselves or our future. Jesus paid the price so that those who have strayed can return to the Father, and that includes all of mankind.

And they remembered his words

"Oh, no! I'm starting to sound just like my parents!" How many of us have said these words? This statement reveals that we really *were* paying attention, as hard as we may have tried not to listen. The corrections and instructions our parents gave us were usually unsolicited and seemingly unnecessary. However, through maturity and life experience, we come to recognize the wisdom in their words.

Jesus told His disciples many times that He would be crucified and rise again. They seem to have been oblivious to the message, even doubtful of its truth. But when they saw Him in His resurrected state, they remembered the words He had spoken to them. Jesus has also said that He will come again to meet us in the air. Let us be watchful and believing, remembering His words to us.

—Beverly Jones.

Golden Text Illuminated

"Remember how he spake unto you when he was yet in Galilee, saying, The Son of man must be delivered into the hands of sinful men, and be crucified, and the third day rise again" (Luke 24:6-7).

The crucifixion and resurrection of Jesus Christ played out like other events in life. Each step and decision was determined by decisions that preceded it. Nobody knew with certainty where it all would lead. Or so it seemed.

The angels who met the women at the empty tomb reminded them that even back in Galilee, Jesus had explicitly declared that these events would take place. He had said first that He would be "delivered into the hands of sinful men." While all people are sinful by nature, and Jesus knew this better than anyone (cf. John 2:24), the reference here is particularly directed to the Gentile Romans (cf. Luke 18:32). The Romans practiced the brutal art of crucifixion, and they alone had the authority to carry it out in Jerusalem.

The angels also reminded the women that Jesus had foretold His resurrection on the "third day." It was now the third day, and the tomb of Jesus, to which the women had come, stood empty.

Jesus actually had foretold His death and resurrection on a number of different occasions. In fact, He had given His followers explicit details of what would happen to Him: He would be betrayed; the chief priests, elders, and scribes would condemn Him; He would be turned over to the Gentiles; and He would be mocked, scourged, spat upon, and crucified. But He also repeatedly foretold His resurrection on the third day (cf. Matt. 16:21; 17:22-23; 20:18-19; Luke 9:22, 44; 18:32-33).

The women and the disciples they would later inform had already witnessed the suffering and death Jesus had foretold. We might think that the fulfillment of Jesus' words regarding these things would have given the disciples hope that He would also rise from the dead on the third day. But the disciples were not at the tomb on the third day expecting Him to appear, and the women who were there were looking for a dead body, not a living Saviour.

With hindsight it is easy to be critical of Jesus' followers. But it seems that their visions of Jesus' kingdom blinded them to the suffering He had to endure before His kingdom comes. Any talk of His suffering and death was put out of their minds. It was too unpleasant to contemplate or even consider for the King of kings.

The brutality of the crucifixion and the beatings that preceded it erased all hope for the disciples. How could anyone—even their King—triumph over death?

The angels reminded Jesus' followers of His words; and in the hours and days ahead, the risen Christ Himself would prove their truthfulness. He would appear to His disciples, teach them, encourage them, and prepare them to take the gospel to the world (Acts 1:3). Essential to that gospel is the death, burial, and bodily resurrection of Jesus Christ (I Cor. 15:1-8).

What we see in the resurrection of Christ is what we so often see in our own lives. Things that take us by surprise are really things that God has planned all along for His own good purposes (cf. Acts 2:23-24).

—Jarl K. Waggoner.

Heart of the Lesson

Concerning the resurrection of Jesus Christ, Dr. Charles Swindoll said, "Let's face it. If Jesus didn't stand up that first Easter morning, lay aside His burial wrappings, and leave the tomb to walk among those who loved Him, nothing really matters. Let me write that another way. If Jesus didn't rise from the dead, or if His resurrection was a hoax, then nothing—absolutely nothing—has any meaning at all.

"Any blessing you enjoy will come to a sudden, heartbreaking end. Any good work we accomplish will either decay or quickly become obsolete. When our life has passed—a mere twinkling of a moment when compared to the eons before and after you—any impact we leave will be washed away like footprints in wave-washed sand" (*The Cemetery Evangelist*," Insight for Living).

In this week's lesson, we learn once again of the reality of our risen Saviour!

1. Challenge to return and serve the Lord (Hos. 6:1-3). Hosea urgently exhorted Israel to return to the Lord. He clearly revealed that the God of all mercy stood ready to welcome and restore His people. The prophet's assurance of God's forgiveness and restoration was presented under the theme of "the third day," which has scriptural significance (cf. Exod. 19:10-16). As a result, the Lord's healing and restoration would be a very special day of victory for God's people.

Hosea's assurances are as certain as the regularity of God-supervised nature itself. God's future blessing upon His repentant and received people is as certain as the coming of the dawn of each new day and the seasonal winter and spring rains.

God delights in giving good gifts to His people (cf. Ps. 37:4; Jas. 1:17). God's people should delight in personal repentance, which restores them to an intimate relationship with God and His blessings for them.

2. Discovery of the empty tomb (Luke 24:1-7). Several special women came to the tomb where Jesus' body had been placed. They entered the tomb and discovered that His body was not there. The women were at a loss for words, but two angelic creatures told them that Jesus had risen from the dead in fulfillment of His prior teaching (cf. Mark 9:30-31).

Followers of Jesus Christ are not immune to emotional distress. In fact, many believers have faced times of despair and devastation when the disappointments of life overwhelm them. But because Jesus lives and because He experienced earthly suffering, He is able to give spiritual aid to His children in distress through His angelic ministers (cf. Heb. 1:14).

3. Contrasting responses to the reports of resurrection (Luke 24:8-12). When the women came to their senses and remembered what Jesus had told them, they left the empty tomb to share their spiritual experience with Jesus' disciples. However, the disciples dismissed the women's testimony as nonsense. Peter, though, was intrigued. He raced to the empty tomb, made an eyewitness discovery, and departed, contemplating the future.

Followers of Jesus Christ should be reflective thinkers. They should embrace the mystery of the risen Jesus Christ and His gospel (cf. Eph. 3:4; 6:19). With a sense of awe and wonderment, believers should also delight in growing in a full assurance of spiritual understanding as the Holy Spirit reveals to them the truth of God's inspired Word (cf. Col. 2:2).

—*Thomas R. Chmura.*

World Missions

Many Christians give up reading the Old Testament because it is hard to understand. But in light of what the prophets had to say, the Old Testament is a document of divine purpose. Without the Old Testament, we would not know what was coming, for it was these Old Testament prophets who pointed to the coming of the resurrected King. While the people of God knew about the coming Messiah, many of those in Jesus' time did not recognize Him when He did show up.

Jesus commanded us to tell the world about His resurrection so that everyone will know that He is alive and that He has already paid the price for our sins. It is a message of redemption. We are told that one day He will return again and take us to be with Him forever. That is good news! Yet there are many in our world who do not yet know of this resurrected Jesus. He conquered death and sin and lived to tell us about it so that we can now reap the benefits of His suffering for us.

Paul reminds us that the Son of Man who was crucified is the same one who has risen again. The day Jesus' death is remembered is often referred to by the Christian church as "Good Friday," even though it reminds us of a terrible crime against the only sinless Man who walked this earth. However, it is still *good* because Jesus ushered us into the good news of the gospel that became manifest to us in the form of a resurrected King. He suffered in shame but was raised for us in glory.

Is this not news worth sharing with the world? In these difficult days, the world could use some really good news. The Bible reminds us that we are to go out into all the world and speak to people who speak all kinds of languages and proclaim the good news in their own languages so that they understand. When we look at the sacrifices that people down through the ages have made to tell the world this simple but wonderful message, we see how important this message is for the world. It provides hope in a lost world.

It is very interesting that Paul reminds us in the epistles that "if Christ be not risen, then is our preaching vain, and your faith is also vain" (I Cor. 15:14). In other words, every missionary effort would be pointless, because it hangs on the resurrection of Jesus. We would be wasting our time if we were only proclaiming a dead Jesus who is still in the grave. What motivates us to tell the world is that this Jesus who died on the cross rose again and showed Himself to many people to prove it.

We can ask ourselves yet another important question: what is it that motivates so many people to spend their lives proclaiming this message about a Jewish carpenter who died and rose again? It was God's way of showing us that the prophets talked about Him many years ago, and now He had fulfilled their prophecies. He was indeed the King they had talked about who would deliver them.

Yes, in our lesson this week, Jesus is referred to as a King. If this King suffered for us, then we must reciprocate with gratitude by telling the world what He has done for us and what He can do for them. The world needs to know that the One who was crucified is the same One who is now on the throne as Lord so that we might have hope in Him.

—A. Koshy Muthalaly.

The Jewish Aspect

The rabbi spoke warmly of Jesus, even approving of much of the Lord's opposition to the Pharisees. I am sure most of those in the Introduction to Judaism course considered rabbis of the Reform movement to be latter-day disciples of the Pharisees. The female rabbi shocked us by saying, "We are Sadducees."

Sadducees are best known for their denial of both bodily resurrection and the reality of angels. In general, they were committed solely to what Moses taught in the Torah, the first five books of the Old Testament. The Sadducees were the wealthy, controlling religious body. The high priests Annas and Caiaphas were Sadducees who were in power during the Lord's ministry.

Alfred Edersheim, a noted Jewish believer and writer, believes the Pharisees incited Herod to take action against John the Baptist. Early in his ministry, John had greeted the Sadducees and Pharisees with the words "O generation of vipers, who hath warned you to flee from the wrath to come?" (Matt. 3:7). John spoke of the ax laid to the roots, a suggestion that a false religious system would not stand (vs. 10).

If Edersheim was correct, the half-Edomite puppet ruler, Herod, smarting under John's attack, may have been pressured to cast John the Baptist into prison, where he was later executed (*The Life and Times of Jesus the Messiah,* Hendrickson).

Our lesson title this week is "The Resurrection of the King." Jesus' triumph over the grave largely spelled an end to Pharisaic opposition. The difficult job of denying the bodily resurrection of the Saviour now was up to the Sadducees. The female rabbi referred to earlier must carry on the masking of the best-known miracle of antiquity in order to keep her Jewish congregants from finding the truth. In our text, we have the marvelous words of Hosea 6:2: "After two days will he revive us: in the third day he will raise us up, and we shall live in his sight." What a remarkable forecast of resurrection! For many, Judaism is a mourner's faith. No hope of a deliverance from death is given.

First on the scene at a death is the Chevra Kadisha Society, those who wash and prepare the body for the funeral. No embalming is permitted. The body is simply washed and placed in the coffin. A small bag of dirt from Israel is placed behind the head of the deceased, signifying that he is figuratively being buried in the Holy Land.

The mourning family prepares the home by covering mirrors, storing pictures of the deceased, and draping the furniture with cloth. Everyone who comes must sit on the floor. No family members attend parties or recreational activities for a considerable time. On the anniversary of the death (called Yahrzeit), the loved one is remembered with prayer and candles.

How sad it is that the people who had a hope of life after death have sentenced themselves to the consistent denial of a blessed reunion through resurrection!

Issy was beside himself at his father's funeral. At the graveside, Issy broke down in tears and made as if to plunge into the open grave. He was restrained. "It's against the Din" (the law covering burial). Plaintively, Issy cried, "Is that all there is to life, rabbi?" "Yes," the rabbi reassured him, "that's all there is."

It will be wonderful to be present at the reunion of Israel with the Messiah. They will look upon the One who was crucified for them, and the entire nation will rejoice.

—Lyle P. Murphy.

Guiding the Superintendent

Some biblical scholars contend that all prophets prophesied about the resurrection of Christ Jesus. This week's lesson contains Hosea's prophecy concerning the resurrection as expressed in the raising of the Israelite nation on the third day from their death-like state.

DEVOTIONAL OUTLINE

1. Portrayal of the resurrection (Hos. 6:1-3). Hosea's message was primarily to the northern kingdom of Israel. He foretold the irrevocable judgment that was certain to befall Israel because of their immorality.

An appropriate response to such a warning is to acknowledge and reject all sinful acts, repent, and turn to God. Although our sins are a stench in His nostrils, our Father's love and mercy will remain unchanged toward His children. In Christ we have confidence that He will not leave us dead in our sins or held captive by our iniquities. He will raise us up out of the pit of our degradation as a renewed people who are prepared to live in the presence of the Most High God.

2. The significance of the resurrection (Luke 24:1-8). As significant as the crucifixion is to the Christian faith, had it not been for the resurrection, Jesus would be remembered as just a man who died after performing many miraculous acts during his lifetime. The women's challenge would then have been the huge stone in front of Jesus' grave, not the fact that His body was not there. There would not have been "two angels in white" (John 20:12) who spoke to them and confronted them for not remembering Jesus' words. Finally, there would have been nothing to tell the disciples. Happily, the story does not end at the tomb! The stone was indeed rolled away, and the body of our Lord was not there—He had risen.

With great determination, Jesus took advantage of every opportunity to prepare His disciples for His death. Though He had spoken of it repeatedly, they lacked understanding. Perhaps these women were present when Jesus told His disciples of the events concerning His suffering and death, and perhaps they too had forgotten.

3. The significance of remembering Christ's words (Luke 24:9-12). It is critical that as believers, we remember Christ's words and, like David, commit to hiding His words in our hearts so that we might not sin against Him (Ps. 119:11). God's Word is His sword to use against the enemy. The Word emboldens us to run to tell others the glad tidings so that they too might come to know Christ and be saved. Although all will not believe our report that Jesus is the Christ, the Son of the living God, and that He came to redeem us from the penalty of sin and death, it remains our duty to declare it. We must constantly pray that, like Peter, lost men, women, boys, and girls will diligently seek Jesus.

AGE-GROUP EMPHASES

Children: Easter is an exciting time for children. Help them become excited about Jesus and the love that led Him to the cross.

Youths: Do not assume that they cannot comprehend the magnitude of Christ's death, burial, and resurrection. Give them time to express what Easter means to them.

Adults: Take time to reflect on this lesson. Challenge each student to examine his faith in the wonder-working power of the Word.

—Jane E. Campbell.

Scripture Lesson Text

ISA. 53:5 But he *was* wounded for our transgressions, *he was* bruised for our iniquities: the chastisement of our peace *was* upon him; and with his stripes we are healed.

6 All we like sheep have gone astray; we have turned every one to his own way; and the LORD hath laid on him the iniquity of us all.

7 He was oppressed, and he was afflicted, yet he opened not his mouth: he is brought as a lamb to the slaughter, and as a sheep before her shearers is dumb, so he openeth not his mouth.

8 He was taken from prison and from judgment: and who shall declare his generation? for he was cut off out of the land of the living: for the transgression of my people was he stricken.

LUKE 24:25 Then he said unto them, O fools, and slow of heart to believe all that the prophets have spoken:

26 Ought not Christ to have suffered these things, and to enter into his glory?

27 And beginning at Mo'ses and all the prophets, he expounded unto them in all the scriptures the things concerning himself.

44 And he said unto them, These *are* the words which I spake unto you, while I was yet with you, that all things must be fulfilled, which were written in the law of Mo'ses, and *in* the prophets, and *in* the psalms, concerning me.

45 Then opened he their understanding, that they might understand the scriptures,

46 And said unto them, Thus it is written, and thus it behoved Christ to suffer, and to rise from the dead the third day:

47 And that repentance and remission of sins should be preached in his name among all nations, beginning at Je-ru'sa-lem.

NOTES

116

From Suffering to Glory

Lesson: Isaiah 53:5-8; Luke 24:25-27, 44-47

Read: Isaiah 52:13—53:12; Luke 24:25-27, 44-50

TIMES: about 700–695 B.C.;
A.D. 30

PLACES: Jerusalem; near Emmaus;
Jerusalem

GOLDEN TEXT—"Beginning at Moses and all the prophets, he expounded unto them in all the scriptures the things concerning himself" (Luke 24:27).

Introduction

One of the hardest realities to accept is that the path upward often leads downward first. Rarely do we achieve our goals without first having to experience hardship or shame.

A pitcher who enters the major leagues as a young marvel suffers an injury that requires surgery and rehabilitation. A company with phenomenal success in marketing a new product founders in economic hard times and has to reorganize and start anew. A couple with great plans for their family suddenly have to cope with the challenges of rearing a Down syndrome child. Our world is full of such experiences.

Perhaps the most difficult truth for the ancient Jews to grasp was that their Messiah would have to experience the same pattern. They envisioned Him as a great Conqueror but could not fathom His hanging on a cross. Even His most loyal disciples, as this week's lesson shows, had to have their minds changed to understand the full scope of His mission.

LESSON OUTLINE

I. A DESCRIPTION OF CHRIST'S SUFFERING—Isa. 53:5-8

II. AN EXPLANATION OF CHRIST'S SUFFERING—Luke 24:25-27, 44-47

Exposition: Verse by Verse

A DESCRIPTION OF CHRIST'S SUFFERING

ISA. 53:5 But he was wounded for our transgressions, he was bruised for our iniquities: the chastisement of our peace was upon him; and with his stripes we are healed.

6 All we like sheep have gone astray; we have turned every one to his own way; and the LORD hath laid on him the iniquity of us all.

7 He was oppressed, and he was afflicted, yet he opened not his mouth: he is brought as a lamb to the slaughter, and as a sheep before her shearers is dumb, so he

openeth not his mouth.

8 He was taken from prison and from judgment: and who shall declare his generation? for he was cut off out of the land of the living: for the transgression of my people was he stricken.

The reason for His suffering (Isa. 53:5-6). Our verses from Isaiah 53 are part of one of several Servant passages in the book. This one begins at 52:13 and concludes at 53:12. The Servant of the Lord is seen first as highly exalted (52:13), but the picture quickly changes, and His humiliation and suffering dominate most of the rest of the passage. Parts of this passage are quoted by New Testament writers, all of whom accepted the premise that the Servant is Jesus.

Isaiah acknowledged the difficulty of accepting the report of a suffering Messiah (Isa. 53:1). Neither His place of origin nor His unassuming manner would impress the nation (vs. 2), and they would despise and reject Him (vs. 3). Though they would think Him "smitten of God" (vs. 4), the reason for His suffering was to bear their griefs and carry their sorrows.

He explained further Christ's substitutionary role: "he was wounded for our transgressions, he was bruised for our iniquities" (Isa. 53:5). This verse is filled with graphic terms. "Wounded" means "pierced," implying a severe bodily wound. "Bruised" means "crushed," implying complete brokenness of body and spirit. All this was for our "transgressions," which speaks of violations of God's standards. It was also for our "iniquities," which refers to crooked, perverse behavior.

"The chastisement of our peace" (Isa. 53:5) means the punishment that brought about our peace with God. It fell on Christ instead of us. Similarly, "with his stripes (blows, scourgings) we are healed." Our souls, broken and marred by sin, have been made whole by this Suffering Servant.

The whole verse speaks of substitution. It pictures sinners, at enmity with God and sick with sin, being reconciled and healed through the suffering of One who is innocent (cf. Rom. 4:25—5:1; II Cor. 5:21; I Pet. 3:18). The suffering described corresponds to what Jesus suffered in His humiliation and crucifixion (cf. John 19:1-3, 34).

Isaiah next illustrated the nature of our sin: "All we like sheep have gone astray; we have turned every one to his own way" (Isa. 53:6). Jesus told a parable to stress God's care for *one* lost sheep (Luke 15:3-7). Isaiah emphasized the waywardness of a *whole flock.* Israel was guilty of spurning the guidance of their loving Shepherd (cf. Isa. 40:11) and stubbornly following their own way.

Wayward sheep are guilty of "iniquity" (Isa. 53:6), for they follow a crooked path. But "the Lord hath laid on him (the Messiah) the iniquity of us all." This could be translated to say that He "has caused the iniquity of all of us to strike him violently." And just as the verse began with "all," so it also ends. All of us have gone astray and deserve punishment for it. But Jesus' substitutionary work is sufficient for the restoration of all (I Pet. 2:25; I John 2:2).

The manner of His suffering (Isa. 53:7-8). Though Jesus' death was a sacrifice for human sin, it was also a travesty of human justice. He was "oppressed" and "afflicted" in each of the trials to which He was subjected. Annas, Caiaphas, Herod Antipas, and Pontius Pilate all misused their authority in condemning a righteous man to death. The soldiers abused Him physically, and the crowds mocked Him.

Yet He bore it all with dignity and opened "not his mouth" (Isa. 53:7). In this He is likened to a lamb going quietly to the slaughter and a ewe being sheared without resistance. While the figure of sheep aptly describes wayward sinners (vs. 6), it also fittingly portrays this righteous Servant as He suffered (vs. 7). John the Baptist called Him "the Lamb of God" (John 1:29), and Peter cited Isaiah's portrayal of Him as an incentive for Christians to bear suffering patiently (I Pet. 2:22-23).

Isaiah continued to describe the Servant's suffering: "He was taken from prison and from judgment" (Isa. 53:8). "Prison" can read "unjust restraint," since Jesus never was imprisoned. From this restraint and judgment He was "taken away" by death. The words following, "And who shall declare his generation?" have received many interpretations. It seems best to take them to mean "And who can speak of His descendants?"

The point would be that Jesus was cut off in the prime of life and left no progeny. This is supported by the phrase "cut off out of the land of the living" (Isa. 53:8). "Cut off" always refers to a violent and premature death (cf. Exod. 12:19; Num. 9:13; Dan. 9:26). And to a normal onlooker, it would appear that Jesus was left without descendants, since He died suddenly. People would not take into account the millions of spiritual descendants brought into the family of God by faith in Him ("seed" in Isaiah 53:10).

The final statement in this section, "For the transgression of my people was he stricken" (Isa. 53:8), returns to the theme of substitution. The speaker here could be either Isaiah or the Lord, but either way "my people" refers primarily to Israel. They had violated God's law and deserved His judgment. But the Just One took their place and received the Lord's punishment (cf. vss. 9-10).

AN EXPLANATION OF CHRIST'S SUFFERING

LUKE 24:25 Then he said unto them, O fools, and slow of heart to believe all that the prophets have spoken:

26 Ought not Christ to have suffered these things, and to enter into his glory?

27 And beginning at Moses and all the prophets, he expounded unto them in all the scriptures the things concerning himself.

44 And he said unto them, These are the words which I spake unto you, while I was yet with you, that all things must be fulfilled, which were written in the law of Moses, and in the prophets, and in the psalms, concerning me.

45 Then opened he their understanding, that they might understand the scriptures,

46 And said unto them, Thus it is written, and thus it behoved Christ to suffer, and to rise from the dead the third day:

47 And that repentance and remission of sins should be preached in his name among all nations, beginning at Jerusalem.

A rebuke for unbelief (Luke 24:25-26). Old Testament references to Christ that seem clear to us were not nearly so clear to New Testament disciples. On the day of His resurrection, many of them did not make the connection between His finished work and Old Testament prophecy. Two of these were walking from Jerusalem to Emmaus, a village about seven miles away. Jesus joined them, and He found them demoralized by His death and confused by reports of the disappearance of His body (vss. 13-24).

After Jesus had heard their woeful story, He took charge of the conversation. He said abruptly, "O fools, and slow of heart to believe all that the prophets have spoken" (Luke 24:25). The Greek word for "fools" means "unthinking ones," or men devoid of understanding. This lack of understanding had made them "slow of heart" to believe the prophets.

It was not that these disciples had rejected prophetic testimony about the Messiah entirely; it was that they had not believed *all* the prophets had said (Luke 24:25). They had used Scripture selectively, focusing on what foretold His glorious reign and neglecting what pointed to His suffering. As we often do, they looked only at the revelation that supported their preconceived ideas. Thus, they could not take seriously even Jesus' own foretelling of His death and resurrection.

Jesus continued, "Ought not Christ to have suffered these things, and to enter into his glory?" (Luke 24:26). "Ought not" means "Was it not necessary?" The necessity of things happening to fulfill God's plan is a recurring theme in Luke (cf. 2:49; 4:43; 19:5; 21:9). Nothing happened by accident—not even Jesus' death.

It was not wrong to believe that He would "enter into his glory" (Luke 24:26). But the prophets had also spoken of the sufferings that had to precede the glory. They did not always understand the message they gave, but they gave it nonetheless (I Pet. 1:10-12). Jesus' death had to occur before He was glorified, and the disciples, like the prophets, should have believed this even though they did not understand.

The glory of Christ commenced with His resurrection (cf. Acts 17:3; Rom. 1:4), but it includes much more. He would yet ascend to heaven and take the most exalted position in the universe (Ps. 110:1; Acts 2:33-36; Heb. 8:1; 12:2). He will achieve the fullness of glory when He returns to reign (Dan. 7:13-14; Matt. 26:64; Rev. 1:7; 19:11-16). But none of this would have been possible without His death.

An exposition of messianic prophecies (Luke 24:27). The two disciples did not grasp this. So Jesus set out to enlighten them about "the things concerning himself." His exposition was wide-ranging. He began "at Moses and all the prophets" and eventually covered "all the scriptures." Luke did not specify any passages, but it is clear that they were found in all three divisions of Hebrew Scripture—the Law, the Prophets, and the Writings.

What a marvelous teaching session it must have been—a flawless exposition of prophecies, types, and parables that foreshadowed His Person and work! And it was exhaustive, including the whole of the scriptual record. The two disciples did not know who He was. Yet they were captivated by His teaching, for afterward they reflected, "Did not our heart burn within us, . . . while he opened to us the scriptures?" (Luke 24:32; cf. Ps. 39:3).

A reminder of Scripture's fulfillment (Luke 24:44). The two disciples reached their destination, invited Jesus to stay with them, and sat down to eat. But after Jesus had given thanks for the food, He vanished, and they knew immediately who He was (vss. 28-32). Filled with joy they could not contain, they returned to Jerusalem and shared the good news with the Eleven and others gathered with them (vss. 33-35).

But even as they talked, "Jesus himself stood in the midst of them" (Luke 24:36). As they sat frozen in fright, He reassured them that it was He, not a spirit, whom they saw. He showed them His wounds and ate in their presence (vss. 37-43). Then, knowing they would be receptive, He began to teach them.

He reminded them that He had told them all of those things while He had been with them. This remarkable statement shows that Jesus' earthly ministry was now ended. He was no longer with them in the way He had been before the Cross. His body, though real, was glorified and fitted for heavenly realms, and His few remaining days on earth were only to confirm His resurrection and prepare His followers for their ministry.

But He called to their attention the statements He had made in those previous days. He had told them then "that all things must be fulfilled, which were written in the law of Moses, and in the prophets, and in the psalms, concerning me" (Luke 24:44). He had revealed how He would fulfill what was in all three divisions of Hebrew Scripture.

An enlightenment of understanding (Luke 24:45-47). Jesus "opened . . . their understanding" to comprehend what they previously had not. He quickened their minds so that the scriptural truths about Him might become clear. He had the power to illuminate the minds of believing disciples, a power He would later assign to the Holy Spirit (cf. John 14:25-26; 15:26). As a result, we know that the apostolic interpretation of the Old Testament is trustworthy.

Once again, Luke reveals no specific content of Jesus' teaching. With "thus it is written" (24:46), he merely summarizes its major themes. "Behoved" reminds us again of all that was necessary to the fulfillment of God's redemptive plan. First, it was necessary for Christ to suffer. This was the truth that had eluded them before in spite of repeated prophecies. Second, He had to "rise from the dead the third day." They previously had not grasped this simply because they had refused to concede that He had to die.

The Scriptures had also indicated "that repentance and remission of sins should be preached in his name among all nations" (Luke 24:47). The gospel was not for Jews alone; people of all nations were included in God's gracious plan (cf. Matt. 28:19; Mark 16:15; Acts 1:8). Though Old Testament writers did not foresee the eradication of all Jew-Gentile distinctions in the church (Eph. 3:5-6), many passages did speak of the extension of salvation to the nations (cf. Isa. 49:6; 56:6-7).

This outreach of the good news would begin at Jerusalem (Luke 24:47). It was imperative that the witness to His death and resurrection begin there. It was where they had occurred but also where the authorities had painted the crucifixion in its most negative light and denied the resurrection altogether. It was therefore important that the city become the center from which the true message should emanate.

Jesus concluded by reminding the Eleven that they were witnesses of all that had occurred, ordained to spread the good news (Luke 24:48; cf. Acts 1:8; 2:32). But He encouraged them with the promise that God's power would come upon them to enable them for their task (Luke 24:49). With this same challenge and promise, let us go forth to share His gospel.

—Robert E. Wenger

QUESTIONS

1. What graphic terms did Isaiah use to describe Messiah's suffering and the causes for it?

2. How does Isaiah's illustration of wayward sheep differ from Jesus' parable of the lost sheep?

3. How is the suffering Messiah likened to sheep?

4. What kind of death is depicted by the phrase "cut off" (Isa. 53:8)?

5. Why did Jesus call the disciples on the Emmaus road "fools" (Luke 24:25)?

6. How was these disciples' view of the Messiah flawed?

7. How thorough was Jesus' teaching of the Scriptures about Himself?

8. Of what previous words did Jesus remind the Eleven as He stood among them?

9. What major themes did Jesus teach the disciples from Scripture?

10. Where was the outreach to the Gentiles to start? Why?

—Robert E. Wenger

Preparing to Teach the Lesson

In this week's lesson we will look at Isaiah's prophecy of the Suffering Servant and at Jesus' meetings with His disciples in which He explained the Old Testament prophecies of His coming.

TODAY'S AIM

Facts: to study how the Old Testament prophecies specifically foretold Jesus' death and resurrection.

Principle: to show that Jesus fulfilled the prophecies that promised the Messiah.

Application: to prove that since Jesus is the Messiah of the Old Testament who died and rose again, we can trust Him for our salvation.

INTRODUCING THE LESSON

When we place our trust in someone, we want to know that he is worthy of that trust. We need to be able to verify the claims he makes. God provided many specific prophecies of a Saviour over a long period of time so that when the Saviour finally arrived, He could be recognized without doubt. Any person claiming to be the Messiah had to provide evidence by fulfilling all of the required prophecies.

The only person in history who actually met the qualifications was Jesus, the Son of David and the Son of God.

DEVELOPING THE LESSON

Help your students understand that the Bible was written over a long period of time. New additions to the Scriptures were given over time as needed. These additions gave additional history and new revelations from God about Himself, the world, and how His overall plan was to unfold. Many of these additions were clues and prophecies and promises concerning the coming of the Messiah. The first promise of the

Messiah was given in Genesis 3:15.

Over time, God gave more specific information about how He was going to provide salvation. By the time Isaiah prophesied, God had revealed that the Messiah would come through Abraham, then Isaac, then Jacob (Israel), and then through the tribe of Judah. Within Judah, the Messiah would come through David, and He would occupy David's throne for eternity.

1. Isaiah's prophecy of the Messiah's death (Isa. 53:5-8). Isaiah prophesied about seven hundred years before his prophecies of Christ would be fulfilled. The prophecies in Isaiah present some of the most specific and significant descriptions of the coming Messiah found anywhere in the Old Testament. Isaiah foretold the virgin birth, the future reign, and the identity of the Messiah as One having both a divine and a human nature—God in the flesh.

Isaiah 52:13 through 53:12 is known as the song of the Suffering Servant because it pictures the Messiah as God's Servant who will suffer as man's substitute for the punishment due for sin. As you present this first portion of your lesson, explain the passage from Isaiah's perspective—looking ahead to the coming of the Saviour. Stress that the prophets did not have the complete picture but only bits and pieces to try to understand.

Help your class appreciate the advantage we have today with the completed New Testament. Jesus' sacrifice and resurrection have now been completed and explained.

Examine with your class the specific details that are contained in Isaiah's prophecy, and realize they are pieces of a developing puzzle. Piece together what Isaiah is saying, and write on the board, with your students' help, what you discover. Try to avoid reading into the prophecy what you already know from the New Testament. On the board, list and number each new fact you discover.

For example, what do you find in Isaiah 53:5? He was wounded. If you explore on a deeper level, you will find that the word "wounded" actually means to be pierced.

Continue this process until you have finished the lesson text. Then summarize your findings. From these facts, what would you look for to help you identify the Messiah when He came?

Remember that hindsight is always better than foresight. Fulfilled prophecy is always easier to explain than prophecies that are awaiting fulfillment.

2. Jesus' explanation of the prophecies (Luke 24:25-27, 44-47). Briefly ask your students whether they have ever anticipated something that did not turn out as they expected. If so, why? Point out how Jesus' disciples often failed to grasp what He had been telling them, particularly when He warned them about the events of His last week. It may help to refer to the following passages: Matthew 26:31-35; Luke 9:43-45; and John 12:12-16; 13:1-7. Point out especially the resurrection account in John 20:1-10.

The disciples were devastated when Jesus was crucified. Then, when the tomb was found empty and the resurrection had taken place, they still did not fully understand what had happened and how to respond to it.

Point out from Luke 24:13-24 that the two disciples on the way to Emmaus reflected the perplexed sentiments of Jesus' followers on the afternoon of the resurrection. Even though the prophecies of the Old Testament spoke of Jesus' birth, nature, ministry, death, burial, and resurrection, it was necessary for Jesus to clarify these things and put them into their proper perspective.

Once the disciples had the complete picture, including how the Messiah had to die and be resurrected, they understood without a doubt that Jesus was the prophesied Messiah.

Divide the remainder of the lesson into two sections—Jesus' meeting with the two disciples on the road to Emmaus and Jesus' meeting with the disciples in Jerusalem.

Luke wrote that Jesus began at Moses and all the prophets and expounded "in all the scriptures the things concerning himself (Luke 24:27)." He was thorough in covering every messianic prophecy. Locate a list of messianic prophecies, and post it on your board.

ILLUSTRATING THE LESSON

Without doubt, the Old Testament prophecies pointed to Jesus.

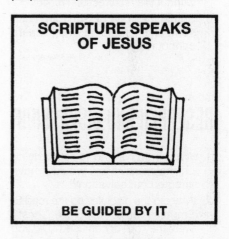

SCRIPTURE SPEAKS OF JESUS

BE GUIDED BY IT

CONCLUDING THE LESSON

When the directions and descriptions are given in advance that will enable you to identify a particular person, it is foolish to miss that person when he arrives.

ANTICIPATING THE NEXT LESSON

In our next lesson we will look at Jesus' temptation in the wilderness and how He used the Scriptures to overcome Satan.

—*Carter Corbrey.*

PRACTICAL POINTS

1. Those who reject Christ must think that they are good enough for God without Him (Isa. 53:5-6).
2. Because He loved us, Christ endured the utmost suffering to achieve His desire, which is our salvation (vss. 7-8).
3. Often we fail to do God's will because we concentrate too much on our own (Luke 24:25-27).
4. We appreciate God's perfect plans for us as we realize how intricate they are (vss. 44-45).
5. Christ's death for our salvation would have been of no benefit for us without His resurrection (vs. 46).
6. Sometimes one person can reach someone for Christ when others cannot (vs. 47).

—Anne Adams.

RESEARCH AND DISCUSSION

1. What if Jesus had resisted dying on the cross? How would it have affected our salvation?
2. Why did the disciples on the road to Emmaus fail to recognize Christ? Were they dull or confused? Did you immediately understand the gospel when you first heard it, or did you need further explanation?
3. What made the disciples suddenly understand Jesus' message when they had previously had difficulty? Which is surer—a quick belief in Christ or a conversion that takes a long time? Discuss.
4. What motivated the disciples to immediately begin preaching as Christ had instructed them? Discuss.

—Anne Adams.

ILLUSTRATED HIGH POINTS

All that the prophets have spoken

A favorite uncle promised his eight-year-old niece that he would buy her a car when she turned sixteen. The little girl embraced his words with wide-eyed expectation. Three years later, her family moved eight hundred miles away from her uncle, but she never forgot his promise. They stayed in touch by telephone regularly through the next few years. On her sixteenth birthday, guess who this young lady called? "Hello, Unc. Remember what you promised?" This man learned that children never forget a promise.

All that God has told His children *is* the truth. He sent His prophets to foretell the arrival, life, and mission Jesus would fulfill on earth. Though He spoke hundreds of years prior to Jesus' appearance, God's words were no less true. What He spoke came to pass, is coming to pass, and will come to pass. We can count on God's Word.

The things concerning himself

An autobiography is a story a person writes about his own life. It reveals information about its subject that the readers may explore with amazement. The author is the prime authority on the facts in the story. Though others were involved in the events depicted in an autobiography, the details are best described by the writer of the account.

The Bible is Jesus' autobiography. He wrote it by His Spirit as He breathed the details into the minds of men. After His resurrection, Jesus explained to His disciples all the recorded facts and prophecies in the Holy Book that pertained to Him. It must have been exhilarating for the disciples to discover that they were listening to the Author of the Scriptures expounding on His own amazing autobiography.

—Beverly Jones.

Golden Text Illuminated

"Beginning at Moses and all the prophets, he expounded unto them in all the scriptures the things concerning himself" (Luke 24:27).

On the evening of the day of His resurrection, the risen Lord appeared and joined two of His followers as they walked from Jerusalem toward Emmaus. The two did not recognize Jesus, and they began to share with Him their perplexity over recent events. They had thought that Jesus was Israel's Messiah and Redeemer, but they could not reconcile this with His crucifixion. Nor could they make sense of the reports of the women who claimed that Jesus' tomb was empty and that angels had told them He was alive (Luke 24:19-24).

Jesus responded by first rebuking these two for their slowness to believe the prophets who had foretold these events (Luke 24:25-26). It was apparent that they either did not understand or did not take literally what the Old Testament said about the Messiah's suffering. In either case, they were foolish.

Jesus therefore began to teach them what the Scriptures said about the Messiah. Our golden text says that Jesus began His teaching with "Moses and all the prophets." "Moses" is a reference to the first five books of the Old Testament, which were all written by Moses.

"The prophets" can refer to the prophetic writings of the Old Testament in distinction from the "psalms," or "writings" (cf. Luke 24:44). However, the word can also refer to all the non-Mosaic writings of the Old Testament. Thus, Moses and the Prophets and the Law and the Prophets are often used to speak of the entire Old Testament (cf. Matt. 7:12; 11:13; 22:40; Luke 16:16,

29, 31; John 1:45).

It seems likely that when our golden text speaks of "Moses and all the prophets," it is referring to the entire Old Testament. Thus, the phrase is synonymous with "all the Scriptures" (Stein, *Luke,* Broadman). The point seems to be that Jesus began with Moses and explained what all the Old Testament said about the Christ.

While Jesus undoubtedly pointed to specific passages that foretold the suffering, death, and resurrection of the Messiah, it is unlikely that He expounded on every messianic passage in the Old Testament. We could imagine that such a task would have taken much longer than the time the three had together on their walk. The emphasis is on *all* the Scriptures; that is, the Old Testament points "to Jesus in all its parts" (Morris, *Luke,* InterVarsity).

The Old Testament spoke clearly of the coming Messiah and foretold His suffering, death, and resurrection; and this Messiah was Jesus. Thus, our text says Jesus saw in the Scriptures those things that concerned "himself."

The Old Testament prophecies not only offer proof of who Jesus is; they also present a warning. Jesus' followers had read the Scriptures, but the Lord said they were foolish. They do not seem to have taken *all* the Scriptures into account. Perhaps, like so many people today, they did not look at *all* the Scriptures but selected those that most appealed to them. The danger of this, of course, is that we create a Jesus to our liking and miss the real Jesus of the Bible.

—Jarl K. Waggoner.

Heart of the Lesson

As I write this lesson, the United States of America has just experienced a tragic mass murder in Aurora, Colorado. As a result, innumerable people are enduring unexplainable suffering. On the Sunday following the shooting, Pastor Lee Strobel said the following words to his congregation:

"If you've never asked why our world is infected with pain and suffering, you will when they strike you with full force or they come to a loved one. And Jesus said they are coming. Unlike some other religious leaders who wrote off pain and suffering as just being illusions, Jesus was honest. He told us the truth. He said in John 16:33, 'You will have suffering in this world.' He didn't say you might—he said it *is* going to happen" (www.BibleGateway.com).

In this week's lesson, we learn about the Suffering Saviour, who is able to compassionately assist His suffering people.

1. Isaiah's description of the Suffering Saviour (Isa. 53:5-8). Using vivid and graphic language, Isaiah described the Suffering Saviour, who was punished for the sins of defiant and disobedient humanity. With a glorious display of humility, the Saviour became the all-sufficient Sacrifice for sin. Under a pretense of justice, His life was taken away in a violent manner. An innocent Person suffered for the transgressions of others.

Graphic television shows and video games are numbing young and old alike to the vicious nature of violence. But the media representations of violence remain imaginary. The violence that the Saviour suffered was real, representing the pervasive wickedness of sinful mankind. Let us be eternally thankful for the willingness of the Suffering Saviour to be made sin for us so "that we might be made the righteousness of God in him" (II Cor. 5:21).

2. Jesus' declaration to some perplexed travelers (Luke 24:25-27). As He traveled with two perplexed individuals toward the village of Emmaus, the risen Lord Jesus Christ spoke perceptive words to His traveling companions. He then opened their understanding and taught them that He was the dominant and pivotal figure in all the Scriptures.

Although it is not God's plan today for the risen Lord Jesus Christ to physically walk alongside His followers, He has sent the indwelling Holy Spirit to be their spiritual Guide to all truth (cf. John 16:13). As a result, believers have the privilege of intimate fellowship and full disclosure that results in "the knowledge of his will in all wisdom and spiritual understanding" (Col. 1:9).

3. Jesus' disclosure to His troubled disciples (Luke 24:44-47). The risen Saviour appeared to an assembled group of anxious and distressed followers. He told them that He was the ultimate fulfillment of the Old Testament messianic prophecies. After opening their spiritual minds, the risen Lord stated the gospel message of forgiveness of sins that would be proclaimed to the world, beginning in the city of Jerusalem.

Jesus Christ had to endure a violent death so that the message of eternal life could be proclaimed to people who are dead in their trespasses and sins. Filled with the Holy Spirit, God's people have the incredible privilege of being ministers of light and life to people who dwell in darkness. Therefore, let us commit ourselves not only to the Word but also to the ministry of reconciliation (cf. II Cor. 5:18-19).

—*Thomas R. Chmura.*

World Missions

The interesting thing about the proclamations of the prophets in the Bible was that they did not stop with talking about the suffering and death of Jesus. They went on to finish the story and spoke about His being glorified. This is good news for the whole world. This same Jesus who died was raised from the grave for all the world to see. So we know that we have a risen Jesus who is now in glory. No other religious leader in the world has ever done anything like this. No prophet ever shared this kind of glory.

Our Lord Jesus is unique because He is the only one we know of who ever conquered death and lived to tell the world about it. In so doing, He has also shown us that we can live with Him eternally. All we have to do is turn our lives over to Him, knowing that the price for our sins has already been paid in full. This is good news for the whole world. It provides hope and encouragement to all who are weary of trying to earn their salvation through their own good works. His suffering did lead to glory.

We need to understand and let the world know that the Old Testament and what the prophets foretold there did come to pass in the life of Jesus. The prophets spoke of this Messiah who would one day be glorified. When we trust in our Lord Jesus for our salvation, we must understand that our pain will eventually turn to power just as it did for Jesus. The people of the world need to know that there is an answer to their pain. That answer is found in Jesus alone, for He alone wipes our tears away and gives us His comfort.

In a world of turmoil, we need to let the world know that the Suffering Servant described by the Prophet Isaiah went through pain so that we might inherit the hope that He has provided for us. We have hope for eternity and the assurance that we will be with Him forever. Such an assurance is not found in any other religion because other religions work their way to salvation. In Christianity, Jesus has already fulfilled for us what we could never do alone. Our suffering too can turn into glory because of Him.

As Christians, we need to remember that there are people all over the world who are trying to find salvation by themselves. They do this by turning prayer wheels, bowing before lifeless deities, doing penance in caves, and other such acts by which they believe that they will achieve a state wherein there is no pain and no punishment for their sins. The good news about the Bible is that our Lord has already met the demands of a righteous God and saved us from punishment.

In many parts of the world, people are yet to hear of Jesus' sacrifice. They need to hear how He was also glorified. They need to hear that He is indeed coming again to receive us to Himself and that they too can be part of that company that will go to heaven with Him. It is interesting that God has entrusted to the body of those who believe in Him, the church, the task of telling the world about this Jesus. We are to leave no stone unturned in proclaiming this gospel of hope to the world.

The prophets pointed to One who was coming so that no one would miss the event when it did happen. Sadly, many of the Jewish people still did. He is coming again, glorified, for us. We need to tell the world this good news. He is worthy of our worship. He is coming as our glorified King.

—A. Koshy Muthalaly.

The Jewish Aspect

The Jewish people simply will not accept the uniform testimony of the Old Testament that the Messiah had to suffer and die for the sins of the whole world. On two separate occasions that we see this week, Jesus had to teach His Jewish followers that a suffering Messiah is the theme of God's Word. "He expounded unto them (the Emmaus pilgrims) in all the scriptures the things concerning himself" (Luke 24:27).

The disciples needed the same message. "Then opened he their understanding, that they might understand the scriptures" (Luke 24:45).

Some Orthodox Jews, unable to grasp the truth that the Bible teaches a suffering Messiah, contrived the idea of two Messiahs. One they called Rabbi Ben David, the genuine Messiah, who could never be wounded or die. A second Messiah, Rabbi Ben Joseph, would be the surrogate, suffering for Ben David. This theory did not receive widespread acclaim in Jewish circles.

One ultraorthodox Jewish sect in New York contended that its late, esteemed rabbi was the Messiah. This belief is notable only for the devotion of its followers, even though it is without factual support.

The reader may be able to imagine the immense problem the local rabbi faces in attempting to keep his congregants from believing, first, that the Messiah has already come. To Orthodox Jews, who are still looking for a first coming of the Messiah, that idea is unscriptural. Reform Jews, who deny any coming of a person called Messiah, would simply shrug it off. *Meshuggeneh* (madness) is the word Jews use to describe Christian teachings that Jews will not accept.

On a second level, a challenge to the local rabbi to lay before the congregation, as Jesus did, the birth claims of Jesus to King David's throne could spell the end of Judaism as a worshipping community. One mission to the Jews has issued that challenge to a synagogue. They replied angrily, but without citing any reason for their concerted effort to keep the people from knowing the truth.

Soul-winning is a thrilling occupation for Christians. Among soul-winners, it is always important to impart the Word of God to the Jewish people. As a first requirement, the one who would minister to the chosen people must be prepared for resistance to the truth. Appeals are made all the time by Jewish sources, asking missionaries to leave them alone. The cry is "If you loved us, you would not try to change us to your religion!"

Rabbi Yechiel Eckstein heads a group of Christians and Jews who raise funds for nonmilitary spending in Israel. Estimates of the sums given by Christians run as high as fifty million dollars each year. But for a mission to the Jews to cooperate in that fundraising, the mission must agree to give up efforts to evangelize the Jews. What mission constituted by the Holy Spirit could agree to such a demand?

Jews will suggest that door-to-door evangelism in a Jewish district is one step removed from open anti-Semitism.

And what of the rabbis themselves? One mission makes a particular effort each year to see that the local rabbis know God's simple plan of salvation. It would be tragic to fail to give the blind leaders of Israel the message they need to know and act upon, but the effort is greeted with cries of "Unfair!" "Unloving!" and "Anti-Semitic!"

Would you ask the Lord if He would use you in reaching the ten million Jews in the world? God has not cast off His people (Rom. 11:2).

—*Lyle P. Murphy.*

Guiding the Superintendent

A full grasp of Christ's glory demands a deep appreciation of His suffering. In a very real sense, before He took on the form of man and came into this sin-cursed world, He understood that suffering would dominate His ministry. However, He willingly endured affliction and humiliation at the hand of His despisers to rescue man from the clutches of the enemy. Because of His love for us, we can share in His glory—that great reward awaiting the faithful.

DEVOTIONAL OUTLINE

1. Suffering for sinful man (Isa. 53:5-8). Christ, the Anointed One, compassionately laid aside His glory—His excellence, beauty, majesty, and grace—to be crushed, beaten, and rebuked for the peace and spiritual renewal of sinful man. The weak-mindedness of man caused him to stray, but Jesus paid the ultimate price of death by the cruelest form. He was nailed to two crossed pieces of wood and made a spectacle of as ignorant men jeered. In meekness and silent submission, He was taken from judgment hall to judgment hall, humiliated, dishonored, and dismissed as a troublemaker and a blasphemer. All this Christ endured not just for the sins of the nation of Israel, but for all humankind.

2. Suffering was Christ's assignment (Luke 24:25-27). Christians often exchange the Lord's blessings for skepticism and unbelief. The Word of God is for our edification, explicitly clarifying who God is, His plan for our redemption, and what we can expect from Him as His blood-bought possessions. Had Christ not paid our ransom, our sin debt would remain ours to bear—a load much too heavy for man to bear alone.

Christ's death completed His earthly mission, which had to be finished before He could return to the glory He possessed before the foundation of the world.

It frustrated Christ that the disciples had heard His word but had not received it in their hearts. Many believers frustrate Him today because of their failure to trust God's Word despite having the entire Bible—every inspired word—together with the abiding Holy Spirit to lead them into understanding and accepting the truth.

3. Christ wants us to know Him (Luke 24:44-47). Jesus no longer walks among us. But the writings of the Law, the Prophets, and the Psalms remain tangible records with insightful words of knowledge and comfort to prepare us for His imminent return. As the Scripture informed the disciples of old, so today it brings new believers into the knowledge of Christ. His Word teaches Christians about the life, works, and saving power of Messiah, who, through the shedding of His own precious blood, saves and convicts us. Those of us who know Him are now called upon to go and declare the truth of the gospel throughout the world.

AGE-GROUP EMPHASES

Children: Contrast Christ's horrific suffering with His excellent glory to demonstrate how great the love of Jesus is.

Youths: Teach the students about the many things that Christ suffered, and remind them that He did it in their stead. Then challenge them to commit to living lives that honor His loving sacrifice.

Adults: Remind them that the trials and tribulations that they endure in their daily walk with Christ will seem as nothing when they see Him in His glory.

—Jane E. Campbell.

Scripture Lesson Text

DEUT. 6:13 Thou shalt fear the LORD thy God, and serve him, and shalt swear by his name.

14 Ye shall not go after other gods, of the gods of the people which *are* round about you;

15 (For the LORD thy God *is* a jealous God among you) lest the anger of the LORD thy God be kindled against thee, and destroy thee from off the face of the earth.

16 Ye shall not tempt the LORD your God, as ye tempted *him* in Mas'sah.

MATT. 4:4 But he answered and said, It is written, Man shall not live by bread alone, but by every word that proceedeth out of the mouth of God.

5 Then the devil taketh him up into the holy city, and setteth him on a pinnacle of the temple,

6 And saith unto him, If thou be the Son of God, cast thyself down: for it is written, He shall give his angels charge concerning thee: and in *their* hands they shall bear thee up, lest at any time thou dash thy foot against a stone.

7 Je'sus said unto him, It is written again, Thou shalt not tempt the LORD thy God.

8 Again, the devil taketh him up into an exceeding high mountain, and sheweth him all the kingdoms of the world, and the glory of them;

9 And saith unto him, All these things will I give thee, if thou wilt fall down and worship me.

10 Then saith Je'sus unto him, Get thee hence, Sa'tan: for it is written, Thou shalt worship the LORD thy God, and him only shalt thou serve.

11 Then the devil leaveth him, and, behold, angels came and ministered unto him.

NOTES

Victory over Temptation

Lesson: Deuteronomy 6:13-16; Matthew 4:4-11

Read: Deuteronomy 6:13-16; 8:3; Psalm 91:11-12; Matthew 4:4-11

TIMES: about 1406 B.C.; A.D. 26   PLACES: Moab; wilderness of Judea

---

GOLDEN TEXT—"It is written, Man shall not live by bread alone, but by every word that proceedeth out of the mouth of God" (Matthew 4:4).

Introduction

The third and final segment of this quarter's study consists of four lessons that examine the way Jesus used Scripture. In His earthly lifetime, of course, Scripture included only what we call the Old Testament. Because we have the additional revelation of the New Testament, we are tempted to neglect the Old. But Jesus' example reminds us that both are important and each has its own purpose, for both came from the same God. Jesus revered the Hebrew Scriptures. He came to fulfill, not destroy, them (Matt. 5:17).

This week we will study how Jesus used Scripture when tempted by Satan. Temptation comes to all of us, and if we are not prepared for it, we can be humiliated and fail God miserably.

When we are tempted, we do well to admit our weakness and to lay hold of all the resources God has given for our success. Above all, we need to so incorporate His Word into our lives that we can call it to mind and immediately apply it when the need arises (cf. Ps. 119:11). If even Jesus saw the need to use Scripture to overcome Satan's tricks, surely we need its protective authority even more!

LESSON OUTLINE

I. THE LAW'S EDICTS—Deut. 6:13-16

II. THE LAW'S APPLICATIONS—Matt. 4:4-11

Exposition: Verse by Verse

THE LAW'S EDICTS

DEUT. 6:13 Thou shalt fear the LORD thy God, and serve him, and shalt swear by his name.

14 Ye shall not go after other gods, of the gods of the people which are round about you;

15 (For the LORD thy God is a jealous God among you) lest the anger of the LORD thy God be kindled against thee, and destroy thee from off the face of the earth.

16 Ye shall not tempt the LORD your God, as ye tempted him in Massah.

Fear the Lord (Deut. 6:13). The people of Israel were camped on the plains of Moab, poised to cross the Jordan into Canaan. Moses was reviewing for them the laws of God. Their obedience to them would ensure that they would continue to inhabit this land and prosper in it (vss. 1-3). Moses thus exhorted them to love the Lord wholeheartedly, take His commands into their hearts, and teach them to their children (vss. 4-9).

Diligence was essential because great temptation lay ahead. They would have in Canaan all things conducive to their prosperity—cities, houses, wells, vineyards, and olive groves—none of which they had labored to produce (Deut. 6:10-11). Yet in their prosperity they would be tempted to become proud and complacent. Instead of thanking the Lord for these blessings, they might take the credit themselves (vs. 12).

Moses therefore commanded them, "Fear the Lord thy God" (Deut. 6:13). This "fear" is a reverential awe that every sinner ought to feel in the presence of a holy God. It does not rule out love (vs. 5), but it does recognize that any favor He bestows comes solely through His grace. It allows no room for human merit or pride.

The person who fears the Lord will serve him. Serving is the outworking of fear. It entails all the acts of worship performed in His name. The reverent person also will swear by God's name. For Israel, this included formal oaths in court as well as private ones used to fortify assertions. Such declarations would reveal the religious loyalties of the oath-taker. Jesus, of course, later ruled out swearing as improper for His followers (Matt. 5:33-37).

Do not follow false gods (Deut. 6:14-15). Moses next commanded, "Ye shall not go after other gods, of the gods of the people which are round about you." If the Israelites forsook Yahweh, they surely would seek out other deities, for human beings are created with a need to worship. In Canaan there would be plenty of false deities from which to choose, for every ethnic group had its own. The fleshly enticements of idolatrous religion made it a perennial temptation for Israel.

The penalty for idolatry would be harsh because "the Lord thy God is a jealous God among you" (Deut. 6:15). The thought of God being jealous may be troublesome to some, but the word indicates zeal for the glory that is due Him (cf. Exod. 20:5; 34:14; Deut. 4:23-24). God demands exclusive worship, refusing to share it with false gods (Isa. 42:8). When His people stray to these false lovers, He, like a forsaken husband, becomes angry and metes out judgment.

The judgment is severe. God will "destroy thee from off the face of the earth" (Deut. 6:15). Idolatry was considered the worst of all sins for Israel. For an individual who engaged in it or seduced others to it, it meant certain death (Exod. 22:20; Deut. 13:6-10). And for the nation as a whole, apostasy would lead to removal from their land (Deut. 4:25-27; 29:24-28).

Do not put the Lord to the test (Deut. 6:16). Moses further warned the Israelites, "Ye shall not tempt the Lord your God, as ye tempted him in Massah." To "tempt" God does not mean to solicit evil from Him, for He cannot be touched by that kind of temptation (Jas. 1:13). It means to put Him to a test to see whether He is faithful. To do this betrays a lack of faith in His promises and power.

Moses knew that those who entered Canaan would sometimes suffer hardship. In those circumstances, they would be tempted to doubt God and ask Him for special signs to prove His goodness. But Moses reminded them of what had happened to their forefathers at Massah (Deut. 6:16; cf. Exod. 17:1-7). When they lacked water, they complained and questioned whether the Lord was with them. He did supply water, but the name "Massah" (test) was a reminder of their unbelief.

THE LAW'S APPLICATIONS

MATT. 4:4 But he answered and said, It is written, Man shall not live by bread alone, but by every word that proceedeth out of the mouth of God.

5 Then the devil taketh him up into the holy city, and setteth him on a pinnacle of the temple,

6 And saith unto him, If thou be the Son of God, cast thyself down: for it is written, He shall give his angels charge concerning thee: and in their hands they shall bear thee up, lest at any time thou dash thy foot against a stone.

7 Jesus said unto him, It is written again, Thou shalt not tempt the LORD thy God.

8 Again, the devil taketh him up into an exceeding high mountain, and sheweth him all the kingdoms of the world, and the glory of them;

9 And saith unto him, All these things will I give thee, if thou wilt fall down and worship me.

10 Then saith Jesus unto him, Get thee hence, Satan: for it is written, Thou shalt worship the LORD thy God, and him only shalt thou serve.

11 Then the devil leaveth him, and, behold, angels came and ministered unto him.

Live by the Lord's Word (Matt. 4:4). Jesus did not just fulfill Old Testament Scripture; He used it repeatedly. An example of this is His appeal to the law in repelling Satan's temptations. God cannot be tempted by evil. But Jesus, through His incarnation, was also human, and this humanity made Him temptable. His temptation was necessary to manifest His obedience to His Father (Heb. 5:8) and to encourage us

who are tempted (2:18; 4:14-16).

His temptation occurred just after His baptism, when the Holy Spirit came upon Him and His Father attested to His divine sonship (Matt. 3:16-17). The first thing the Spirit led Him to do was to go into the wilderness and fast for forty days (4:1-2). This made Him vulnerable to the devil's first temptation to turn stones into bread (vs. 3). Surely this was not unreasonable. Was it fitting for the Son of God to endure such hunger? If He but spoke, He would have food!

But Jesus answered, "It is written, Man shall not live by bread alone, but by every word that proceedeth out of the mouth of God" (Matt. 4:4). He knew that to act independently of the Father's will, even for the legitimate purpose of feeding Himself, would be sin. He was in this condition, at the leading of God's Spirit, for a divine purpose. To thwart this purpose would be a flagrant violation of God's Word. To Jesus, obeying God's Word was more important than having bread to eat.

The scriptural passage Jesus chose to refute Satan (Deut. 8:3) could not have been more apt for the occasion. Moses was reminding the Israelites of the lessons the Lord had taught them in the wilderness. He had tested their faith and obedience, humbling them so that they would not trust themselves. In particular, He had provided no food except the manna He gave. Food was less important than the divine Word they learned to believe and obey.

Trust in the Lord wholly (Matt. 4:5-7). In a second temptation, the devil "taketh him up into the holy city, and setteth him on a pinnacle of the temple." Whether this occurred physically or in a vision is not clear. The reference is to the temple of Jerusalem. "A pinnacle" is "the pinnacle" in Greek, referring to some well-known point. The word means a wing, edge, or extremity. It could have been the temple's highest point or the porch towering on the edge of the Kidron Valley.

Here Satan issued a second challenge: "If thou be the Son of God, cast thyself down" (Matt. 4:6). Some have interpreted this as a temptation for Jesus to prove His deity through a spectacular display (Walvoord and Zuck, eds., *The Bible Knowledge Commentary,* Cook). Malachi 3:1 does mention the Lord suddenly coming to His temple, and a rabbinical writing claims that the Messiah will come and stand on the roof of the temple.

But it is not clear whether this tradition was held in Jesus' day. In addition, Jesus' answer does not seem to address this issue. So Satan more likely was tempting Jesus to jump from the temple simply to test God's faithfulness in protecting Him. After all, He would not let harm befall His Son—would He?

Satan even fortified his temptation by quoting Scripture (Matt. 4:6). From Psalm 91:11-12 he reminded Jesus that God promised angelic protection. But even apart from his omission of a phrase—"to keep thee in all thy ways"— Satan also misapplied the text. Even though it pertained to the protection of a righteous man (and Jesus was certainly that), it made no mention of testing God by doing something foolish. It therefore did not apply to this situation at all.

Jesus therefore countered Satan's misuse of Scripture through another quotation: "Thou shalt not tempt the Lord thy God" (Matt. 4:7). These words, as already seen, come from Deuteronomy 6:16 and forbid putting the Lord to a test to see whether He will do what He has promised. In this instance, He had promised preservation from harm. To deliberately create danger to test this promise would have been a refusal to believe Him.

Jesus' response holds an important lesson for us. Scripture texts can be used for illegitimate purposes. Using isolated texts, Satan's emissaries trick the untaught and gullible into false doctrine or moral failure. To combat this danger, we must educate ourselves thoroughly in the Word of God. We need to look at every Scripture in its context and compare all passages that deal with the same subject. We also need to ask if our response will honor our Saviour.

Worship the Lord only (Matt. 4:8-10). Satan's third temptation took place on "an exceeding high mountain," from which he showed Jesus "all the kingdoms of the world, and the glory of them." We do not know if the mountain was literal or in a vision. Perhaps the mountain was literal, but the view of the world's kingdoms "in a moment of time" (Luke 4:5) was visionary, since no mountain affords such a view naturally.

Satan's proposition was this: "All these things will I give thee, if thou wilt fall down and worship me" (Matt. 4:9). There was now no appeal to Jesus' divine sonship, no pious pretense of quoting Scripture. Satan threw off his mask, appeared as the archrival to God, and issued a naked bribe: worldwide dominion in exchange for worship.

Were the kingdoms really his to give? According to Luke's Gospel, Satan claimed that they were: "For that is delivered unto me; and to whomsoever I will I give it" (4:6). In a temporal sense, he was correct. He is "the prince of this world" (John 16:11) and "the god of this world" (II Cor. 4:4). The world is said to lie in Satan's power (cf. Eph. 2:2; I John 5:19), but he holds this dominion only under the greater dominion and forbearance of God (cf. Job 1—2).

All that Satan offered (and more) would someday belong to Jesus by another route (cf. Rev. 11:15). But the temptation was to reach that goal by a shortcut that eliminated the need for the Cross. However, this would have thwarted God's plan of redemption and entailed for Jesus the unthinkable idolatry of worshipping God's rival.

And He ultimately would have had only a vassalage under God's dominion, doomed to be swept away when Satan was overcome.

It is no wonder, then, that Jesus abruptly terminated the conversation: "Get thee hence, Satan" (Matt. 4:10). And it was no accident that later, when Simon Peter tried to dissuade Him from the cross, Jesus turned on him with the words "Get thee behind me, Satan" (16:23). "Satan" means "adversary." Jesus used the title aptly in both cases, for He recognized opposition to God's plan for Him and for mankind.

One more time Jesus appealed to Scripture: "It is written, Thou shalt worship the Lord thy God, and him only shalt thou serve" (Matt. 4:10). This quote was from the Septuagint (Greek) translation of Deuteronomy 6:13 and 10:20. God had demanded sole allegiance and worship from the Israelites who were about to enter Canaan, and He demanded no less from His own Son. To try to reach the kingdom without suffering and death would have been an intolerable, idolatrous compromise.

Experience the Lord's victory (Matt. 4:11). Satan had tempted Jesus in all the ways he had tempted Eve in Eden (Gen. 3:1-6). He had appealed to the lust of the flesh, the lust of the eyes, and the pride of life (cf. I John 2:16); but he had found nothing in Jesus that could be seduced. In each case, Jesus had countered with scriptural principles that kept Him focused on God's will.

As a result, the devil left Him (Matt. 4:11), although Luke states that it was only "for a season" (4:13). Temptation would return later in other guises. Jesus had established a pattern of obedience and trust that would characterize His ministry to the end.

There was immediate provision: "Behold, angels came and ministered unto him" (Matt. 4:11). Just as an angel had been sent to provide for Elijah (I Kings 19:5-8), so angels now supplied Jesus' needs. He had refused to turn stones to bread; now they gave Him bread. He had refused to call on them to rescue him from a jump from the temple; now they ministered to Him unasked. Later they would again assist Him in His time of greatest need (cf. Luke 22:43).

We, like our Saviour, will persevere in temptation if we apply God's Word at our point of need. And whatever straits may have brought us into the tempting situation will be more than counterbalanced by the rewards that will follow.

—Robert E. Wenger.

QUESTIONS

1. What were the circumstances that prompted Moses to give the commands in this week's text?

2. What is fear of the Lord? How will it affect one's life?

3. When does God's jealousy lead Him to anger?

4. Under what circumstances might Israel have "tempted" God?

5. Why was Jesus especially vulnerable to Satan's first temptation?

6. How did Satan's second temptation put God to an unnecessary test?

7. Should we give credence to everyone who quotes Scripture? Explain.

8. How was Satan's third temptation of Jesus less subtle than the first two?

9. How would Satan's proposition to Jesus have thwarted God's plan?

10. How did God respond to Jesus' resisting temptation?

—Robert E. Wenger.

Preparing to Teach the Lesson

Christians are often tempted to turn to popular but false teachings instead of to God and the Bible for spiritual help.

In this week's lesson we will see how Jesus Himself, the Author of Scripture, relied on the Bible when faced with His own time of temptation. It is noteworthy that He used a portion of Scripture, the book of Deuteronomy, that many believers today largely ignore.

TODAY'S AIM

Facts: to show that when He was tested by Satan, Jesus responded with God's Word, the source of His strength.

Principle: to show that the Scriptures are important for our spiritual strength during times of temptation, testing, and spiritual warfare.

Application: to show that when we are tempted and tested, we need to follow Jesus' example and rely on God and the Bible.

INTRODUCING THE LESSON

When Jesus faced His three great temptations in the wilderness, He turned to and applied passages from the book of Deuteronomy, a book that few Christians today can quote. This week's lesson should inspire us to study and learn all of Scripture so that we will be ready to use it when we need it.

DEVELOPING THE LESSON

1. Give God alone your obedience (Deut. 6:13-16). The book of Deuteronomy contains laws and guidelines that were practical and necessary for the welfare and spiritual health of Israel and its people. It was a practical guidebook for the nation as they took possession of Canaan.

Primary to every commandment and instruction was the command that the Israelites were to worship God and Him alone. Every commandment, ritual, and practice depended on that commitment and truth.

This passage in Deuteronomy was designed for those moments when Israel, both as a nation and individually, would be tempted to stray from God due to prosperity and comfort. When we are in trouble, we usually seek help. At times, Israel sought help from sources other than God.

God warned about another danger. When we are successful and credit ourselves with our success, we may lose our sense of need for Him. We trust in our own efforts. In times of comfort and wealth, we tend to take God for granted and forget that He is the one who provided our blessings. If we rely on Him in the best of times, we will also be ready to trust Him in the worst of times as Satan tries to lure us away from God.

Since Jesus is the Son of God, the only way He could be tested was in the flesh of His human body. The Holy Spirit placed Him in a situation in which His body experienced the weaknesses that would enable Satan to test Him. At the climactic moment of this test, Jesus quoted Deuteronomy 6:13 to point out that regardless of the circumstances, one must always serve and trust God only.

Discuss with your class how a person's physical environment can lead to the temptation to turn to sources other than God for help.

2. Trust God's Word (Matt. 4:4). When Israel wandered in the wilderness, God provided manna for the people to eat. This provision was a miracle that lasted until their wilderness journey came to an end. As Jesus was tempted by Satan, He too was in the wilderness, and He drew from that parallel situation to succeed in His confrontation with Satan. Israel wandered in the wilderness for forty years. Jesus' temptation lasted forty days.

Point out to your class how a wilderness in the Middle East is not a forested land but a desert region that is barren and dry. Without food and water, a person's life can be in genuine danger. There are times when we face circumstances that threaten our welfare. These dangers may take several different forms. The common element is that they force us to make the conscious commitment to trust in God alone.

3. Trust God's plan (Matt. 4:5-7). Satan's challenge was not whether Jesus was the Son of God. He already knew that to be true, as did the demons who rebelled against God with him. Point out how the demons responded to Jesus prior to His casting them out (Matt. 8:29; Mark 3:11; Luke 4:41).

Satan attempted to lure Jesus into fulfilling the prophecies Satan's way rather than according to God's plan. Malachi had foretold that after the forerunner to the Messiah (John the Baptist) had arrived to prepare the way, the Messiah Himself would "suddenly come to his temple" (Mal. 3:1). Satan also misapplied Psalm 91:11-12 to assure Jesus that the angels would protect Him. For Jesus to step off the corner of the temple and be publically delivered by angels would have been a dramatic way to appear to fulfill Malachi's prophecy.

Discuss with your students how Satan will twist Scripture to try to deceive us. By using the Bible, he makes it appear that we are obeying the Lord. This is why it is so important to understand the Scriptures in context.

4. Worship God only (Matt. 4:8-11). Because of the Old Testament prophecies, Satan knew that Jesus would one day reign from David's throne over all the kingdoms of the world. He said that if Jesus would worship him, he would give Him the kingdoms and bypass the cross. The irony here is that Satan, the created and fallen creature, asked for worship of himself from the incarnate Son of God, the very One who had created him.

Discuss with your class the idea that Satan's lures are often completely contrary to logic. There may be cost and sacrifice to doing things God's way, but we must always look beneath the surface at the alternatives that Satan may present.

ILLUSTRATING THE LESSON

We face the temptation to give in to temporary needs, temporary desires, and temporary glories rather than depend on God and His Word for what is best in our lives.

SAY NO TO TEMPTATION

Temptation

KNOW GOD'S WORD

CONCLUDING THE LESSON

It is significant that Jesus was tested by Satan, who himself had failed to serve only God. In Jesus' time of temptation, He was the world's greatest success against the world's greatest failure.

ANTICIPATING THE NEXT LESSON

In our next lesson we will study the mission that Jesus carried out in His earthly ministry.

—Carter Corbrey.

PRACTICAL POINTS

1. Focusing on God alone keeps us from being distracted by what might be spiritually harmful (Deut. 6:13-15).
2. When we "test," or defy, God, we are saying that we know better than He does (vs. 16).
3. Contentment with the divine food of God's Word means we will be spiritually satisfied with nothing else (Matt. 4:4).
4. We cannot expect God to conform His superior plans to our human ideas (vss. 5-7).
5. Successful service for God comes when we see His Word as more real than anything else (vss. 8-10).
6. God always sustains us in whatever circumstances we serve Him (vs. 11).

—Anne Adams.

RESEARCH AND DISCUSSION

1. Why does God say He is a jealous God? What does it mean for us that God has this quality? Is it comforting or frightening?
2. Is it OK to do something dangerous if you feel sure that God will protect you from injury? Why or why not? How does this tempt God? Discuss.
3. Does worldly success always cause distraction from serving God? Can someone be prosperous but remain faithful to God? Discuss.
4. Have you struggled with temptation? How did you feel? If you know someone who is struggling in this way, how can you help him?

—Anne Adams.

ILLUSTRATED HIGH POINTS

Man shall not live by bread alone

A popular relief pitcher for a professional baseball team had a stellar career. This athlete accomplished much for which to be proud. But he publicly admitted that the best decision he ever made was to devote his life to Jesus Christ. He regularly read the Bible before games to find his inspiration. It is reported that "I can do all things through Christ which strengtheneth me" (Phil. 4:13) was inscribed on his pitching glove. This gifted man understood that life is not about the fame, talent, money, or success. Rather, life is in God and in His Word.

Many people spend their lives pursuing material wealth and popularity, only to discover that they are still unsatisfied and empty. During His wilderness temptation, Jesus showed us that even with all that the world has to offer, nothing can bring true life except the Word of God.

And him only shalt thou serve

While pursuing my master's degree in college, I became friends with a young woman who embraced belief in many gods. Her religion had gods for education, fertility, health, wisdom, and many other categories of life. According to my friend, the worshippers performed specific rituals to honor each god.

One evening as we sat at dinner, our conversation turned again to our differing faiths. Feeling a deep desire for my friend to know salvation in Jesus, I whispered a prayer, asking God to lead the discussion. Then I asked her a question she could not answer: "Do any of your gods love you?"

Our God is the only God, and our worship should be only of Him. There is no fulfillment of purpose for our lives until we respond to the only true God, our Creator, who made us to worship Him.

—Beverly Jones.

Golden Text Illuminated

"It is written, Man shall not live by bread alone, but by every word that proceedeth out of the mouth of God" (Matthew 4:4).

These words of Jesus came in response to Satan's first temptation. Matthew 4:2 tells us that after fasting for forty days in the wilderness, Jesus was "hungred" (clearly an understatement!). At this time, the devil came to Him and said, "If thou be the Son of God, command that these stones be made bread" (vs. 3).

The Holy Spirit had led Jesus into the wilderness (Matt. 4:1). This was a place where food was not readily available and where He could fast without distraction. Given this divine leading, it was clearly God's purpose that Jesus suffer hunger.

The devil saw Jesus' weakened physical state as an opportunity. He too recognized Jesus' hunger as God's will for Him at this time, so in offering Him a way to satisfy His hunger, Satan was also offering Him a way to reject the Father's will. This was an attempt "to destroy the Son's confidence in his Father's will and power to sustain him. What the tempter was asking Jesus to do was to distrust his Father, and to take matters entirely into his own hands" (Hendriksen, *Exposition of the Gospel According to Matthew,* Baker).

Jesus, of course, had the power to do what Satan suggested. But He would not use that power to avoid the suffering that was God's will for Him (Pfeiffer and Harrison, eds., *The Wycliffe Bible Commentary,* Moody).

Jesus' response was to quote from Deuteronomy 8:3. In that verse, the Lord reminded His people, who had spent forty years in the wilderness, that while He had allowed them to suffer hunger for a time, He had also faithfully supplied manna for them to eat throughout the many years of wandering. The Lord said that this was designed to teach them that they did not live by "bread alone" but by every word that comes from the mouth of God. They were dependent on the Lord and His promise to provide for them in the wilderness.

In quoting this, Jesus was affirming that it is of far greater importance that we trust the Lord and obey His Word than seek to satisfy even the most basic needs of life. Ultimately, it is not physical food alone that sustains us but God's eternal Word. Christ was "declaring that no man's whole life can be fed by bread that perishes. He needs more, that his spirit shall be fed, and its strength sustained by feeding upon the word proceeding from the mouth of God, and its safety ensured by abiding within the will of God" (Morgan, *The Crises of the Christ,* Revell).

Jesus' answer to this first temptation of Satan came from Scripture. He likewise responded to the devil's other temptations by quoting Scripture (Matt. 4:5-10).

While Satan's attacks often make use of physical weaknesses and pleasures, they are really spiritual attacks that must be confronted with the spiritual power of the Word of truth. If this was Jesus' method of handling temptation—and the temptation He faced was surely greater than anything we experience—we certainly should follow His pattern. We overcome temptation not by self-will or reason but by knowing, applying, and obeying the Word of God.

—*Jarl K. Waggoner.*

Heart of the Lesson

In his book entitled *Mere Christianity,* C. S. Lewis wrote, "A silly idea is current that good people do not know what temptation means. This is an obvious lie. Only those who try to resist temptation know how strong it is . . . A man who gives in to temptation after five minutes simply does not know what it would have been like an hour later. That is why bad people, in one sense, know very little about badness. They have lived a sheltered life by always giving in."

Jesus Christ did not lead a sheltered life. As the God-Man, He fully and perfectly engaged temptation without yielding to it (cf. Heb. 4:15). As a result, our Great High Priest is able to support His followers when they encounter temptation (cf. 2:18).

1. An injunction to worship (Deut. 6:13-16). Moses spoke strong and concise words to God's people about their relationship with Him, who would not tolerate the presence or admiration of any rival deity. If God's people followed pagan deities, God promised that His furious anger would annihilate His people "from off the face of the earth."

God's people had previously put Him to the test when they doubted His kindness and presence among them (cf. Exod. 17:1-7). God remembered their rebellion and was not pleased. He restated His demand that His people not provoke Him by doubting His goodness and mercy.

In earthly relationships, a person who demands undivided attention is called controlling and egocentric. Such a relationship dynamic is not healthy. The believer's spiritual relationship with God requires his undivided attention and commitment. God, though, cannot be called controlling and egocentric. He is called jealous and loving, and the relationship dynamic is healthy and sound.

Followers of Jesus Christ should not shy away from total commitment to their Saviour. Instead of experiencing abuse, they will experience unspeakable joy and glorious fulfillment (cf. I Pet. 1:8).

2. An illustration of temptation (Matt. 4:4-11). The Holy Spirit directed Jesus into the wilderness to be tempted by Satan (vs. 1). The Lord did not shy away from this experience but faced the tempter and his accusations with full and firm resolve.

Jesus responded to Satan's threefold temptation with the authority and truth of Scripture. Following his third effort and realizing that he was a defeated foe, Satan gave up and left the victorious Saviour. After Satan's departure, God the Father sent His ministering spirits to affirm His Son's resolve and sustain and strengthen Him.

I am left with two distinct impressions from this portion of this week's lesson text. First, the Lord Jesus Christ was fully tempted and emerged from the temptation with a holy victory. As a result, the Lord perfectly empathizes with the weaknesses of His followers and overwhelms them with His mercy and grace (cf. Heb. 4:14-16).

Second, God the Father was perfectly aware of His Son's ordeal and did not abandon Him. When the temptation was over, the Father demonstrated His compassion. When believers experience temptation's power, the Father will provide an exit path that will enable the Christian to patiently endure the temptation (cf. I Cor. 10:13).

—*Thomas R. Chmura.*

World Missions

There are many religions of the world that revere their holy books. The Sikhs respect the Granth Sahib and the Muslims their Koran. We Christians have our Bibles. The sad part is that we often do not put the needed emphasis on studying the Bible as we ought to, for it is the Word of God that gives us power through the Holy Spirit. Every word in the Bible came through "holy men of God [who] spake as they were moved by the Holy Ghost" (II Pet. 1:21).

In our lessons for this unit, we focus on the importance of Scripture in the overall mission of our Lord Jesus on earth. Jesus often spoke of this. In John 6:63 He said, "The words that I speak unto you, they are spirit, and they are life." The Bible is therefore the Book that has life-giving words and so is different from any other book that we may have. Other books can contain knowledge, but the Word of God gives us life. Jesus Himself used the Word to show how He overcame temptation.

The good news for the world is that we have the Word of God in a language that we can read and understand. Now we have to make sure that, through our efforts, the rest of the world will also be able to have the Word in their own languages. The founding of the British and Foreign Bible Society was inspired by the zeal of a Welsh girl named Mary Jones to have her own Bible in Welsh. Bible societies now work untiringly to initiate the distribution of Bibles to the world.

The world also needs to know that the Word of God gives us the resources to fight against temptation. Jesus Himself used the Word for this purpose and set an example. Now we have the same power over sin, and we need to share this with the world. The same methods that Jesus used to win against the temptations that faced Him are now available to all of us. The Bible has the power to help transform people from within; so we have to share this Word with the world.

The promises of God are available to us in His Word; so we all can fight against and resist temptation. Again, we need to see that the remedy for sin begins with God's Word. If Jesus used it to fight His battles with the devil, then we must follow His example. He never lost a single battle. We can be victorious too. As Christians, we are to share this good news with the world. Down through the ages, we see how the Word of God has transformed individuals from sin to eternal life.

Martin Luther was one individual who was transformed when he discovered the power of God's Word. He found that he did not have to earn his salvation but that salvation came through grace. This is a message that the world needs to hear. Jesus has already given us the victory we need over temptation. This was done through His death on the cross. This message of the Cross needs to be proclaimed to the whole world so that everyone might have the same hope of victory over sin.

Jesus' death shall not be in vain. We need to help the world see that the Word proclaims this salvation message so that we might have life and victory. We do not need any more roller-coaster spiritual journeys, for we have the ultimate Victor with us in our Lord Jesus Christ. It is His Word that proclaims Him to us. We dare not keep this victory to ourselves.

—A. Koshy Muthalaly.

The Jewish Aspect

Perhaps the most important spiritual victory in the history of Israel was overcoming the worship of false gods. In our text this week, Moses reminded the people of the enormity of this apostasy (Deut. 6:14). God is jealous. It is right for God to be jealous about His own things—the people who were to be committed to His service alone.

Moses knew the Israelites' weakness for false gods. The false gods were not gods, of course, but the Jews understood that the idol of stone represented a real demon. The Jews worshipped demons in the wilderness (Deut. 32:17).

Gideon struck down the altar of Baal on orders of the Lord (Judg. 6:25-32). Up to that time, Gideon's father had followed Baal; but with the idol's destruction, he saw that it had no real divinity. It was simply fashioned by men.

In a very colorful passage, Isaiah described what an idolater must go through to fashion his god. First, a fine craftsman takes wood from cedar, cypress, or oak and fashions it (Isa. 44:14). If he is cold, he uses a portion of the wood for warmth (vs. 15). Another portion is used for roasting his meat (vs. 16). "And the residue thereof he maketh a god, even his graven image: he falleth down unto it, and worshippeth it, and prayeth unto it, and saith, Deliver me; for thou art my god" (vs. 17).

God has made idolatry look foolish in countless passages of the Old Testament. Yet idolatry has a degrading persistence in the affairs of men. In the freeing of the children of Israel from Egypt, the plagues were directed against the gods of the Egyptians.

Paul traveled to the advanced Hellenistic culture of Athens. He found the city "wholly given to idolatry" (Acts 17:16). He told the Athenian philosophers that he had found an altar "TO THE UNKNOWN GOD. Whom therefore ye ignorantly worship, him declare I unto you" (vs. 23).

Satan failed miserably in his attempt to have Jesus abandon the worship of His Father. The temptation in the wilderness (Matt. 4:3-10) went for naught. Jesus said, "It is written, Thou shalt worship the Lord thy God, and him only shalt thou serve."

Idolatry of a formal kind is no longer a Jewish problem. The *frum* (careful) Jewish synagogue member will have only one plaque on the wall called a *mizrach*. It is placed on an eastern wall of the home, the direction for prayer.

What might be termed an informal kind of idolatry seems to take place in the Jewish tendency to deify learning and other achievements. Undeniably, Jews are among the most gifted people on earth, far above their numbers in the general population. They have received more than 20 percent of all the Nobel prizes ever awarded. Albert Einstein, through his theoretical framework, provided the Allies the background for a workable atomic bomb, thereby shortening World War II.

In our city, a Hebrew Academy of superior students annually sends its eleven or twelve graduates to the finest colleges in the nation. They rarely return to this city, for they are employed by leading technical, educational, and medical concerns. In general, they are justly proud of their Jewish heritage, but they follow their parents in a concerted disregard for what God has given them. Clearly, Jewish success in every field is a muted testimony to the grace of God upon His chosen people.

We must redouble our efforts to rescue the Jews from their own gods.

—*Lyle P. Murphy.*

Guiding the Superintendent

This new unit invites us to take a look at the various ways Jesus used Scripture. This week's lesson includes Scripture that Jesus used very effectively when the Spirit directed Him deeper into the wilderness to face Satan and his vain offerings. Every believer will find Jesus' example useful in his personal battles against the enemy and his destructive attacks.

DEVOTIONAL OUTLINE

1. Be aware of temptations (Deut. 6:13-16). There are so many worldly things that seem to capture man's imagination, causing him to stand in awe. Someone recently said that the term "awesome" should be reserved for God and God alone, for He exceeds the Seven Wonders of the World and anything else man can conceive of. He therefore must be revered, and our deepest devotion must be pledged to Him.

Christians must be strong in their knowledge of the one true God and His teachings and not easily swayed by the eloquence of those who "lie in wait to deceive" (Eph. 4:14) with their feel-good doctrine. Thanks to modern technology, these deceivers have easy access to the saints via radio, television, Internet, and cell phone. But let us remember how jealous our God is and be careful not to challenge His patience. He will not always withhold His wrath as He did despite the blatant haughtiness of the nation of Israel during their wilderness journey.

2. Victory through Christ's example (Matt. 4:4-11). Jesus was hungry and probably very weak, but He had not forgotten who He was and whom He represented. John 1:1 reminds us that from the beginning, Jesus "was the Word, and the Word was with God, and the Word was God." It follows that He knew when and how to apply Scripture. Jesus has shown us how to fend off the enemy with the power of "the sword of the Spirit, which is the word of God" (Eph. 6:17).

This text also teaches us just how cunning Satan can be. He is "the prince of the power of the air" (Eph. 2:2), and he uses things that we know and love—bright lights, beautiful colors, status, and daring exploits—to distract us. He devises wicked traps to ensnare our hearts and minds; he negatively influences the world around us in an attempt to divert our affection from the Saviour and get us to yield to his control.

Jesus said that it is wrong to tempt, test, or try to seduce God. If we pattern our counterattack against evil after our Saviour's example, we are guaranteed victory in every situation.

It is ill-advised to attempt to take on Satan the way Jesus did, for Jesus was directed by the Holy Spirit. Until Jesus returns, we must guard our souls with the power of the Word and learn to triumph gloriously in this unfriendly world.

AGE-GROUP EMPHASES

Children: Teach them that being tempted is not a sin but that yielding to that temptation is sin. When God allows us to be tempted, He always gives us a way of escape.

Youths: Make Sunday school relevant to them by giving examples of how a working knowledge of the Word can positively impact their world.

Adults: Assure them that their dedication to prayerfully reading and studying the Bible is not in vain. It sharpens their "weapon" and prepares them for battle against the enemy.

—Jane E. Campbell.

Scripture Lesson Text

LUKE 4:14 And Je′sus returned in the power of the Spir′it into Gal′i-lee: and there went out a fame of him through all the region round about.

15 And he taught in their synagogues, being glorified of all.

16 And he came to Naz′a-reth, where he had been brought up: and, as his custom was, he went into the synagogue on the sabbath day, and stood up for to read.

17 And there was delivered unto him the book of the prophet E-sa′ias. And when he had opened the book, he found the place where it was written,

18 The Spir′it of the LORD *is* upon me, because he hath anointed me to preach the gospel to the poor; he hath sent me to heal the brokenhearted, to preach deliverance to the captives, and recovering of sight to the blind, to set at liberty them that are bruised,

19 To preach the acceptable year of the LORD.

20 And he closed the book, and he gave *it* again to the minister, and sat down. And the eyes of all them that were in the synagogue were fastened on him.

21 And he began to say unto them, This day is this scripture fulfilled in your ears.

NOTES

144

Jesus' Mission on Earth

Lesson: Luke 4:14-21

Read: Leviticus 25:8-55; Isaiah 61:1-2; Luke 4:14-21

TIME: A.D. 27   PLACE: Nazareth

GOLDEN TEXT—"He began to say unto them, This day is this scripture fulfilled in your ears" (Luke 4:21).

Introduction

Although Jesus was born in Bethlehem and was from the tribe of Judah, He spent most of His earthly life in Galilee. From the time His family returned from Egypt, Nazareth was His home. And when He began His public ministry, He spent most of His time in Galilee.

Galilee was close to the Gentile world and influenced by it. Because of this influence on them and because of their distance from Jerusalem, Galileans were generally despised by the more orthodox Jews of the south (John 7:52). Even their accent was considered peculiar (Matt. 26:73; Acts 2:6-8). The prevailing prejudice was reflected by Nathanael's question when told of Jesus' home:

"Can there any good thing come out of Nazareth?" (John 1:46).

Yet Jesus chose to spend most of His time with these people, who lacked the spiritual smugness of Judea and were more inclined to recognize their need for salvation. In this week's lesson we find Him in a synagogue of Nazareth, His hometown, expounding one of the prophecies that He Himself fulfilled.

LESSON OUTLINE

I. A MINISTRY IN GALILEE—Luke 4:14-15

II. A SABBATH IN NAZARETH—Luke 4:16-21

Exposition: Verse by Verse

A MINISTRY IN GALILEE

LUKE 4:14 And Jesus returned in the power of the Spirit into Galilee: and there went out a fame of him through all the region round about.

15 And he taught in their synagogues, being glorified of all.

Jesus' return (Luke 4:14a). Luke records that "Jesus returned in the power of the Spirit into Galilee." If we had only the information in Luke's Gospel, we might assume this happened immediately after Jesus' temptation. But John tells of events that most Bible scholars believe occurred before this Galilean visit.

Jesus left the place of temptation and went to where John the Baptist was baptizing—Bethany, east of the Jordan. There He gathered the first five of His disciples (John 1:35-51). With them He returned to Galilee, where He performed His first miracle (2:1-12). Then He attended a Passover in Jerusalem, where He performed other miracles and spoke to Nicodemus (2:13—3:21). After spending more time baptizing in Judea (3:22-36), He left to return to Galilee. As He passed through Samaria, He evangelized the Samaritans (4:1-42).

Only after this did Jesus and His disciples return to Galilee as recorded by Luke (Luke 4:14; cf. John 4:43-45). He came "in the power of the Spirit." The Holy Spirit, who had endowed Him at His baptism, led Him to the place of temptation, and given Him power to perform miracles, now rested on Him for His Galilean ministry. Indeed, it was by the Spirit's power that He would do all His mighty works (Matt. 12:24-32).

Jesus' influence (Luke 4:14b-15). The initial response to Jesus in Galilee was favorable: "There went out a fame of him through all the region round about." Luke does not specify the places He visited or the deeds He did. But this early Galilean ministry must have included the healing of the nobleman's son recorded in John 4:46-54. Many other unrecorded miracles no doubt contributed to Jesus' fame as well.

These deeds merely enhanced a reputation Jesus had already begun to build before He arrived in Galilee. He had performed many miracles at Jerusalem while attending the Passover (John 2:23). When He returned to His home province, Galileans who had attended the feast welcomed Him back (4:45). He had quickly become a Galilean celebrity, and His countrymen expected Him to perform

there the same deeds He had done in Jerusalem.

The center of Jesus' ministry was "in their synagogues" (Luke 4:15), where He engaged in teaching. It is noteworthy that His miracles were never ends in themselves. He used them as teaching tools to call attention to God's truth, notably truth that upheld Jesus' messianic claims. His teaching was fresh and original. He did not spend time debating the viewpoints of rabbis. He spoke on His own authority, arousing amazement and spiritual hunger (cf. Luke 4:32, 36; Matt. 7:28; John 7:46).

Thus, Jesus was "glorified of all" (Luke 4:15). Later in His ministry, He would be severely opposed by the religious establishment and even abandoned by erstwhile disciples (cf. Luke 19:47; 20:19; John 6:60, 66). But at this early stage, opposition had not yet hardened. He was popular with the crowds and the leaders, though they might have had questions and misgivings. They were still investigating His claims.

A SABBATH IN NAZARETH

16 And he came to Nazareth, where he had been brought up: and, as his custom was, he went into the synagogue on the sabbath day, and stood up for to read.

17 And there was delivered unto him the book of the prophet Esaias. And when he had opened the book, he found the place where it was written,

18 The Spirit of the LORD is upon me, because he hath anointed me to preach the gospel to the poor; he hath sent me to heal the brokenhearted, to preach deliverance to the captives, and recovering of sight to the blind, to set at liberty them that are bruised,

19 To preach the acceptable year of the LORD.

20 And he closed the book, and

he gave it again to the minister, and sat down. And the eyes of all them that were in the synagogue were fastened on him.

21 And he began to say unto them, This day is this scripture fulfilled in your ears.

Attending the synagogue service (Luke 4:16). Jesus now returned to His boyhood town of Nazareth, located among the hills of Lower Galilee. It is not mentioned in the Old Testament or other early Jewish writings, and it would no doubt have remained obscure were it not for its New Testament associations. It was the home of both Joseph and Mary, who again took up residence there after their return from Egypt with the Child Jesus. The town apparently did not have a good reputation.

On the Sabbath, Jesus entered the synagogue with other worshippers. "As his custom was" (Luke 4:16) emphasizes the fact that Jesus had been brought up in a devout atmosphere. Apparently the family of Joseph and Mary worshipped regularly according to the prevailing Sabbath laws. By New Testament times, the Sabbath had become a day of worship and instruction as well as rest from weekly labors.

The function of the local synagogue was to teach and to facilitate worship. The Greek word for "synagogue" means, simply, a place of assembly. There is no mention of synagogues in the Old Testament, so they must have originated in the intertestamental age. They might well have started with Babylonian exiles who gathered to pray and build themselves up in their faith. Ezra's emphasis on teaching the law in the restored Judah may also have furthered their prominence. By Jesus' day, they were found in both Palestine and places of Jewish dispersion.

A typical synagogue service began with the Jewish confession of faith (the Shema), which was followed by prayers. Then came Scripture readings from the Law and the Prophets. Following this was a sermon, usually based on the Scripture that had been read. The service closed with a benediction. Any Jew could read the Scripture, standing while reading. Likewise, any competent person could be asked to give the sermon, being seated while doing so. So it was that Jesus was asked to participate (Luke 4:16).

Reading the prophecy (Luke 4:17-19). As Jesus rose to read, "there was delivered unto him the book of the prophet Esaias (Isaiah)." Whether this was the assigned reading for this Sabbath or Jesus Himself chose the passage is not clear. But, as shown already, Isaiah was a fertile field for messianic prophecies, and Jesus made the most of His opportunity to call attention to His fulfillment of them.

The book from which Jesus read was a scroll. Pieces of skin were sewn together to form a complete volume. The two ends were attached to two wooden sticks, and a person rolled the scroll from one to the other as he read the successive columns. Jesus unrolled this scroll to Isaiah 61:1-2 and began to read the first part of a messianic prophecy.

The text began, "The Spirit of the Lord is upon me, because he hath anointed me to preach the gospel to the poor" (Luke 4:18). It was one of several that referred to the Messiah's anointing with the Holy Spirit (Isa. 61:1; cf. 11:2; 42:1; 48:16). This anointing enabled Him "to preach the gospel (good news) to the poor" (Luke 4:18). "Poor" here implies more than economic poverty; it points to all those who are in special need of God's help (cf. Matt. 11:5; Luke 7:22).

God also anointed the Messiah "to heal the brokenhearted" (Luke 4:18).

Being "brokenhearted" is an emotional state in which one feels utterly ruined. The Messiah came to heal such, or to "bind up" their hearts, as Isaiah 61:1 states. Jesus met many brokenhearted people. Mary Magdalene was possessed by seven demons. Jairus and his wife had lost a daughter. A man with a demon-possessed son had given up hope. The Samaritan woman had given up on marriage. Jesus bound up all their wounds.

The Messiah was also sent "to preach deliverance to the captives" (Luke 4:18). In Isaiah's original prophecy, "captives" may have referred, in part, to those who would be taken captive to Babylon. But Jesus' fulfillment includes all those who are held captive to sin. Jesus' contemporaries argued that they had never been in slavery to anyone, but He pointed out that all who live in sin are enslaved by it. And only He can set them free (John 8:32-36; cf. Rom. 6:16; II Pet. 2:19).

Jesus was also sent for "recovering of sight to the blind" (Luke 4:18). This phrase is not found in Isaiah 61, but the idea exists in several other passages in his prophecy (cf. 42:7, 16). Jesus restored the physical sight of many during His ministry (cf. Matt. 11:5; 15:30-31; John 9:1-7). But He also recognized a spiritual blindness that could be cured only through the enlightenment regeneration brings (Matt. 15:14; 23:16-17; cf. II Cor. 3:14-16; 4:3-4).

The Messiah was also sent "to set at liberty them that are bruised" (Luke 4:18). The word translated "bruised" means shattered, broken in pieces, or oppressed. Jesus met many such shattered people in His day. Some were demon possessed; others were made helpless by long illnesses or were oppressed by the unbearable requirements of legalism. Still others were outcasts from their society. Jesus set them free and gave their lives new joy, meaning, and purpose.

The final thing the Messiah was sent to do was "to preach the acceptable year of the Lord" (Luke 4:19). We could also translate this "the year of the Lord's favor." This was alluding to the Hebrew Year of Jubilee, which was to be observed every fiftieth year. It was a year of release for both persons and property. The land rested, debts were forgiven, and slaves were set free (Lev. 25:8-17). Jesus used it to illustrate the special season of spiritual deliverance He was introducing (cf. Isa. 49:8; II Cor. 6:2).

It is noteworthy that in reading from Isaiah 61:1-2, Jesus stopped in the middle of a Hebrew sentence. The Isaiah text continues, "and the day of vengeance of our God," but He stopped short of this. The reason is clear: His first coming was the season of God's favor, when He purchased and offered salvation for all. God's vengeance will be manifested only when Christ returns to reign (cf. John 3:16-17; 12:47-48; Acts 17:30-31).

The long season of grace mankind has enjoyed since Jesus' first coming tends to lull many into complacency. Yet Scripture warns that this can be deadly, for a day of reckoning will surely come (cf. Rom. 2:4-6; II Pet. 3:3-10). When God's favor is extended to us, we ought to grasp it quickly, humbly, and thankfully, knowing that it could be withdrawn at any time (I Thess. 5:2-3).

Applying the Scripture (Luke 4:20-21). Having finished His reading, Jesus rolled up the scroll. Then He "gave it again to the minister." "Minister" here refers to an attendant. Every synagogue had at least two officials—a ruler and an attendant. While the ruler was responsible for the building, property, and oversight of worship, the attendant maintained the building and furnishings, including the sacred scrolls. These were kept in a chest or cabinet, to which he returned them after the reading.

Jesus sat down, as was the custom for the sermon (Luke 4:20). As He did so, "the eyes of all them that were in the synagogue were fastened on him." The Greek verb translated "fastened on" is used by Luke one other time in his Gospel (22:56) and ten times in Acts. It occurs in circumstances of strong emotion—anticipation, fascination, or hostility. In our passage it indicates intense anticipation. How would Jesus interpret this passage? The anticipation was heightened by the teaching reputation He already had (Luke 4:15).

The words "and he began to say unto them" (Luke 4:21) indicate that what follows is only the beginning of the sermon. But these opening words give the gist of the whole message: "This day is this scripture fulfilled." Only at one other place in Luke do we find "fulfilled" used in connection with biblical prophecy. Jesus used it in 24:44 to convince the disciples gathered in Jerusalem that He had risen. Thus, He punctuated His mission at both the beginning and the end of His ministry.

We are apt to miss the full impact of Jesus' words on His audience. They knew enough to realize that this Isaiah passage was part of a messianic prophecy. In its entirety it foretold not only miracles such as those He had already been doing but also judgment on the wicked and restoration of the glory of Israel (Isa. 61:1-6). So Jesus was claiming to be the Messiah, and they were seeing proofs of it before their very eyes!

Isaiah's prophecy had been given seven centuries earlier, and during that time Jews had been waiting for this moment. Now Jesus was telling them that it had finally arrived. Would they be open to this revelation and accept His claim?

The verses that follow (Luke 4:22-30) reveal that, sadly, most of them would not. At first they were filled with won-der at His gracious words. But then they remembered that He had grown up in the town; He could not possibly be the Messiah! Their wonder turned to skepticism, hostility, and murderous rage. And Nazareth became a microcosm of what Jesus would experience in all Israel (John 1:11).

Jesus' mission on earth was to declare this season of God's favor and to make it possible through His death and resurrection. But only those who trust Him can experience its blessings. For those who do not, the day of God's vengeance is the only remaining prospect.

—Robert E. Wenger.

QUESTIONS

1. What occurred between Jesus' temptation and the events in this week's lesson?

2. What was the early response to Jesus' ministry in Galilee?

3. What do we know about the town of Nazareth?

4. What was a synagogue? What was a typical synagogue service like?

5. From what prophetic book did Jesus read in the Sabbath service?

6. Where did the power for the Messiah's ministry originate?

7. From what kind of bondage does Jesus set us free, and what kind of blindness does He heal?

8. How did the Year of Jubilee illustrate Jesus' mission?

9. What was Jesus claiming when He said Isaiah's prophecy had been fulfilled by Him?

10. How did the people of Nazareth respond to Jesus' teaching?

—Robert E. Wenger.

Preparing to Teach the Lesson

This week's lesson will show that Jesus identified Himself as the Messiah, whose mission He was to accomplish. As you begin class, be sure everyone understands that the Jewish Messiah was also to be the Saviour of the world, as John 3:16 explains.

TODAY'S AIM

Facts: to show that Jesus clearly revealed His identity and mission as the anointed Messiah who had come to fulfill Isaiah's prophecy.

Principle: to show that Jesus was the Messiah and that He carried out His mission according to biblical prophecy and under the power of the Holy Spirit.

Application: to show that since Jesus clearly identified His mission as Israel's Messiah, we are responsible for the way we respond to Him.

INTRODUCING THE LESSON

Critics will say that Jesus was nothing more than a simple yet wise itinerant preacher. However, the Bible is consistently clear in presenting Jesus as the Son of God and the promised Messiah.

In this week's lesson we will see that Jesus clearly stated that He was the Messiah foretold by the Old Testament prophets. As you lead the class in this study, help them see that Jesus' ministry was clearly in fulfillment of what the prophets foretold the Messiah would do.

DEVELOPING THE LESSON

1. Ministering in the power of the Spirit (Luke 4:14-15). Jesus had submitted Himself to John's baptism in the Jordan River, followed immediately by His forty days of testing in the wilderness of Judea. Luke noted three important points in the progression of the events surrounding the beginning of Jesus' ministry. As Jesus prayed at the conclusion of His baptism, the Holy Spirit descended upon Him in bodily shape like a dove (3:22). Immediately after that, being filled with the Holy Spirit, He was led by the Spirit into the wilderness to be tested (4:1). Immediately after His testing was completed successfully, He returned to Galilee in the power of the Holy Spirit (vs. 14). From the moment of His baptism forward, the Holy Spirit was the indwelling and empowering personal force that characterized Jesus' ministry. Even though Jesus was the Second Person of the Trinity, His ministry was carried out in the strength and under the guidance of the Holy Spirit. From this perspective it can be seen that at the minimum, two Persons of the Trinity were directly involved in Jesus' earthly ministry.

A map of first-century Israel would be helpful to enable your class to understand the area that has been discussed. Point out the area of the Jordan River around Jericho (believed to be near the site of Jesus' baptism), the Judean wilderness west of the Dead Sea, and Galilee.

Jesus' ministry was well received initially. News about Him spread quickly, and He taught in the area synagogues.

2. Revealing His mission from God (Luke 4:16-21). In keeping with the Holy Spirit's central role, Jesus' quote from Isaiah 61:1 began, "The Spirit of the Lord is upon me" (Luke 4:18). Jesus would later warn that blasphemy against the Holy Spirit is unforgivable (Matt. 12:31). The Spirit is the one who provides the evidence of Jesus' identity.

Jesus' normal practice as a Jewish man was to attend the synagogue on the Sabbath. He chose to reveal His identity at the synagogue in Nazareth, His hometown. Locate this on the map.

The person who read from the Prophets was appointed to that office by the synagogue ruler. The reader would stand, read no less than twenty-one verses, and then sit down to teach from the passage. Jesus was either selected or approved as that day's reader. He was given the book of Isaiah, from which He selected chapter 61. He would be able to choose the passage.

Breaking with synagogue custom, Jesus read only two verses, and He stopped short of the second part of verse 2. He gave the book back to the attendant and sat down to expound upon what He had read.

Read Isaiah 61:1-2 to the class, and point out what Jesus left out. In His initial ministry, Jesus fulfilled only the first part of the prophecy. At His second coming He will fulfill the remainder dealing with God's vengeance.

Number each of the separate elements of the prophecy on the board, and discuss each one briefly.

Be sure to discuss the role of the Holy Spirit in Jesus' mission. Jesus made it evident that He was not acting on His own. He also claimed that the Holy Spirit had anointed Him for His mission. The title "Messiah" and its Greek equivalent, "Christ," refer to the anointing of God. The Messiah was to be the Anointed One.

Although His ministry of preaching and the miracles involved in authenticating His ministry were critical, His role of proclaiming "the acceptable year of the Lord" (Luke 4:19) was especially significant for Israel. This was synonymous with saying that He was bringing the kingdom of God to them at that time. This is also the consistent message of the Gospel of Matthew, in which Matthew showed that while Jesus made a genuine offer of the kingdom to Israel, Israel ultimately rejected it.

Everyone in the synagogue stared intently to see what Jesus would say next. His reputation had spread throughout the region, and they perhaps were hoping for something dramatic to happen. It did.

In a simple and short declaration, Jesus explained that He was fulfilling Isaiah's messianic prophecy in their presence. They were eyewitnesses to the Messiah's arrival, and they were hearing Him declare His presence. His claim was unmistakable.

Compare Jesus' declaration in the synagogue with His later response to John the Baptist when John sent messengers to Him from prison (Matt. 11:1-6). John wanted a confirmation that Jesus was indeed the promised Messiah. Jesus' answer was that He was performing the very things Isaiah had prophesied the Messiah would do.

ILLUSTRATING THE LESSON

Jesus revealed that He was the subject of Isaiah's messianic prophecy. Come to Him in faith.

CONCLUDING THE LESSON

Ask your class to imagine how they would react to Jesus' claim if they were people from His hometown.

ANTICIPATING THE NEXT LESSON

In our next lesson we will study how Jesus reacted to the Pharisees' criticism of His disciples concerning their failure to observe the traditions of the elders.

—Carter Corbrey.

PRACTICAL POINTS

1. An encouraging and supporting church is a blessing to all (Luke 4:14-16).
2. Because God often directs us through His Word, we should always be open to what He is telling us as we read the Bible (vs. 17).
3. Christ's message of salvation provides comfort and encouragement no matter what we are facing in life (vs. 18).
4. The good news of Christ endures because it is timeless (vs. 19).
5. Others can see how we live and speak for Christ even though we may be unaware that they are observing us (vs. 20).
6. Personal arrogance has no part in our witness for Christ (vs. 21).

—Anne Adams.

RESEARCH AND DISCUSSION

1. Did Jesus' fame in Galilee come from His messages or His miracles? Can famous people truly serve God? How might they inspire someone in a way that someone else might not?
2. Why was this specific passage read? Has a randomly chosen Scripture ever had a message you needed at that moment? Discuss.
3. If you have a guest speaker at your church, do you listen more carefully to him than to your regular pastor? If so, why? Discuss.
4. Jesus showed authority in what He said. How can we witness with self-assurance but without arrogance? Discuss.

—Anne Adams.

ILLUSTRATED HIGH POINTS

Being glorified of all

I am not much of a television viewer, but I try to catch a daily newscast just to keep abreast of the latest happenings. It is fascinating to see reports of people saved from accidents, disasters, and other near-death experiences. I watch, wondering what they will say is responsible for their survival—luck or God.

No matter what occurs in our lives, we must remember that God deserves the glory. Jesus understood that His mission on earth was to glorify the Father. Wherever He taught, His words caused God to be glorified. It should be the mission of every believer to give God the glory in all he experiences and in all he does.

To preach the gospel to the poor

A wealthy family hired a young Christian handyman to do yard work and fix-it jobs around their home. The husband owned a lucrative law firm and lavished his teenage children with all the material desires of their hearts. The wife often flew to other continents to shop for clothing. They appeared to have what every family would want.

But the handyman saw the extreme lack this family experienced. He mourned for the children, who craved love and attention. He prayed for the father, who hopelessly pursued esteem through his work. And he prayed for the mother, whose emptiness was never filled. This family was spiritually poor without God in their lives.

Jesus promised to preach good news to the spiritually poor, those who needed to know God in a personal way. No matter how much they owned, without the richness of knowing Christ, they were poor.

—Beverly Jones.

Golden Text Illuminated

"He began to say unto them, This day is this scripture fulfilled in your ears" (Luke 4:21).

Jesus' public ministry began in Judea shortly after His baptism and temptation. However, He soon returned to His home area of Galilee. Luke 4:14 tells us that He returned "in the power of the Spirit" and that His "fame" spread throughout the region. His teaching in the synagogues of Galilee brought praise from everyone (vs. 15). This, along with miraculous healings, created great anticipation when He finally came to His hometown of Nazareth.

When He entered the synagogue in Nazareth on the Sabbath, Jesus "stood up for to read" (Luke 4:16), probably at the invitation of the synagogue leader. He read a portion of the book of Isaiah (61:1-2), and then, in accordance with custom, He sat down to expound on the passage. As people eagerly waited to hear from the now-famous rabbi, "He began to say unto them, This day is this scripture fulfilled in your ears," or "in your hearing."

These first words from Jesus' mouth were shocking. The passage He had read spoke of the coming Messiah, the One who would be anointed to preach the gospel and to bring freedom and deliverance. Now Jesus was plainly saying that this messianic passage was fulfilled that very day in Him. He was claiming to be the fulfillment of the messianic prophecies of the Old Testament. Jesus was saying that the "era of salvation" (Marshall, *The Gospel of Luke,* Eerdmans) Isaiah spoke of was now present because the Messiah had come.

In quoting Isaiah, Jesus also made a fine distinction that could be understood only later. He read Isaiah's prophecy regarding the Messiah's work of preaching the gospel to the poor and bringing healing to the brokenhearted and deliverance and freedom to the captives, the blind, and the bruised (Luke 4:18). All these things characterized Jesus' ministry.

Jesus also preached "the acceptable year of the Lord" (Luke 4:19). While the meaning of this is probably equivalent to preaching the kingdom of God (vs. 43), the Year of Jubilee may be in the background. If so, Isaiah—and therefore Jesus—was comparing the Messiah's ministry to the fiftieth year in the Jewish calendar, when all debts were to be forgiven and all slaves freed. This served as an apt illustration of the spiritual freedom He would bring.

Jesus ended His quotation in the middle of a sentence. Isaiah, however, went on to speak of the "day of vengeance of our God" (Isa. 61:2). This speaks of the Messiah's work in His second coming. Since this would not be fulfilled in Jesus' first coming, He did not read these words.

Jesus was keenly aware of who He was and why He had come. His mission in His first coming was to "seek and to save that which was lost" (Luke 19:10). His work of judgment awaits His second coming.

While many in the synagogue were no doubt looking *for* the Messiah, it was startling to hear one of their own claiming to *be* the Messiah. Their initial pride and amazement soon turned to skepticism and rejection and even led to an attempt on His life (Luke 4:22-30). Such rejection in His hometown foreshadowed the rejection of Jesus by the entire nation.

—Jarl K. Waggoner.

Heart of the Lesson

"So popular and effective was Campbell Morgan's ministry that he was given all kinds of offers from many different places and people. John Wanamaker, the great merchant of Philadelphia, offered to build Morgan a million dollar church if he would become its pastor. Morgan turned him down, something the wealthy Wanamaker was not accustomed to in his dealings with people. 'I am God's man,' said Morgan. 'If I did that I would become John Wanamaker's man'" (Wiersbe, *The Wycliffe Handbook of Preaching & Preachers,* Moody).

Not only was Jesus Christ God's Man, but He also was the God-Man. As the fulfillment of every Old Testament messianic prophecy, Jesus was God's chosen Minister to proclaim the message of good news. In this week's lesson, we learn about Jesus' mission on earth—a mission that provided hope and salvation to those who lived in darkness and despair.

1. Jesus, the powerful, Spirit-filled Minister (Luke 4:14-15). Following His season of temptation and His subsequent season of spiritual renewal (vss. 1-13), Jesus returned to Galilee filled with the power of the Holy Spirit. His presence in Galilee and His teaching ministry in the region's synagogues quickly became newsworthy. At the beginning of His public ministry, Jesus was "glorified of all" (vs. 15).

Spiritual ministry is never dull or boring; in fact, serving the Lord often involves the reality of spiritual conflict, with all its elements of triumph and failure. Jesus' servant-ministers often experience seasons of powerful victory following seasons of powerful temptation.

The challenge for servant-believers is to remain anchored to the Person of Jesus Christ. When evil enticement seems overwhelming, Jesus will provide the patience to endure. When spiritual activities are accompanied by the praise of men, God will extend to us the grace needed to humbly and devotedly glorify Him.

2. Jesus, the perfect, Scripture-based Messiah (Luke 4:16-21). Following His teaching ministry in the Galilean synagogues, Jesus returned to His hometown of Nazareth. On the Sabbath, Jesus went to the synagogue, where teachers would read, interpret, and explain the weekly Torah passages. When it was Jesus' time to teach the concluding Sabbath lesson, He was handed a scroll that contained the second portion of the book of Isaiah.

After Jesus had read Isaiah 61:1 and the first part of verse 2, He closed the scroll, returned it to the synagogue attendant, and sat down. He had the full attention of all who attended the synagogue, and they were eager to hear what He had to say. Jesus proceeded to explain how the Scripture He had read would be fulfilled in His ministry as the Messiah.

One of the notable tenets of the Christian faith is the ability believers have to know, understand, and apply the Scriptures under the guidance of the Holy Spirit, who reveals truth (cf. John 16:13). But how can a follower of Jesus Christ be assured that he is being guided by the Holy Spirit and not by his own agenda?

A believer can be assured that the Holy Spirit is guiding him toward truth when he believes that Jesus Christ is the ultimate fulfillment of every messianic prophecy. In an age in which spiritual charlatans and spirits of deception abound, Jesus Christ remains the Way, the Truth, and the Life!

—*Thomas R. Chmura.*

World Missions

The name Jesus means "God saves" and is indicative of His mission here on earth. Jesus never lost sight of that mission. He Himself said that He always did what His Heavenly Father wanted Him to do (John 8:29). He was sent here for a purpose, and He never wavered from that mission. When He, as the Messiah, finally revealed Himself to His own people, He boldly declared that the Old Testament Scriptures found their fulfillment in Him. He was the Messiah for the world.

In this hurting world, people need to know that this Messiah is the one who saves them from their sins. Every other way is futile and powerless to save them from their sins. Jesus was unique in that He showed through His use of the Scriptures how He was to die for the whole world. Anyone who wishes to have his sins washed away needs to simply look to the Cross to find redemption. This is truly good news for all! It involves repentance and turning to Jesus to receive what He has already finished.

Sometimes this message is too simple for many. Some feel that they have to do something to "earn" their salvation. Jesus showed through the Scriptures that His mission on earth was one of redemption. He paid the price for all our sins, and this was accepted in heaven as appropriate payment for everything we have done wrong before the Father. Jesus' mission was to pour out His lifeblood as payment for our sins. Even though this was a bitter cup to drink, He carried through with faithfulness.

Luke recounts for us the time when Jesus read the Scriptures publicly in the temple at Jerusalem. There was something wonderful about that moment when He had finished. He had come to fulfill His mission. Jesus affirmed that He was the fulfillment of what Isaiah was talking about. The people could hardly believe it. They had been waiting for all these years, and now He was there in the flesh. Jesus showed them who He was by opening up the Old Testament before them and showing that He was, indeed, that Messiah.

Since this is the true Messiah shown to us by Luke and Jesus proved how He fulfilled that office, we ought to be spreading this good news to the whole world. A hurting world needs such a Messiah, and He has indeed come. As Christian believers, we know that the Bible is certainly true; and if the Bible backs up Jesus' description of Himself, should we not be telling the world about this Messiah and His mission? He came to save. Sadly, there are still so many in the world who have not yet heard of Jesus.

Part of our task as followers of Jesus is to remember that it is through us as a body of believers in Jesus that the message about why Jesus came to earth will go around the globe, one conversion at a time. One of the last commandments He gave His disciples was to spread this good news. The Scriptures talk about Him, and we ought to spread that good news. In a world of technology, this good news can spread quickly if we show how Jesus used the Scriptures to back up His claims as our Saviour.

The danger for those of us who live in urban societies is that we can easily forget that there are people who do not even own a copy of the Scriptures in their own language. We must help those who are involved in the mission of Scripture distribution so that the lost can hear of Him.

—A. Koshy Muthalaly.

The Jewish Aspect

This week's lesson offers a preview of the great kingdom of Messiah to come. Jesus preached from a portion of Isaiah 61:1-2. It was a message for the Jews—and at this point, it was a message for them alone. When Jesus sent His disciples out with the kingdom message, they were instructed, "Go not into the way of the Gentiles, and into any city of the Samaritans enter ye not: but go rather to the lost sheep of the house of Israel" (Matt. 10:5-6).

The kingdom was offered in the covenants. Abraham was promised descendants and land (Gen. 12:2, 7; 15:18). David was promised a kingdom forever (II Sam. 7:8, 23-24).

The kingdom was proclaimed at Sinai (Exod. 19:1, 4-6) and illustrated dramatically in the stone that struck the figure representing four major worldly kingdoms (Dan. 2:31-35, 44-45).

God preserved the kingdom truth through the ages (Isa. 65:17-25; Amos 9:11-14). Dr. Alva J. McClain said of the Isaiah 61 passage, "In all the literary masterpieces of the world there is probably nothing comparable for beauty to a single verse in Isaiah's picture of the joy which will prevail in the coming kingdom of our Lord" (*The Greatness of the Kingdom,* BMH Books).

Did the kingdom message register with the Jews in Jesus' day? Apparently it did not, for in His home area of Galilee, five thousand were fed on loaves and fish. Significant numbers were healed of every disease, demonic oppression, and other ailments. But the apathy of Chorazin, Bethsaida, and Capernaum earned them judgment more severe than that promised to Tyre and Sidon and Sodom (Luke 10:12-15).

In an extended discussion of *tz'dakah,* the acts of kindness of responsible people, Rabbi Arthur P. Nemitoff said,

"Tz'dakah is a tree of life" (*A Basic Judaism Reader,* Congregation Beth Israel). He went on to define *tz'dakah* with these words: "to aid the poor, care for the sick, teach the ignorant, and extend a helping hand to those who have lost their way in the world."

It would be wonderful to be able to say at this point that Judaism is extending the plan and purpose of the coming of the Messiah, but the fact is that the Messiah has been replaced.

The Jews practice tremendous feats of giving. The rabbis concluded centuries ago that poor women should receive aid in preference to men and that poor relatives are to receive help before strangers. The poor of the land of Israel take precedence over everyone (Nemitoff).

It may be truthfully said that the State of Israel is the only nation in history that survives on the freewill offerings of her people and other charitable nations. American Jews give huge sums of money each year for the defense and the welfare of the people of the land. Efforts to interest American Jews in migrating to the Holy Land have been fruitless. At the same time, Jews the world over realize that the survival of Israel is tied to their own welfare in other parts of the world.

In our city of 20,000 Jews, the health of our economy depends in large measure on Jewish economic health. Most of our major business firms are Jewish-owned or the result of their investment. In turn, they give generously to every community need. When revival comes to Israel, the *tz'dakah* practiced today will be put to good use in the kingdom of the Messiah. Great days lie ahead for the Jews when they mix faith with wisdom and hard work in the service of the King-Messiah Jesus.

—Lyle P. Murphy.

Guiding the Superintendent

Before embarking on any venture, some preparation or training will prove beneficial to the success of that venture. Jesus' wilderness testing was His initiation as He began His earthly ministry. Christ's period of fasting and temptation caused Him much suffering and despair, but we can be certain that just as the power of God protected and sustained Him, so that same power is available to every believer in his pursuit of his purpose.

DEVOTIONAL OUTLINE

1. Announcement of Jesus' earthly mission (Luke 4:14-17). There was not a second that the Spirit of God was not with Jesus, watching over Him after leading Him into the wilderness. That same Holy Spirit then led Jesus into the towns and villages in the region of Galilee. Traveling on foot, Jesus had the opportunity to encounter many of the townspeople. It was not uncommon for Him to minister to the needs of those He came in contact with as well as to share the love of God with them. This contributed to the reputation that preceded Him into the cities to which He traveled and ministered.

It is generally agreed that bad news travels fast. But when a man named Jesus declared glad tidings and performed miraculous deeds, good news spread quickly throughout the countryside.

During this early stage of Jesus' ministry, the Jewish leaders did not object to His teaching in their places of public worship; many even praised Him. How fitting that Jesus announced His call to the ministry in the town where He grew up! It was no accident that He read from the book of Isaiah, for He was also announcing what He had been called to do. Like Jesus, every Christian has a ministry—a purposeful use of the God-given gifts that lie within him. Any Christian who is unsure of his appointment can seek God through prayer and His Word. He will then reveal the assignment clearly and specifically.

2. Declaration of Jesus' prophetic mission (Luke 4:18-21). In reading the passage from Isaiah, Jesus confirmed that His mission was to bring the message of hope to those who were neglected and discounted, to mend shattered lives, to bring the message of freedom to those entangled in bondage, to deliver souls from darkness and bring them into the light of life, and to restore those broken under life's pressures. Christ further proclaimed that God's favor and goodwill are readily available to all who will hear His Word and receive His free gift of salvation.

The next order of service was the expounding of the Scripture that Jesus had read. The eyes of all focused intently on Christ, waiting to hear His explanation of that Scripture. How absolutely amazed they must have been to hear Him say that He was anointed and appointed to be the fulfillment of Isaiah's prophecy!

AGE-GROUP EMPHASES

Children: Children have a place in kingdom work. Use this lesson to assure them that even as young children, their job is to represent Christ well in the world.

Youths: They may think of the word "mission" as an ancient, irrelevant term. Teach them that God gives a specific mission, purpose, or calling to each of His saints. Challenge them to learn theirs.

Adults: Encourage the adults to look to Jesus for support as they do the work God has called them to.

—Jane E. Campbell.

Scripture Lesson Text

MATT. 15:1 Then came to Je'sus scribes and Phar'i-sees, which were of Je-ru'sa-lem, saying,

2 Why do thy disciples transgress the tradition of the elders? for they wash not their hands when they eat bread.

3 But he answered and said unto them, Why do ye also transgress the commandment of God by your tradition?

4 For God commanded, saying, Honour thy father and mother: and, He that curseth father or mother, let him die the death.

5 But ye say, Whosoever shall say to *his* father or *his* mother, *It is* a gift, by whatsoever thou mightest be profited by me;

6 And honour not his father or his mother, *he shall be free.* Thus have ye made the commandment of God of none effect by your tradition.

7 *Ye* hypocrites, well did E-sa'ias prophesy of you, saying,

8 This people draweth nigh unto me with their mouth, and honoureth me with *their* lips; but their heart is far from me.

9 But in vain they do worship me, teaching *for* doctrines the commandments of men.

10 And he called the multitude, and said unto them, Hear, and understand:

11 Not that which goeth into the mouth defileth a man; but that which cometh out of the mouth, this defileth a man.

18 But those things which proceed out of the mouth come forth from the heart; and they defile the man.

19 For out of the heart proceed evil thoughts, murders, adulteries, fornications, thefts, false witness, blasphemies:

20 These are *the things* which defile a man: but to eat with unwashen hands defileth not a man.

NOTES

158

Jesus' Teaching on the Law

Lesson: Matthew 15:1-11, 18-20

Read: Exodus 20:1-17; Isaiah 29:13-14; Matthew 5:17-48; 15:1-20

TIME: A.D. 29   PLACE: Galilee

GOLDEN TEXT—"This people draweth nigh unto me with their mouth, and honoureth me with their lips; but their heart is far from me. But in vain they do worship me, teaching for doctrines the commandments of men" (Matthew 15:8-9).

Introduction

Ever since human beings first became corrupted by sin and aware of their separation from God, many of them have been trying to regain His favor by their own devices. From ancient times, pagan religions have involved practices ranging from nonsensical and silly to disgusting, nauseating, and unspeakably vile.

Today, most "civilized" people detest such practices and observe more "enlightened" religion. But the great majority still seek to reach God through their own merits. By church attendance, neighborly kindness, charitable giving, or community activism they hope, somehow, to gain God's favor. They do not understand the depth of either human sin or divine grace.

Sadly, the Jewish religious leaders of Jesus' day had fallen into this same arrogant frame of mind. So zealous were they to keep the law that they had hedged it in with an unbelievable array of rabbinical traditions. These brought them into conflict with Jesus, as we see in this week's lesson.

LESSON OUTLINE

I. **THE CHALLENGE**—Matt. 15:1-2

II. **THE REJOINDER**—Matt. 15:3-9

III. **THE LESSON**—Matt. 15:10-11, 18-20

Exposition: Verse by Verse

THE CHALLENGE

MATT. 15:1 Then came to Jesus scribes and Pharisees, which were of Jerusalem, saying,

2 Why do thy disciples transgress the tradition of the elders? for they wash not their hands when they eat bread.

The challengers (Matt. 15:1). The event detailed in this week's study occurred more than halfway through Jesus' public ministry. Opinions about Him, both positive and negative, were becoming solidified. The religious officials had hardened their opposition and found more and more occasions to find fault.

Since Jesus was spending most of His time in Galilee, they came there from Jerusalem to critique His actions.

Those who came were "scribes and Pharisees" (Matt. 15:1). These two groups are often mentioned together in the Gospels. By New Testament times, scribes had become the recognized experts in the study of the law. They interpreted it and set it forth as the rule for Jewish daily life. In their zeal for its sanctity, they filled in presumed gaps with a complicated body of tradition. The Pharisees were the strictest and most influential sect in Judaism. Many of the scribes were also Pharisees, so the two terms overlapped.

The fact that these men came from Jerusalem is significant. Scribes and Pharisees existed all over the country, but only these sought to interrogate Jesus. They were probably from among the most respected, and their visit was a semiofficial investigation.

The issue (Matt. 15:2). The scribes and Pharisees charged Jesus' disciples with transgressing "the tradition of the elders." Tradition was not part of the Mosaic Code but a collection of oral teachings that interpreted it and prescribed its observance through detailed rules. It took form through the teachings of many rabbis. Though it was still in oral form, it was considered almost as authoritative as Scripture.

The disciples' alleged transgression was that "they wash not their hands when they eat bread" (Matt. 15:2). In his account, Mark used the words "defiled" and "unwashen" to describe the charge against the disciples (7:2). The issue was not cleanliness but ceremonial purity. The word for "unwashen" means that their hands were unclean—that is, not purified from spiritual contamination.

Mark explained that the Jews washed whenever they came from the marketplace, where their commerce placed them in contact with "unclean" Gentiles (Mark 7:3-4). They also ap-plied ritual cleansing to other objects related to eating—cups, pots, vessels, and tables. All this was thought to win them merit before God.

THE REJOINDER

3 But he answered and said unto them, Why do ye also transgress the commandment of God by your tradition?

4 For God commanded, saying, Honour thy father and mother: and, He that curseth father or mother, let him die the death.

5 But ye say, Whosoever shall say to his father or his mother, It is a gift, by whatsoever thou mightest be profited by me;

6 And honour not his father or his mother, he shall be free. Thus have ye made the commandment of God of none effect by your tradition.

7 Ye hypocrites, well did Esaias prophesy of you, saying,

8 This people draweth nigh unto me with their mouth, and honoureth me with their lips; but their heart is far from me.

9 But in vain they do worship me, teaching for doctrines the commandments of men.

Jesus' counterchallenge (Matt. 15:3). Jesus did not directly answer the Pharisees' question. Instead, He dealt with underlying issues their question reflected. The first involved the spiritual authority a person should follow—human tradition or divine revelation. They had emphasized the rules of the rabbis, which were not commanded in Scripture.

The problem was that these rules were not only *unnecessary* but also often *contradictory* to Scripture. So Jesus asked, "Why do ye also transgress the commandment of God by your tradition?" (Matt. 15:3). The critics had condemned the disciples for violating rabbinical tradition; Jesus accused them of violating God's command in order to keep this tradition. Such a charge no doubt horrified them, for they professed to be *protecting* the law through tradition.

God's command (Matt. 15:4). Jesus gave an example of how they did this. He stated the fifth commandment, "Honour thy father and thy mother" (Exod. 20:12). He also included the corollary, "He that curseth father or mother, let him die the death" (cf. Exod. 21:17; Lev. 20:9). These statements had come from God's direct revelation to Moses, which Jewish leaders claimed to revere and obey.

The Pharisees' evasion (Matt. 15:5-6). Rabbinical tradition had found a way to circumvent the Mosaic command. "But ye say" places special emphasis on "ye," as opposed to "God" (vs. 4). Normally, honoring parents included supporting them financially in old age. But a son could say, concerning property that might be used for their support, "It is a gift" (vs. 5)—that is, a gift devoted to God for sacred use and thus no longer available to them.

The technical Hebrew term for such a gift was "Corban" (Mark 7:11). It originally referred to any offering a person might give (cf. Lev. 1:2-3; 2:1; 3:1). Once so dedicated, the offering could not be withdrawn or changed. Tradition allowed a person to pronounce as "Corban" any wealth that might have been used to benefit parents, and the vow could not be rescinded. Ironically, the property could remain in the possession of the one who dedicated it, so he was actually giving up nothing.

This was a convenient way for greedy children to evade the command to honor their parents (Matt. 15:6). And while they might not have gone so far as to curse their parents, their heartless disrespect approximated the same thing. Thus, by their tradition they had negated God's command.

The error into which the scribes and Pharisees fell is common today as well. Religious people often add enough layers of tradition to the Bible to overlook the Bible completely. And as it is overlooked, it is contradicted. Seeking God's favor through recitation of creeds, liturgical observances, or family practices in itself violates biblical teaching on salvation by grace alone. And who knows how many more biblical teachings we contradict when we forsake them for human tradition?

Jesus' condemnation (Matt. 15:7-9). Jesus described His critics with one word—"hypocrites." This term comes from a root meaning "to act out a part in a play." A hypocrite is a play actor, one who pretends to be someone he is not. The New Testament uses the word for one who professes devotion to God but has no substance behind it.

Jesus asserted that Isaiah had prophesied of the hypocrisy of these men (Matt. 15:7-8). He quoted the Septuagint (Greek) version of Isaiah 29:13 for His condemnation. The prophet's words were originally directed against his contemporaries, who were in a spiritual stupor and unable to comprehend God's revelation. They had boldly professed religion with their lips, but their hearts were far from Him because they had substituted the teachings of men.

Jesus' critics could be described the same way. They drew near to God with their mouths and honored Him with their lips. They made pontifical pronouncements and paraded their learning in the synagogues. They made long, loud, flowery prayers in public places. They quoted the rabbis with ease. To the average Jew, they were paragons of godliness.

But despite their words, they were far from God (Matt. 15:8). Jesus warned that unless a person's righteousness exceeded that of the scribes and Pharisees, he would not enter God's kingdom (5:20). They robbed widows (23:14); led

Gentile converts astray (vs. 15); and overlooked justice, mercy, and faith (vs. 23). Jesus likened them to cups that were clean on the outside but detestable inside (vss. 25-26) and to whitewashed tombs full of bones (vs. 27).

Their worship, therefore, was "vain" (futile, fruitless) (Matt. 15:9). Their teachings consisted of "the commandments of men" instead of the revelation of God. Jesus reminded them that their tradition regarding Corban was but one example of many traditions that violated His law: "and many such like things do ye" (Mark 7:13). This had become such a way of life to them that they now assumed their traditions were really God's commands.

Their empty religion should cause us to examine our own motives for religious observances. How many of them are really commanded by God? Have we taken accumulated church traditions and given them an authority only the Bible deserves? And even if they are in themselves wholesome traditions, why do we practice them? Are we seeking to obtain or increase God's favor through them? Have we turned the gospel of grace into a collection of legalistic rules? Paul reminded the Galatians that that was no gospel at all (Gal. 3:1-5).

THE LESSON

10 And he called the multitude, and said unto them, Hear, and understand:

11 Not that which goeth into the mouth defileth a man; but that which cometh out of the mouth, this defileth a man.

18 But those things which proceed out of the mouth come forth from the heart; and they defile the man.

19 For out of the heart proceed evil thoughts, murders, adulteries, fornications, thefts, false witness, blasphemies:

20 These are the things which defile a man: but to eat with unwashen hands defileth not a man.

A word for the multitude (Matt. 15:10-11). Having addressed the issue of spiritual authority—Scripture or tradition—Jesus turned to the immediate question the scribes had raised—the nature of spiritual defilement. Was it possible to be defiled by the things one ate with unwashed hands? He first gave a general answer to the crowd.

"And he called the multitude" (Matt. 15:10) tells us that Jesus' previous words had been spoken to the scribes and Pharisees privately. The crowd nearby apparently knew what the controversy was about but had not been privy to Jesus' comments about authority. So He now called on them to address them directly. "Hear, and understand" makes it clear that He wanted them to be enlightened, not confused, about this subject.

Jesus' lesson was straightforward: "Not that which goeth into the mouth defileth a man; but that which cometh out of the mouth, this defileth a man" (Matt. 15:11). Jesus did not further explain to the crowd what He meant by this; He reserved that for His disciples when they pressed Him later. So the statement here was general, and it was left to the hearers to interpret it.

Thus, as Peter recognized, it was spoken as a "parable" (Matt. 15:15; cf. Mark 7:17). A parable compares two objects or concepts to teach a lesson. Jesus used this method only after His nation had rejected His messianic claims. He explained to the disciples why He did so: to reveal truth to those who were spiritually ready to receive it while concealing it from those who had closed their hearts (Matt. 13:10-16).

Here Jesus spoke to the multitude in parabolic terms because He knew it was a mixed group. Some had open hearts; others were spiritually dull. So He did not explain what He meant by "that which cometh out of the mouth" (Matt. 15:11). Those with spiritual insight would either understand or seek further light; to the rest, it would remain an enigma.

A word for the disciples (Matt. 15:18-19). The disciples' first concern was that the Pharisees were offended (vs. 12). Jesus assured them that this did not matter, since they were spiritually blind and not qualified to teach (vss. 13-14). But then Peter asked for an explanation of the parable. After rebuking the Twelve for their lack of insight, Jesus began to explain (vss. 15-17).

He declared that "whatsoever entereth in at the mouth goeth into the belly, and is cast out into the draught" (Matt. 15:17). Foods only pass through the digestive system and do not affect one's inner spiritual condition. This does not address food's physical benefit or harm; it merely states that it does not defile spiritually. Mark's account, which adds "purging all meats" (7:19), indicates that Jesus was thenceforth declaring all meats clean and legitimate for the use of His people.

But there is a more important lesson here; we need to beware of what comes forth from the wicked heart (Matt. 15:18). The source of defilement is *within* us, and that defilement becomes evident through our words and deeds.

Matthew lists several sins Jesus enumerated as coming from the heart (15:19). The first is "evil thoughts"— corrupt reasonings that produce any and all of the sins that follow. "Murders, adulteries, fornications, thefts, false witness" violate the sixth, seventh, eighth, and ninth commandments. "Blasphemies" refers to slander against either God or man. They are therefore violations of the two comprehensive commandments to love God and neighbor (22:35-40). Mark's list of sins is even more extensive (7:21-22).

A final summary (Matt. 15:20). Jesus concluded that the sins that defile a person come from within, not without. And for this truth He appealed to Scripture itself, not to tradition. He treated the law with the greatest respect even as He set aside the accumulated traditions of men. Since He fulfilled all that the law foreshadowed (cf. 5:17), He was free to abolish the dietary practices that had now served their purpose (cf. Rom. 10:4; 14:3; I Tim. 4:3-5).

Human traditions have their place, and they can be helpful if we use them intelligently. But we must not confuse them with or substitute them for biblical teaching. Wise is the person who has studied the Bible enough to know the difference!
—*Robert E. Wenger.*

QUESTIONS

1. Who were the scribes and Pharisees? Why did they question Jesus?

2. How was the tradition of the elders related to the Mosaic Law?

3. What did the Jews hope to accomplish through ceremonial washing?

4. What example did Jesus give of the tradition of the elders contradicting the command of God?

5. What is a hypocrite?

6. How did the scribes and Pharisees manifest their hypocrisy? How might we manifest it today?

7. In what sense was Jesus' statement to the multitude a parable?

8. Why is it not possible for foods to defile a person spiritually?

9. What is the true source of spiritual defilement?

10. How did Jesus treat the law? Why could He set parts of it aside?
—*Robert E. Wenger.*

Preparing to Teach the Lesson

As we have seen in our previous lessons, Jesus was constantly referring to the Scriptures. His appearance in Israel and His present and future ministry are in fulfillment of biblical prophecy.

In this week's lesson we will examine Jesus' teachings on the law of God as given in the Scriptures and how He dealt with the teachings and traditions of the rabbis and elders when they came into conflict with that law.

TODAY'S AIM

Facts: to show that Jesus upheld the inspired Scriptures as the ultimate and final authority on how a person should think and behave.

Principle: to show that God's Word is superior to the writings of men and is the only and final authority for proper thought and action.

Application: to show that we need to know, understand, and apply the Bible to our lives above any other writing or teaching.

INTRODUCING THE LESSON

We are faced with constant decisions in life. In the twenty-first century, the media and the Internet have become overwhelming influences. We are constantly introduced to new experts in fields that we were unaware even existed—experts who advise us on what to eat, how to shop, and what to think. On the other hand, we struggle with traditions that may have directed our lives since we were born. In fact, there is a trend among churches now to return to church traditions from the Middle Ages—at the expense of the truth of the Bible.

As you begin, ask everyone to think about what their greatest influence is and where they get their rules for life.

God's laws were given not because He wanted to limit how much fun we could have in life but to protect us from individual and social sin and to show us boundaries that reveal our own sin nature. As Paul wrote, the law served as a tutor to show us our need for Christ.

DEVELOPING THE LESSON

1. Superficial obedience (Matt. 15:1-9). As a reference point, place a copy of the Ten Commandments in a prominent place in the classroom. Comment on the simplicity of the list, yet observe the practical aspect of them.

The religious leaders were careful to obey a narrow set of rules that previous generations of scholars had established as a hedge around God's law. To keep a person from breaking God's laws, these improvised rules served as a protective fence to keep the people at a distance. For example, to protect the Sabbath, specific rules that went beyond what God had revealed were devised. They defined the nature of work and specified what could and could not be done. God's laws became hidden behind man's laws. The religious leaders then felt it was their duty to intimidate others into keeping those rules. It became a sin to break these man-made laws.

Notice that the scribes and Pharisees were not concerned about God's laws but only with tradition.

The issue brought up about the behavior of Jesus' disciples was not about cleanliness and its practical benefits but about ritual and tradition. Mark explained the elaborate ritual that the Pharisees practiced based on tradition (Mark 7:1-5). These traditions were oral and written sayings of famous rabbis. While these sayings were only commentaries on the written law, they were regarded as equal to the law of God. The rabbinical traditions took precedence over God's Word!

If the Pharisees and scribes had truly understood God's Word as opposed to their traditions, how do you think they would have responded to Jesus and His disciples?

In the beginning of His ministry, Jesus had given His interpretation of the law of God with specific examples in the Sermon on the Mount (Matt. 5:17-48). He made it clear that He had not come to destroy the law but to fulfill it.

Ask the class whether they are aware of any traditions that have developed within the church that contradict the Scriptures.

Explain Jesus' answer in Matthew 15:3-9. Notice His use of Isaiah 29:13. Why is it dangerous to put human teachings on the same level as God's Word? How can this be avoided?

2. False defilement (Matt. 15:10-11). In this passage Jesus was not talking about germs or the dangers of food poisoning. Defilement meant that someone or something was unclean in a ritual sense. It is best understood in contrast to God's holiness. There were two distinctions: the holy and the common. That which was not holy was not set apart for God. The traditions of the elders had become a superficial substitute for the inner condition that God required to be clean, or holy.

3. True defilement (Matt. 15:18-20). There is a place for personal cleanliness. There are several places in the law that deal with personal hygiene. As Jesus mentioned, whatever enters the mouth goes through the intestinal system and is soon gone.

What is important is the nature of a person's heart and character. Because of the sin nature, a steady stream of evil proceeds from a person's heart and finds expression through his speech.

Look at the specifics of the evils that begin in the heart. Compare this list with the Ten Commandments.

Jesus' final statement directly contradicted the argument of the scribes and Pharisees and, beyond them, the writings and traditions of the revered elders.

ILLUSTRATING THE LESSON

Man-made traditions and outward actions cannot make us what we need to be before God and others. What is most important is what we are inside.

WHAT LEAVES YOUR MOUTH?

THAT SHOWS WHO YOU ARE

CONCLUDING THE LESSON

No one is saved by keeping the law. We are saved by God's grace through faith in Christ and His sacrifice on the cross. However, we rely on the Bible for guidance and instructions on how to conduct our lives as Christians. It is becoming very unpopular to view the Bible as our authority. Society, with all of its secular experts and opinions, complains that the Bible is an obsolete standard that should be discarded by thinking people.

It is important for the Christian to discern properly, keeping the Scriptures as the central and only written authority for how he thinks and conducts himself.

ANTICIPATING THE NEXT LESSON

In the next lesson we will learn what Jesus identified as the greatest commandment of the Bible.

—Carter Corbrey.

PRACTICAL POINTS

1. Finding fault with others prevents us from concentrating on loving and serving God (Matt. 15:1-3).
2. When we avoid following God's Word, we miss its blessings (vss. 4-6).
3. If we lack a close relationship with God, we often feel lost and helpless just when we need Him most (vss. 7-8).
4. Substituting our own ideas for God's Word implies we want to be independent of Him (vs. 9).
5. Unkind words are often the result of harboring envious and jealous thoughts (vss. 10-11).
6. Even when we fail, God is always ready to forgive us (vss. 18-20).
—Anne Adams.

RESEARCH AND DISCUSSION

1. Why were the Pharisees so concerned about the actions of Jesus' disciples? Are you concerned about someone's conduct? How should you deal with it?
2. Jesus called the Pharisees hypocrites because they taught rules that they themselves did not follow. Do such people serve God or only themselves? Does their hypocrisy affect others? How? Discuss.
3. Jesus condemned teaching merely human rules in place of God's. Can you think of current examples?
4. Is sinning in action worse than sinning only in thought? Is it harder to do the right thing or to think the right thing? Discuss.
—Anne Adams.

ILLUSTRATED HIGH POINTS

Honoureth me with their lips

Children, particularly siblings, can have differences of opinion. Often these disagreements escalate to quarrels and even physical fights. To stop such conflicts, a parent will separate the combatants and promote a reconciliation. The discussion, directed at helping the children understand each other's feelings, usually concludes with the order "Say you're sorry." The children usually respond by rote. Though the parent cannot judge the children's hearts, it would be fair to assess that their apologies may be less than genuine.

God knows His children's hearts. He is aware of our intentions and motives. When our words honor Him but our hearts disobey Him, He is insulted and disappointed. As we worship our God, let us always examine our hearts so that our words honor Him.

Hear, and understand

A couple purchased a well-trained German Shepherd dog that had been retired from a law enforcement agency in their area. His new owners were confident that their pet would be gentle, observant, and obedient.

But the dog would not respond to any of the couple's commands—no sitting, no heeling, no fetching—nothing. This continued for several weeks. Bewildered, the husband called the law enforcement agency to complain about the dog's apparent obstinance. "Oh, yes," replied the officer, "we forgot to tell you. The dog was trained for a specific area, and he only understands Spanish."

Jesus knew the people around Him could hear His words but did not always understand. It is His desire today, as it was during His earthly ministry, that we understand His words and apply them to our lives.
—Beverly Jones.

Golden Text Illuminated

"This people draweth nigh unto me with their mouth, and honoureth me with their lips; but their heart is far from me. But in vain they do worship me, teaching for doctrines the commandments of men" (Matthew 15:8-9).

The words of Jesus in our golden text were a stinging rebuke to the scribes and Pharisees of His day. These religious leaders had charged Jesus' disciples with not observing "the tradition of the elders" (Matt. 15:2) because they did not wash their hands when eating bread. This criticism of Jesus' disciples was also an implied condemnation of Jesus Himself.

Jesus met this attack with a far more scathing condemnation of the scribes and Pharisees. He noted that while they concerned themselves with such trivialities as hand washing, which was a matter of mere human tradition, they were ignoring or circumventing the expressly stated law of God to honor one's parents.

In order to avoid using their resources to help needy parents, they piously "dedicated" those resources to God and thus declared them off-limits to their fathers and mothers. In reality, it was merely a scheme to hold on to money and property they did not want to share with their parents.

Jesus rightly called these critics hypocrites (Matt. 15:7). He then quoted Isaiah 29:13. The Lord's words to the people of Isaiah's day accurately described the scribes and Pharisees who stood before Jesus. These hypocrites drew near to God "with their mouth" and honored Him "with their lips." In other words, what they said suggested they were committed to the Lord and were honoring Him.

The scribes and Pharisees said the right things and flaunted their piety, and people considered them godly followers of the Lord. However, like the Jewish people in Isaiah's time, their hearts were far from God. Their religion was solely external. Their worship did not come from the heart and did not affect the heart. What they considered worship was utterly "vain," or empty, because they had elevated their man-made traditions, "the commandments of men," above biblical truth.

Jesus' harshest criticism was not aimed at the tax collectors, the harlots, the drunkards, or those known simply as the "sinners" (Matt. 11:19; cf. 21:31-32). Rather, His sharpest words were directed at the scribes and Pharisees, the most religious people in the society of His day (cf. chap. 23). We should take warning from this. All are sinners, but only those who hide their sinful hearts behind a facade of religion are hypocrites.

Obedience to the Lord's commands and worship of Him are natural expressions of love that flow from redeemed hearts. But if these things become merely an outward show to impress people or a means of justifying our own selfish desires, they mean nothing at all.

Likewise, if our hearts have deceived us into following man-made traditions that take precedence over the Word of God and a genuine relationship with the Lord, we have become hypocrites, and our worship is a sham. The Lord seeks those who will worship Him "in spirit and in truth" (John 4:24). That leaves no room for hypocrisy.

—Jarl K. Waggoner.

Heart of the Lesson

"A rather pompous-looking deacon was endeavoring to impress upon a class of boys the importance of living the Christian life. 'Why do people call me a Christian?' the man asked. After a moment's pause, one youngster said, 'Maybe it's because they don't know you'" (www.bible.org).

Ouch! That one hurt! Maybe it is fitting that the illustration should hurt. The body of Christ has suffered enough damage from believers whose hearts are not fully devoted to following Jesus Christ. The time for personal revival and repentance has come. Let hypocrisy diminish and authenticity abound, and let the truths of this week's lesson text be the catalyst for this spiritual revitalization.

1. Exposing the hypocrisy of spiritual leaders (Matt. 15:1-9). Some spiritual leaders approached Jesus and questioned Him about the nontraditional actions of His followers. Jesus seized the opportunity to pose a piercing question to the two-faced leaders. Jesus then compared Old Testament commands to then-current practices to expose the blatant hypocrisy of the Pharisees and scribes who nullified the sacred Scriptures for the sake of human ritual.

Jesus then leveled a penetrating charge of spiritual hypocrisy against the spiritual leaders. He strengthened His charge with a reference to Isaiah's prophecy concerning the dishonorable hearts and impotent worship of God's people (cf. Isa. 29:13). The silence that followed was condemning.

One of the consistent responses unregenerate people give for not trusting in Jesus Christ as their Saviour by faith is the hypocrisy of God's people. Now, we all understand that hypocrisy is not peculiar to Christians; it saturates all humanity. Believers, though, must be held to a higher spiritual standard.

Simply stated, followers of Jesus Christ must practice what they preach. Our lifestyles must correspond with our personal beliefs. With a view toward eternity, therefore, let us cast off the selfish and damaging mantle of hypocrisy and replace it with the sacred and edifying mantle of spiritual authenticity.

2. Revealing the source of spiritual defilement (Matt. 15:10-11, 18-20). Following His scathing indictment of the religious leaders, Jesus summoned the multitudes and challenged them to open their hearts and minds to His words. Jesus clearly taught the people that the spiritual leaders' emphasis on externals and their exclusion of an emphasis on internals were immoral. He wanted His listeners to comprehend and employ the truth that degrading actions originate in deceitful hearts.

An American author and humorist once said, "Everyone is a moon, and has a dark side which he never shows to anybody" (Twain, *Following the Equator, Pudd'nhead Wilson's New Calendar*). For believers in Jesus Christ, that dark side has been redeemed! The precious blood of Jesus Christ has cleansed our hearts from sin and its curse. As a result, believers have the incredible advantage of demonstrating lives that originate in hearts that have been eternally purified.

Although the spiritual struggle between the flesh and the Holy Spirit will remain until Jesus returns, believers do not need to be enslaved by that struggle. Hypocrisy is defeated; spiritual victory is a present reality for God's people (cf. Rom. 7:21-25)!

—*Thomas R. Chmura.*

World Missions

As a teacher of the Bible in a Christian university, I hear this from students all the time: "Why should we believe in the Jesus you proclaim when Christians are such phonies?" This speaks to the issue of credibility in the world of missions and the proclamation of the gospel. The question is a very valid one. My usual response to such skeptics is something like this: "The fact that some Christians are not faithful does not undermine the truth of Jesus and what He has done for us." Our Lord always remains faithful.

We must remember that Jesus was a Jew. However, He was a Jew with a mission—a mission that was spelled out in the Bible centuries before the incarnation, when He walked this world as a man. As a Jew, Jesus knew the teaching of the Law, the Torah. The Law clearly spoke out against religious hypocrisy.

Our lesson this week attests to this truth. But Jesus stood above all of this. They could not find one single fault against Him. The worship of the one true God—the God of Abraham, Isaac, and Jacob—was a big part of the Torah. Jesus Himself spoke out against the religious hypocrisy of the religious leaders of His day.

If we, as those who bear the name of Jesus, are to become credible in the world in which we live, our lives must fall in line with the message of Jesus that we proclaim. We need to show people that we mean business about Jesus and His message at the cost of that which is truly important to us. Many missionaries in the remote parts of this world are a testimony to the fact that our message is true. In 1956, Jim Elliot and four others were murdered for this message.

On October 28, 1949, Elliot had written in His personal diary, "He is no fool who gives what he cannot keep to gain that which he cannot lose." This was true sacrifice and an unmistakable validation of the truth and power of the gospel for which they were willing to die. Is Jesus worth dying for? If the answer is in the affirmative, then we must show the world more than lip service. We have to tell the world about this Jesus. This takes some soul-searching on our part.

As a result of the gospel message, that particular tribe of natives for whom these missionaries sacrificed their lives are now turning to our Lord Jesus. It is now obvious that the message proclaimed there was worth believing. Our Lord Jesus did not come in vain. It really does not matter so much what those around us who call themselves Christians do or do not do. This is not a matter of following the letter of the law; it is a matter of the heart.

The message of Jesus is still powerful. There is power in the precious name of Jesus, and His name must be proclaimed at all costs. His blood was shed for us so that the whole world might have the opportunity to receive Him as Lord and Saviour. Our Lord is preparing the church to be received as His bride. One day He is coming back again to receive us into His kingdom. But we must be prepared for that great event. Will our hearts be found pure before Him?

The practice of our faith should draw others to Him as Lord and Saviour. The Scriptures open the door for this to happen.

—A. Koshy Muthalaly.

The Jewish Aspect

Jesus put the case to the scribes and Pharisees regarding the difference between the Word of God and the traditions of the elders (Matt. 15:2-3). It is no different today.

In the evolution of the Jewish Law, the Jews recognize the Torah, the first five books of the Bible, as "written law." This divine record is honored as it is read from every Sabbath morning in the synagogue in a plan designed to complete the reading in one year.

However, in the Scripture text this week, we see that the process of undermining the written law in favor of man-made commandments was well underway in Jesus' day. This oral law, as it is called, continued to grow as the Bible became more and more neglected. The Mishnah, a collection of these oral laws, was published two hundred years after Christ.

The Mishnah, in turn, became part of the Babylonian Gemara, published by Jews in Babylon in the fourth century A.D. This was called the Babylonian Talmud, or simply Bavly. Another collection, called the Jerusalem Talmud, was produced in Jerusalem but lacked the honor bestowed on the Bavly.

A page of the Talmud requires a knowledge of Hebrew, of course. In an effort to systematize the reading of opinions accumulated over eighteen centuries, a method of reading the Talmud was set forth in 1520. It is still in use today. The page will show the Bible passage to be interpreted in the center of the page. On the left side of the passage will be the key words under discussion by Rabbi Rashi (1040–1105). Then the balance of the page will be opinions pro and con rendered through time (Nemitoff, ed., *A Basic Jewish Reader,* Congregation Beth Israel).

A Jewish physician related that he hosts a Talmud study each week in his home. They have a very scholarly Jewish rabbi who leads the discussion, but he really does not like the Talmud. He conducts the study to please his friends. In general, the study mostly includes boring, nonsensical situations that rarely affect the way a pious Jew should deal with life as he finds it.

It is clear that Talmudic studies serve the purpose of keeping the Jew out of the Old Testament and, particularly, away from the writings of the prophets, for they are rich in messianic prophecy that would be devastating to anyone obsessed with issues and problems that are largely irrelevant.

Jesus cited the failure of the religious elite to observe the requirement of the Ten Commandments, especially the fifth—"Honour thy father and mother" (Matt. 15:4). Tradition held that it was proper for the pious to withhold support from parents in order to give to their religious practice—in other words, to use a parent's money for a gift that brought honor only on themselves.

In Matthew 5:21-48, Jesus pointed out particular issues in which the leaders of Israel added to Scripture in such a way as to change its substance or its purpose. For example, the seventh commandment forbids adultery, but it must also include looking upon a woman with lust (vss. 27-28). Similarly, divorce is a violation of God's one-flesh principle, but Jewish leaders allowed for putting away a wife on the provision of a bill of divorcement.

American rabbis lament the fact that roughly 50 percent of Jewish marriages are with non-Jews. This demonstrates clearly that Judaism has not made its case as a true faith to the Jewish people.

—Lyle P. Murphy.

Guiding the Superintendent

In today's judicial system, some laws are difficult to understand and interpret, resulting in more confusion than justice. For the believer, to understand and obey God's commands means the sweet, heavenly rest with God.

DEVOTIONAL OUTLINE

1. Choose to follow God's law (Matt. 15:1-6). Hebrews 4:16 says that we may "come boldly unto the throne of grace," but we certainly are not to do so in arrogance and pretext as did the scribes and Pharisees when they came to Jesus. Jesus knows the heart of humankind and discerns through His Word the very intent of every heart (cf. vs. 12). He immediately recognized that the religious leaders from Jerusalem were not seeking Him for good, and He had a ready response to their ridiculous question. This teaches Christians to devote themselves to prayerfully studying God's Word so that the Holy Spirit can bring up in them a powerful defense of their love, obedience, and unwavering faith in God and His Son, Jesus (cf. I Pet. 3:15).

"It is better to trust in the Lord than to put confidence in man" (Ps. 118:8). Man's carnal laws and traditions can be twisted, distorted, and manipulated to communicate whatever is convenient for man. God's "commandments are not grievous" (I John 5:3); they are immutable expressions of truth that guide the lives of God's people.

2. Follow God's law in worship (Matt. 15:7-9). How vain of man to think that God will not take notice of disingenuous worship! If Isaiah detected it, why would our all-knowing God not recognize false veneration? True worship is a combination of spirit, soul, and body; we must bring our total being into His presence. Every believer must strive to worship God as He desires to be worshipped, "in spirit and in truth" (John 4:24).

3. God's laws lead to eternal life (Matt. 15:10-11, 18-20). Jesus taught almost exclusively in parables, using analogies to common, familiar things to teach spiritual lessons. It is critical to our salvation that our fleshly minds hear, understand, and receive the message of Jesus.

Jesus responded to Peter's request for an explanation of the parable on the subject of defilement, despite what appears to us to be the obvious meaning. Jesus wanted His followers to have clear, unambiguous knowledge of God's statutes—unlike the legalistic teachers, who would have them bound by uncommon law or well-preserved traditions that neither edified nor led to everlasting life. "A good man out of the good treasure of the heart bringeth forth good things: and an evil man out of the evil treasure bringeth forth evil things" (Matt. 12:35). The heart produces hateful words, wicked thoughts, and immoral deeds that contaminate the soul. These things are offensive to God.

AGE-GROUP EMPHASES

Children: When encouraging the children to keep their hands clean, teach them that God expects them to have clean hearts by showing love in words and deeds.

Youths: Encourage them to pray and to study the Scriptures daily and not to hesitate to ask any questions that they may have. That is how we all learn.

Adults: Teach them that doing something the same way it has always been done does not mean it is the best or the only way to do it. Challenge them to consider whether it is God's way.

—Jane E. Campbell.

Scripture Lesson Text

LEV. 19:18 Thou shalt not avenge, nor bear any grudge against the children of thy people, but thou shalt love thy neighbour as thyself: I *am* the LORD.

DEUT. 6:4 Hear, O Is'ra-el: The LORD our God *is* one LORD:

5 And thou shalt love the LORD thy God with all thine heart, and with all thy soul, and with all thy might.

6 And these words, which I command thee this day, shall be in thine heart:

7 And thou shalt teach them diligently unto thy children, and shalt talk of them when thou sittest in thine house, and when thou walkest by the way, and when thou liest down, and when thou risest up.

MARK 12:28 And one of the scribes came, and having heard them reasoning together, and perceiving that he had answered them well, asked him, Which is the first commandment of all?

29 And Je'sus answered him, The first of all the commandments *is,* Hear, O Is'ra-el; The LORD our God is one LORD:

30 And thou shalt love the LORD thy God with all thy heart, and with all thy soul, and with all thy mind, and with all thy strength: this *is* the first commandment.

31 And the second *is* like, *namely* this, Thou shalt love thy neighbour as thyself. There is none other commandment greater than these.

32 And the scribe said unto him, Well, Master, thou hast said the truth: for there is one God; and there is none other but he:

33 And to love him with all the heart, and with all the understanding, and with all the soul, and with all the strength, and to love *his* neighbour as himself, is more than all whole burnt offerings and sacrifices.

34 And when Je'sus saw that he answered discreetly, he said unto him, Thou art not far from the kingdom of God. And no man after that durst ask him *any question.*

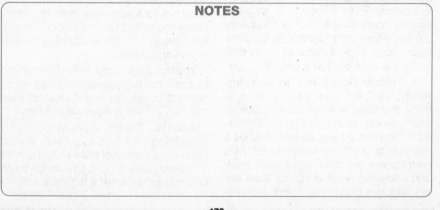

NOTES

The Greatest Commandment

Lesson: Leviticus 19:18; Deuteronomy 6:4-7; Mark 12:28-34

Read: Leviticus 19:18; Deuteronomy 6:1-9; Mark 12:28-34

TIMES: 1445 B.C.; about 1406 B.C.; A.D. 30

PLACES: Sinai wilderness; Moab; Jerusalem

GOLDEN TEXT—"Thou shalt love the Lord thy God with all thy heart, and with all thy soul, and with all thy mind, and with all thy strength: this is the first commandment. And the second is like, namely this, Thou shalt love thy neighbour as thyself" (Mark 12:30-31).

Introduction

We often focus on the details instead of the big picture, the procedures instead of the purpose behind them. Employees of large organizations, for example, are more aware of the multiplicity of internal policies than of their organization's purpose.

Christians are not exempt from this tendency. Too often we do things we have been taught are right without a thought of the One we are to glorify thereby. Churches can easily go through their weekly round of programs and lose sight of their calling to represent their Saviour.

The nation of Israel also had to be reminded often of the reason for the many commandments they strove to keep. In this week's text, Jesus called attention to the two commandments that bind all the rest together.

LESSON OUTLINE

I. THE SOCIAL MANDATE PRESCRIBED—Lev. 19:18

II. THE SPIRITUAL MANDATE PRESCRIBED—Deut. 6:4-7

III. THE DUAL MANDATE CONFIRMED—Mark 12:28-34

Exposition: Verse by Verse

THE SOCIAL MANDATE PRESCRIBED

LEV. 19:18 **Thou shalt not avenge, nor bear any grudge against the children of thy people, but thou shalt love thy neighbour as thyself: I am the LORD.**

A prohibition (Lev. 19:18a). The Law of Moses is a comprehensive system that governed not just worship practices but the whole fabric of social life. This was based on the premise "Ye shall be holy: for I the Lord your God am holy" (vs. 2). As the Lord was set apart from all evil, so the Israelites should be in their social relationships.

Leviticus 19:9-18 deals exclusively with dealings with one's neighbor. Israelites were commanded to provide for the poor and the stranger in the time of harvest (vss. 9-10). They were to refrain from stealing, lying, and swearing falsely (vss. 11-12). They were not to defraud a worker of his wages, take advantage of the handicapped, or show favoritism in governing (vss. 13-15). They were not to spread malicious gossip or bring false charges against a neighbor (vs. 16).

But the law looks beyond external actions to motives. A person is not to harbor hatred for a brother but to deal openly with him as the occasion requires (Lev. 19:17). This means he should not store up a desire for revenge or hold a grudge (vs. 18).

A command (Lev. 19:18b). Most of the foregoing injunctions were given as prohibitions, telling what *not* to do to a neighbor. Even the command not to hate him is negative. But the key to treating a neighbor equitably is a positive command: "Thou shalt love thy neighbour as thyself." This assumes that everyone has an innate love for himself that leads him to expend great care on his own needs. He was to have the same concern for the needs of his neighbor (cf. Matt. 7:12; Rom. 13:8-10).

But who, exactly, is a neighbor? We think of neighbors as those who live near us; to the ancient Israelite, a neighbor was one of the same family, tribe, or country. However, God did not intend that neighborly love be limited to Israelites. He included the "stranger" (Lev. 19:10) as someone whose needs should be supplied, and He specifically commanded Israelites to love strangers as themselves (vs. 34). In His parable of the good Samaritan, Jesus left no doubt that a neighbor is any fellow human being (Luke 10:25-37).

THE SPIRITUAL MANDATE PRESCRIBED

DEUT. 6:4 Hear, O Israel: The LORD our God is one LORD:

5 And thou shalt love the LORD thy God with all thine heart, and with all thy soul, and with all thy might.

6 And these words, which I command thee this day, shall be in thine heart:

7 And thou shalt teach them diligently unto thy children, and shalt talk of them when thou sittest in thine house, and when thou walkest by the way, and when thou liest down, and when thou risest up.

Love of God's Person (Deut. 6:4-5). The ideal of loving a neighbor as oneself cannot be fulfilled unless a person is walking with God in a loving relationship. Moses understood this as he gave his final words to the Israelites. He was about to review with them "the commandments, the statutes, and the judgments" (vs. 1) of the Lord. But before he did, he reacquainted them with the God who had given these commands. Their relationship with Him was crucial to their well-being in Canaan.

The call to love God is based on who He is: "Hear, O Israel: The Lord our God is one Lord" (Deut. 6:4). This verse, called the Shema (the Hebrew word for "hear"), is probably the most-quoted verse in the Bible, since devout Jews recite it at least twice daily. Several different translations of it are grammatically possible, but in my view it is probably best to understand it as "Yahweh our God is one Yahweh." It teaches the dual truths that He is the only true God and that He is the God of Israel.

He stands apart from all the imagined deities invented by mankind. And He is only one Lord. Though He may have revealed Himself in various ways, it is always the same God who has revealed Himself. Moreover, this unique God has chosen to identify Himself with the nation of Israel. He has done this not because He ignores the rest of mankind but because He wants to manifest His attributes to the whole world through Israel (Exod. 19:5-6; I Kings 8:41-43; Ps. 67:1-2; Zech. 8:20-23).

The Lord's relationship with Israel was one of love and covenant loyalty (cf. Deut. 7:7-10). Therefore He asked for their unconditional love in return. They were to love Him with heart, soul, and might (6:5). The terms "heart" and "soul" overlap somewhat in meaning, but both are related to the nonmaterial aspect of man. Mind, emotions, and will are included in the love commanded.

"Might" implies that all of one's energy and strength is committed to the outworking of this love. Taken together, all three terms denote loving obedience to every aspect of God's will. They leave no room for compromise with other religions or even mental reservations while worshipping Him.

Stewardship of God's words (Deut. 6:6-7). Wholehearted love for God would determine how one treated His words. Moses declared that "these words, which I command thee this day, shall be in thine heart." The commands of God's law were not only to be committed to memory and practiced out of fear or duty; they were also to be in the heart (cf. 11:18). They were to become so internalized that they would become the focus of the way in which one conducted the affairs of daily life (cf. Pss. 37:31; 40:8; 119:11).

But the people were to do more: "Thou shalt teach them diligently unto thy children" (Deut. 6:7). The generation to whom Moses was speaking had witnessed the consequences of apostasy in their parents. Surely they understood what might happen to a new generation that had not been taught to cherish God's law. His covenant blessings on them could continue only if they remained obedient. Thus, they were not just to teach their children but to do so *diligently.*

This meant giving instruction "when thou sittest in thine house, and when thou walkest by the way, and when thou liest down, and when thou risest up" (Deut. 6:7). Parents were to use every daily activity as an opportunity to teach their children God's law. To do this, of course, they would have to incorporate it into their own daily routines. Children were to grow up thinking of God's words as a normal part of life and loving Him as their parents did.

THE DUAL MANDATE CONFIRMED

MARK 12:28 And one of the scribes came, and having heard them reasoning together, and perceiving that he had answered them well, asked him, Which is the first commandment of all?

29 And Jesus answered him, The first of all the commandments is, Hear, O Israel; The Lord our God is one Lord:

30 And thou shalt love the Lord thy God with all thy heart, and with all thy soul, and with all thy mind, and with all thy strength: this is the first commandment.

31 And the second is like, namely this, Thou shalt love thy neighbour as thyself. There is none other commandment greater than these.

32 And the scribe said unto him, Well, Master, thou hast said the truth: for there is one God; and there is none other but he:

33 And to love him with all the heart, and with all the understanding, and with all the soul, and with all the strength, and to love his neighbour as himself, is more than all whole burnt offerings and sacrifices.

34 And when Jesus saw that he answered discreetly, he said unto him, Thou art not far from the kingdom of God. And no man after that durst ask him any question.

The scribe's question (Mark 12:28). During the last week of His public ministry, Jesus faced intense questioning from hostile critics. The Pharisees and the Herodians tried to trap Him by asking whether it was lawful to pay tribute to Caesar (vss. 13-14). The Sadducees asked Him about marital status in the resurrection (vss. 18-23). Jesus answered both questions so admirably that He silenced them (cf. Luke 20:26, 39-40).

But a group of scribes and Pharisees had still another question (Matt. 22:34), and one of their numbers, a scribe, approached Jesus with it (Mark 12:28). Though the question was meant to test Him, the questioner came with some admiration, "perceiving that he had answered them (the Sadducees) well."

He asked, "Which is the first (most important) commandment of all?" (Mark 12:28). The rabbis had recognized 613 separate statutes in the law, 365 of them negative and 248 of them positive. They also had attempted to establish which of these were "heavy" and which were "light." So the question was asked in this context, attempting to get Jesus' point of view in a current debate.

Jesus' response (Mark 12:29-31). Without hesitation, Jesus answered that the greatest commandment was that of Deuteronomy 6:4-5, which we have analyzed. While Matthew's account (22:37) includes only the command itself, Mark quoted Jesus as giving the theological rationale for it as well. It was because Israel's Lord God was one Lord that He was to be worshipped wholeheartedly. And because He was Israel's covenant God who loved them supremely, they were to return that love.

Whereas the original command (Deut. 6:5) spoke of love with heart, soul, and might (strength), Jesus also included the mind (Mark 12:30). In this He was following the Greek translation, which included "mind" but not "heart." Jesus combined both Hebrew and Greek texts. But His declaration means the same as the original: Love the Lord with all that is in you.

Jesus went further than the question required. He also named the second greatest commandment (Mark 12:31). "The second is like, namely this" reads in Matthew as "the second is like unto it" (22:39). The two are inseparable; the second, "Thou shalt love thy neighbour as thyself" (Mark 12:31; cf. Lev. 19:18), is the logical extension of the first.

It would be inappropriate to call for a love of neighbor with the same wholehearted commitment one gives to God; that devotion is reserved for Him alone. But to love a neighbor as sincerely as one loves himself makes sense, for we all share the same nature. And since we are all image bearers of God, our love for Him should carry over to our love for mankind. To say we love God while withholding love from a neighbor is a blatant lie (I John 4:20-21).

Jesus concluded His answer: "There is none other commandment greater than these" (Mark 12:31). He also added, "On these two commandments hang all the law and the prophets" (Matt. 22:40). He chose these two because they are the principles on which all the rest are based. "The law and the prophets" was the Jewish term for all their Scriptures. Truly, love for God and neighbor sums up the teaching of all Scripture (cf. Deut. 10:12; Mic. 6:8).

The scribe's reaction (Mark 12:32-33). The scribe, whatever the motive behind his question, was genuinely impressed by Jesus' answer. "Well, Master," he said, "thou hast said the truth." "Well" means "fine," or "well done." It is an exclamation of approval. "Master" is, literally, "Teacher." He recognized Jesus as the equal of any rabbi.

It all made sense to him. He repeated the major points Jesus had made, as if running them through his mind again. In his statement that "there is one God; and there is none other but he" (Mark 12:32), the best Greek manuscripts do not include the word "God." This would reflect the Jewish reluctance to pronounce the divine name unnecessarily out of reverence for it. But the scribe did acknowledge the truth of this cornerstone of Jewish faith.

He also saw the logic in the dual mandate to love God supremely and to love neighbor as self (Mark 12:33). Fulfilling this "is more than all whole burnt offerings and sacrifices." "Burnt offerings" were sacrifices totally consumed when offered; "sacrifices" were those partially consumed and partially eaten by worshippers. This sacrificial system was strictly regulated and occupied much attention. Yet this scribe recognized its secondary place when compared to these two great commands.

This should not have been a new revelation to him, for the Old Testament prophets had often stated the same truth (cf. I Sam. 15:22; Jer. 7:21-23; Hos. 6:6; Mic. 6:6-8). But this scribe, steeped in a religious culture of external observances, was awakening to the fact that they meant nothing apart from a heart and life motivated by love for God and man. For him, this was the beginning of a potential spiritual enlightenment.

Jesus' observation (Mark 12:34). Jesus recognized this from the fact that the scribe had "answered discreetly." "Discreetly" means intelligently. The scribe's answer revealed a level of insight that was lacking in the confirmed legalists. So Jesus responded, "Thou art not far from the kingdom of God." This kingdom is His spiritual rule over those who have trusted Him. To enter it, one must be born anew (John 3:3) through the work of the Holy Spirit (vss. 5-6) when one trusts Jesus as Saviour (vss. 14-17).

Whether this scribe ever took that saving step we do not know. Some religious leaders did become believers after Jesus' resurrection (cf. Acts 6:7; 15:5), and we could hope that he was among them. But whatever the case, he is an example of the many who stand on the threshold of salvation because they see that the gospel makes perfect sense. God demands unreserved love for Him and one's neighbor, which no sinner can give. They can then only accept Christ's sacrifice for their sin and be saved.

When the scribe returned to his group, reevaluating the whole legal system, they probably feared Jesus would make converts of some of them if they prolonged their debate. So "no man after that durst ask him any question" (Mark 12:34). Jesus had ensnared them in their own traps, but this was only because they had set the traps. He desires not to entrap people but to bring them into His kingdom.

—Robert E. Wenger.

QUESTIONS

1. How were the ancient Israelites to display love for a neighbor?

2. In light of Jesus' teaching, what is a neighbor?

3. How did Israel's view of God differ from that of other peoples?

4. How complete is the love the Lord demands of us?

5. In what settings were Israelites to instruct their children?

6. What was happening to Jesus on the day the scribe asked Him about the great commandment?

7. In what way did Jesus' answer go beyond the scribe's question?

8. How are love for God and love for one's neighbor related?

9. How did the scribe respond to Jesus' answer? Why was this like a new revelation to him?

10. How did Jesus evaluate the scribe's spiritual condition?

—Robert E. Wenger.

Preparing to Teach the Lesson

The multitudes of people who heard Jesus teach were often amazed because He taught with authority, unlike the religious leaders they were accustomed to hearing (cf. Matt. 7:29). His reverence for and obedience to the Scriptures, and His concise and accurate interpretations of what the Bible said, stood in stark contrast to the mere opinions and traditions of the scribes and Pharisees. Jesus went directly to the point of a text and let God's Word speak for itself. The Bible is authoritative. This week's lesson is one example of this.

TODAY'S AIM

Facts: to show that Jesus viewed and applied the Scriptures as the authority for a person's life.

Principle: to show that Jesus conducted His life and ministry in light of the Scriptures.

Application: to show that we should accept the teaching of the Bible with the same authority and reverence given to it by Jesus and that we should seek to live by what it says.

INTRODUCING THE LESSON

The scribes and Pharisees often tried to trap Jesus with difficult questions. Some of their questions they could not answer consistently themselves. When one scribe approached Jesus with a sincere question, he did not demonstrate the hostility exhibited by his fellow scribes. He appears to have treated Jesus with respect.

As an aside, use this as an opportunity to show the proper way to approach someone if you are sincere about receiving an answer.

As the Second Person of the Godhead, Jesus fully understood the Scriptures because He inspired them and gave them to His servants (like Moses) who wrote them down.

The scribe's responsibility was to copy and know the Scriptures well. When questioned by the scribe, Jesus gave a brief yet complete answer without hesitation.

DEVELOPING THE LESSON

1. Love your neighbor (Lev. 19:18). If you ask a roomful of Christians to name their favorite book of the Bible, rarely, if ever, will you find someone who mentions the book of Leviticus. Regrettably, this critical book is too often bypassed, or if one is attempting to read through the entire Bible, it is read as rapidly as possible. However, when Jesus answered the scribe's question, the answer came partially from Leviticus. This is an important opportunity to stress to your students that every book of the Bible is important and needs our attention.

As you teach this first section, approach the passage by asking questions of your students. There are two actions that the Lord prohibits His people from taking. What are they? Instead, how is a person to treat his neighbor? Discuss how this can be done. Jesus addressed this in Matthew 5:43-45 and Luke 10:25-37.

Why do you think it is important that Leviticus 19:18 closes with the phrase "I am the Lord"? By adding that closing, He was lending His authority to keeping this action.

2. Love God (Deut. 6:4-7). The first part of the answer Jesus gave to the scribe's question about the most important commandment came from the book of Deuteronomy. This commandment is what the Jews call the Shema, which comes from the Hebrew word in verse 3 meaning "hear." In the context of the passage in Deuteronomy, it was central to the welfare and blessings of Israel as they settled in the Promised Land.

As the Lord prepared the people to enter Canaan, He gave them His directions for a second time, commanding how they should live as they occupied their new home. Every commandment and instruction that God gave to Israel could be summed up in this commandment. If the people loved God with all their hearts and taught each succeeding generation to do the same, all of the other commandments would fall into place.

In many Jewish homes one can find a small, ornate decoration attached diagonally to the upper part of the doorposts. It may be ceramic or brass, perhaps colorfully painted with a biblical scene. It is called a "mezuzah," meaning "doorpost." Within this hollow case is a parchment scroll containing the Shema. The presence of the mezuzah serves as a constant reminder of this commandment.

Some Christian bookstores carry them, and they are usually not very expensive. Discuss with your class the impact such a constant reminder might have on a person's daily life.

Discuss how the commands in Deuteronomy 6:7 could be applied in a practical way in the home. Why is this such a good idea? Ask how your students might apply this in a practical way in their own homes. Would this constant reminder make a difference in the way they lived?

3. The two greatest commandments (Mark 12:28-34). Jesus' response to the scribe summarized the commandments of the Jewish law as given by God. We normally think of the Ten Commandments when we think of the Old Testament law. However, the scribes counted 613 commandments in the Mosaic Law. There were 365 negative laws and 248 positive laws that God had given. Even so, these laws could be easily summed up in the two that Jesus identified.

Post a copy of the Ten Commandments on the wall of your classroom. Ask your students to classify each commandment as directed toward a person's relationship with God or toward his relationship with other people. Next, ask them to apply Jesus' two greatest commandments to each of the ten.

Discuss the scribe's response to Jesus' answer. Notice especially how he seemed to be sincere in his interaction with Jesus. Discuss how Jesus reacted to the scribe's answer.

ILLUSTRATING THE LESSON

Shine a light on what God requires. If you truly love God and genuinely show love to your neighbor, then all of the other commandments take care of themselves.

THE GREATEST COMMANDS

Love God

Love Your Neighbor

ARE YOU OBEYING THEM?

CONCLUDING THE LESSON

Challenge your students to study the Bible for themselves and to regard all of the Bible as inspired Scripture, as Jesus did. Encourage them to be precise in explaining what they believe, as Jesus showed precision in summarizing the commandments.

ANTICIPATING THE NEXT LESSON

Read Haggai 1:1-11 in preparation for next week's lesson. We will discuss the importance of obeying God.

—Carter Corbrey.

PRACTICAL POINTS

1. When we hate others, it hardens us to God's love (Lev. 19:18).
2. Just as God is one God, so He should always be number one in our lives (Deut. 6:4).
3. Experiencing God's love makes us want to share it with those around us (vss. 5-7).
4. Loving God means we should always seek His will and not our own (Mark 12:28-30).
5. As we love others, we reflect God's love for us (vs. 31).
6. Kind deeds to others do not replace the need to love God first (vss. 32-33).
7. When we recognize the importance of loving God, we often seek to serve Him better (vs. 34).

—Anne Adams.

RESEARCH AND DISCUSSION

1. Do we demonstrate God's love by what we say or by what we do? Explain and discuss your answer.
2. Is it more important to love God or to love others? Discuss. Which reveals more clearly how we feel about God?
3. Have you ever had to choose between doing God's will or showing love for others? Did it involve a witnessing situation? Discuss.
4. Do you know someone who is more concerned about godly conduct than about loving others? Does this show that he thinks he is better than others? How might it interfere in his witness to others?

—Anne Adams.

ILLUSTRATED HIGH POINTS

Love the Lord thy God

"I love purple." "I love football." "I love pizza." "I love you." We hear the word "love" in so many contexts that its meaning is almost diminished by overuse. Love can be demonstrated as physical or emotional attraction, friendly affection, or sincere appreciation. But if the intended object of love is a person, he or she would not be fulfilled by any of these vague exhibitions of love. People seeking love, true love, want devotion. God placed in people the desire to be cherished, to benefit from loyal companionship. This desire is a characteristic of God Himself, who formed us in His likeness and enabled us to communicate our love to Him.

God is love. He is the Giver of love, but He also is the Receiver of love. As we love God, we are forming a communion with the One who has always loved us. That strengthens our bond with Him and gives us peace, joy, and all the other benefits we can enjoy as the beloved of God.

This is the first commandment

I saw on a T-shirt the phrase "Second is just the first loser." In our work, sports, entertainment, and even in our shopping, we tend to covet first place. "First" connotes the fastest, the smartest, and the most talented. The first is the best.

A man asked Jesus to reveal to him the first commandment, the one foremost on God's agenda. Without hesitation, Jesus told him to love God with everything he had to offer. God expects no less of His people today. Each of us should consider his level of commitment to obeying this first and most important commandment. We should make sure our love for God is thorough and complete—heart, soul, mind, and strength.

—Beverly Jones.

Golden Text Illuminated

"Thou shalt love the Lord thy God with all thy heart, and with all thy soul, and with all thy mind, and with all thy strength: this is the first commandment. And the second is like, namely this, Thou shalt love thy neighbour as thyself" (Mark 12:30-31).

The golden text was Jesus' answer to an honest inquiry from a scribe. He wanted to know which of God's commandments is the greatest. Jesus first quoted Deuteronomy 6:4-5, which is a portion of what is called the Shema (vss. 4-9). The Jewish people recognized the central importance of this command, and many still continue the practice of reciting the Shema daily.

Jesus also cited the truth that introduces the command to love God (Mark 12:29; cf. Deut. 6:4). The truth that the "Lord our God is one Lord" emphasizes His unity and His uniqueness as the one and only, self-existent God. It also reminds us that He is *our* God, our Creator and Redeemer.

The natural—commanded—response to such a great God is love. We are to love with all our heart, soul, mind, and strength. "Heart" and "soul" together speak of our inner being and life. "Mind" points not only to the intellect but also to attitudes. "Strength," of course, speaks of our ability. The distinctions between the terms are not sharp or especially important. Together they signify that we are to love God with "all the 'faculties' with which God has endowed [us]" (Hendriksen, *Exposition of the Gospel According to Mark,* Baker). Complete, wholehearted love for the Lord is called for.

After quoting the Deuteronomy passage, Jesus stated, "This is the first commandment," or the most important one. Jesus had answered the scribe's question, but He was not through. He added "the second" greatest commandment: "Thou shalt love thy neighbour as thyself." Here too Jesus was quoting from the Old Testament (Lev. 19:18).

Genuine love for God necessarily results in love for people. Love for God is demonstrated by obedience to Him (John 14:15, 21). To claim to love Him while rejecting His command to love others calls our claim into question (cf. I John 4:20). When we truly love God with all our being, we will delight in obeying His commands.

Jesus does not command us to love ourselves here. He commands us to love others as we *already* love ourselves (cf. Eph. 5:29). In following Christ, the focus is never on ourselves but on the God we love.

Unlike many of the scribes, who were intent on discrediting Jesus, this one seemed to have a genuine desire to understand what God requires of His people. He wanted to know which of the 613 laws in the Old Testament was most crucial. Jesus pointed to the two central commands that summarize the entire law. The command to love God sums up the first four of the Ten Commandments, and to love one's neighbor sums up the final six of those commandments. Indeed, Jesus Himself said that "on these two commandments hang all the law and the prophets" (Matt. 22:40).

The Bible sets forth many duties of God's children, but these two commands—to love God and to love others as ourselves—apply to them all and serve as guiding principles for everything we do in life.

—Jarl K. Waggoner.

Heart of the Lesson

"When Rosemary, my youngest child, was three, she was given a little rag doll, which quickly became an inseparable companion. She had other toys that were intrinsically far more valuable, but none that she loved like she loved the rag doll. Soon the rag doll became more and more rag and less and less doll. It also became more and more dirty. If you tried to clean the rag doll, it became more ragged still. And if you didn't try to clean the rag doll, it became dirtier still.

"The sensible thing to do was to trash the rag doll. But that was unthinkable for anyone who loved my child. If you loved Rosemary, you loved the rag doll—it was part of the package" (Pitt-Watson, *A Primer for Preachers,* Baker).

In this week's lesson, we learn about the greatest commandment in all of life—to love God and one another with an unselfish love.

1. A command to demonstrate merciful love (Lev. 19:18). The Lord spoke directly to His servant Moses about the need for merciful love. This type of love, which was to dominate Israelite relationships, was to be devoid of retribution. This dynamic love was also to be without resentment. On the other hand, this God-ordained love was to be others-centered.

From the very beginnings of social interactions, God required His people to demonstrate a peculiar love that placed a priority on the needs of other people. Today, followers of Jesus Christ are responsible to perpetuate a unique spiritual heritage of self-sacrificing love. This distinctive love heads the list of the fruit of the Spirit (cf. Gal. 5:22-23) and is accomplished only as believers yield themselves to the Spirit's filling and control.

2. A command to communicate merciful love (Deut. 6:4-7). Moses summoned Israel to hear what God had revealed to him (5:1). The Israelites were to place God first in their commitment. All other commitments were to take a backseat to their love for God. In fact, they were to love God alone and to do so with all their being.

Moreover, God's people were to safeguard their unbridled love for generations to come. They were instructed to communicate God's words, especially His words about love, to their children. This communication was not to be just verbal; it was to be noticeable in the natural activities of life.

Love for God, for ourselves, and for others has immense worth and value. It deserves to be reproduced from generation to generation. Parents must teach and exemplify this dynamic love.

3. A command to apply merciful love (Mark 12:28-34). A scribe questioned Jesus about the greatest commandment. Jesus responded by quoting Old Testament Scriptures. The scribe responded in kind. Jesus acknowledged his astuteness and revealed that the scribe was close to entering God's kingdom by faith. This lively dialogue affected those who heard it. They would no longer question Jesus.

Intelligent assent to God's commands is commendable; however, it is not sufficient for entrance into God's kingdom. Believers realize that faith that leads to eternal life is an issue of the heart, not merely of the mind. Therefore, let us demonstrate our saving faith by loving our God and loving others. This animated love will silence those people whose only desire is to participate in worthless debate and questions.

—*Thomas R. Chmura.*

World Missions

Most of the world's religions teach about love. The main difference with what is taught in Christianity is that God is love personified in our Lord Jesus. The Bible reminds us that there is no love like that which Jesus demonstrated to us when He gave His life for us (cf. John 15:13). Love demands sacrifice. Many of us sacrifice a lot of things for our children, so we already know about this concept. Jesus taught us that this is the greatest commandment.

It is interesting to note that in our lesson this week, we have two important Old Testament passages to consider. Leviticus 19:18 tells us that love does not take revenge on others. Instead, we are to love our neighbors as ourselves. Deuteronomy 6:4-7 is part of what is known as the Shema to the Jews. It is a prayer that reminds us that we are to love God first with all our hearts. The overflow of our faith is demonstrated in love for our God and for our fellow men in our everyday lives.

Jesus showed us what true love is when He stayed true to His mission to save the world. But this meant that He had to die on the cruel cross for the sins of all of mankind. The Old Testament law stated that blood had to be shed for the sins of the people. Jesus fulfilled this stipulation by meeting the demands of the law and through it set us free. This is good news for us. The law was set up for failure, for no one could keep all its demands. Jesus set us free from bondage.

Out of this freedom from the bondage to the law stems the law of love. Jesus set us that example when He showed us how much He loved the whole world and met the demands of the law on our behalf at the very same time. He was our Passover Lamb, slain for us. In a world where many are searching for freedom and love, Jesus has shown that He is the answer to our deepest needs. He loved us enough to die for us. Paul reminded us that Jesus died for us while we were stuck in our sins (Rom. 5:8).

The world desperately needs to hear the story of Jesus, who loved us so much that He was willing to sacrifice Himself for us. Sacrifice is the mark of true love. Yet there are many religions around the world that teach good works and a way to earn one's way out of sin through good deeds. That can only lead to frustration, for we are a sinful people. Only someone who is absolutely perfect in every way could meet the demands of a righteous God. Jesus cared enough for us to keep us from punishment.

If Jesus is the ultimate example of love, then the world needs to be told of such a loving Saviour. We are His messengers in this divine task. He could have sent angels to do this task easily, but He has chosen us as His messengers of the good news. That should be a source of encouragement to us. Consider this: He has chosen us to be coworkers with Him in His great work to tell the world what He has done for us! There is no greater love.

There is yet one more way to look at this. If we have truly experienced His love in His saving us from our sins, should we not then want to share that same path with others so that we can take them with us into the kingdom? It would be selfish of us not to share such great love!

—A. Koshy Muthalaly.

The Jewish Aspect

Many times in the course of a day, Jews recite the watchword of Judaism: "Hear, O Israel: The Lord our God is one Lord" (Deut. 6:4). But do they go on to say, "And thou shalt love the Lord thy God with all thine heart, and with all thy soul, and with all thy might" (vs. 5) as Moses commanded them?

Judaism has a great deal to say *to* God but very little to say *about* God. Some of their rare expressions about God seem to be less than proper in addressing the God of all creation, the God of all glory. The result is a people who find it hard to talk about the divine Founder of their faith. In the article "Speaking of God," Rabbi Jakob J. Petuchowski pointed out that Jews have a helpful word, "keveyakhol," that means "If we really could say anything about God, it might work to say it this way." This excuses the natural inability of man to say anything truly defining about God (Nemitoff, ed., *A Basic Jewish Reader,* Congregation Beth Israel).

A synagogue will accept as members Jews who do not believe in God. By so much they fail the very first commandment!

When you have the pleasure of knowing a born-again Jew, you find that biblical salvation has made the love of God with heart, soul, and might a reality for him. Martin Meyer Rosen, known now to millions as Moishe Rosen, the founder of Jews for Jesus, was not a very nice man before he met the Messiah Jesus. The incessant struggle against anti-Semitism kept him in a state of semibelligerence. All that changed when he truly met God for the first time.

In the 1980s Rosen was challenged to speak to German Christians, many of whom had cooperated with the Nazis in the persecution of Jews in the 1930s and 1940s. Grace enabled him to speak to them in love, a love that God has for the sinner.

Rachmiel Frydland, a Polish Christian Jew, was turned in to the Nazis by Gentile Polish Christians, who felt constrained by the message of Romans 13 to be loyal to their rulers in spite of their murderous intent. Frydland had the grace to take this without bitterness from the God he honored with all his heart, soul, and strength. It would have been easy to feel otherwise.

And what shall we say of the second commandment, "Thou shalt love thy neighbour as thyself" (Mark 12:31)? Today there is an almost complete breakdown of relationships between neighbors compared to the experience of a half century ago. With the invention of central air-conditioning, homes are closed up tight. Television completed the separation between neighbors. It is no longer rare to be unacquainted with the people next door.

That complicates our obligation, but it does not eliminate it. The only truly practical way to love our neighbor as ourself is to give him the thing we treasure most—our love for the One who saved us, Jesus Christ, the Righteous (John 17:3). When we take a simple gospel message next door, the Holy Spirit can provide the impetus for an invitation to trust the Saviour for salvation.

One other mournful fact about our isolation from our neighbors lies in the fact that many of us do not invite people to go to church with us. Faithful missionary churches spend money on door hangers, attractive invitations, and advertising in an appeal for visitors. Dear reader, did you invite a neighbor to church lately? You did? Well, your love is showing! You are the gospel's best advertisement.

—Lyle P. Murphy.

Guiding the Superintendent

In terms of their importance, commandments can be great, greater, or greatest. When one of God's commandments is considered the greatest, it requires man's truest reverence. That status implies that to God, nothing can be more important than obeying it.

DEVOTIONAL OUTLINE

1. Love for our neighbor enjoined (Lev. 19:18). The Bible exhorts believers to have fellowship with their neighbors—even the more difficult ones—and to live in harmony with them. Key to godly relationships is relying on God to fight our battles for us. Our duty is to follow the principles of the Golden Rule (cf. Matt. 7:12).

2. Venerating and teaching God's law enjoined (Deut. 6:4-7). As the Israelites approached Canaan, Moses again set forth God's law given at Mount Sinai. He got the people's attention by saying, "Hear," meaning "Listen" or "Pay close attention." He stressed that the Lord with whom they were entering into covenant was the one and only God. He alone was worthy of their exclusive love and devotion, having loved them above all other nations. In return, they were to honor and love God only and keep the entire covenant in their hearts.

God's teachings have generational value. Moses urged Israel to conscientiously teach these same laws and judgments to each ensuing generation at every opportunity.

3. The great commandment excels them all (Mark 12:28-34). Jesus was accustomed to the scribes and Pharisees' taunts and challenges to His teachings, and He used these occasions to teach them spiritual truths. As followers of Christ, when we meet those who would question our zeal for God, like Jesus we must view such encounters as evangelistic opportunities and share the gospel of Jesus Christ.

True believers trust every word that Jesus spoke, but this scribe appeared pleasantly surprised to hear Jesus expound the Scriptures with depth of knowledge and authority. Perhaps his prior interactions had been with dull-minded men such as the Sadducees he had heard ask Jesus the nonsensical question about marriage in heaven (cf. Mark 12:18-25). Jesus did not entertain their absurd inquiry but quickly corrected these supposedly learned religious leaders.

The scribe's question allowed Jesus to again stress the enormity of the greatest commandment and the scribe to openly acknowledge that Jesus very eloquently spoke the truth. The scribe referred to Old Testament teaching (I Sam. 15:22; Hos. 6:6) in support of the weight of this commandment; it is paramount above any other sacrifice we may offer God. Their exchange silenced the crowd. Jesus commended the scribe's discretion and encouraged him to draw even closer to God. To gain a seat in God's kingdom, we must hear, receive, and live the principles of God's Word.

AGE-GROUP EMPHASES

Children: Give them examples of sharing. Children have a predisposition to self-centeredness and may not find it easy to show love to others.

Youths: Antibullying programs are receiving a lot of press. Teach the young people how to handle themselves God's way—that is, to treat others the way they wish to be treated.

Adults: Remind them of the dangers of holding a grudge, and offer to pray with those who are dealing with bitterness that they might release it to God.

—*Jane E. Campbell.*

please God. He demonstrated how we should respond in many different situations.

Regarding our enemies, we are admonished, "Love your enemies, do good to them which hate you, . . . pray for them which despitefully use you" (Luke 6:27-28).

He gave us a guarantee on how we could have all the desires of our heart. The method is to "seek . . . first the kingdom of God, and his righteousness; and all these things shall be added unto you" (Matt. 6:33).

Jesus assured us that if we obey and trust Him, no harm or danger intended by our enemies will ever overwhelm us. "No weapon that is formed against thee shall prosper; and every tongue that shall rise against thee in judgment thou shalt condemn. This is the heritage of the servants of the Lord, and their righteousness is of me, saith the Lord" (Isa. 54:17).

Our Saviour reminded us of the high priority God places on forgiveness. He told us, "For if ye forgive men their tres-passes, your heavenly Father will also forgive you: but if ye forgive not men their trespasses, neither will your Father forgive your trespasses" (Matt. 6:14-15).

Jesus showed us by example how God expects us to treat one another. He said, As I have loved you, . . . ye also love one another. By this shall all men know that ye are my disciples, if ye have love one to another" (John 13:34-35).

Our Saviour told us that love is the Father's greatest commandment. In addition, He was, is, and always will be the embodiment of that commandment.

Love was the motivating factor that enabled Jesus, who knew no sin, to be willing to suffer excruciating pain and unimaginable agony to give mankind the opportunity to be reconciled to God. This was the plan when He created Adam and Eve. Christ's sacrifice remains an act of love that can never and will never be duplicated.

Jesus fulfilled His mission on earth by being an infallible example that we must choose to follow. We also have access to the Scriptures, which document all that Jesus said and did.

Our mission is hear God's Word and obey it. Jesus told His disciples—and He is also telling us today—"If ye love me, keep my commandments" (John 14:15).

Covenant Blessings

JOYCE M. SIMON

Suppose you were allowed to hear a conversation between God and Satan (cf. Job 1:6-12). As you listen, you realize the conversation is about you. God tells Satan you are a man or woman after His own heart. Would that not be wonderful to hear? That is exactly what God said about David when He made the covenant with him: "I have found David the son of Jesse, a man after mine own heart, which shall fulfill all my will." Paul stated, "Of this man's seed hath God according to his promise raised unto Israel a Saviour, Jesus" (Acts 13:22-23).

God's promise to David that the Saviour would be born through his lineage expanded His covenant with the children of Israel. Jesus would be the ultimate sacrifice to atone for the sins of mankind. The Saviour would be the means to give every individual direct access to God the Father.

In spite of their character flaws and human failures, God extends the same love and patience to His children today as He did to David.

David's life story provides a great example of the frailties and complex nature of human beings and of God's love for us. It is a love that knows no bounds and a love that will never fail.

David had a quick temper. However, when the moment of anger passed, he was always willing to listen to reason. One excellent example is the I Samuel 25 account of his confrontation with Nabal and his decision to kill him.

David became enraged with Nabal when he did not show respect to him, and he decided to kill him. However, he was willing to listen to Nabal's wife, Abigail, and he allowed himself to be persuaded not to give in to his anger. He quickly recognized and acknowledged (as he always did) that the Lord intervened on his behalf. He told Abigail, "Blessed be the Lord God of Israel, which sent thee this day to meet me: and blessed be thy advice, and blessed be thou, which hast kept me this day from coming to shed blood, and from avenging myself with mine own hand" (I Sam. 25:32-33).

Like David, many of us are quick to get angry. Some folks let it be known they have a "short fuse" that makes them prone to becoming angry at anything they view as an insult.

David's life story is a study in triumphs, failures, and the inevitable consequences of our actions. Nevertheless, he had two admirable qualities that pleased the Lord. First, he loved the Lord totally, sincerely, and without reservation. David's other quality that delighted the Lord was his willingness to always confess his sin before asking for God's forgiveness. Psalm 51 illustrates the point. This was David's plea for forgiveness after the incident with Bath-sheba. This example could be considered a blueprint for repentance.

David began his prayer by first asking for mercy. Then he acknowledged that he had sinned. And—what some of us may, at times, be reluctant to admit—he said sin is evil (Ps. 51:4).

He asked the Lord, "Create in me a clean heart" (Ps. 51:10). Regrettably, many of us really do not believe our hearts are evil. In spite of whether we believe it or not, God Himself says, "The heart is deceitful above all things, and desperately wicked: who can know it?" (Jer. 17:9).

In the repenting process, we are often tricked by Satan into thinking it is not necessary to confess our sins in detail before the Lord, as David did every time before he asked for God's forgiveness.

Satan encourages us to rationalize. The opposing thought the devil gives us is that since God knows everything, He is already aware of our sin; so there is no need to tell Him about it when we ask His forgiveness. However, God did not leave us in the dark about any part of His Word. Leviticus 5:5 tells us clearly that God requires that we name the sin when we ask His forgiveness.

In fulfilling God's covenant with David, Jesus was willing to be the final sacrifice God would accept as atonement for the sins of mankind. Jesus opened the door that allowed us the privilege of direct contact with the Father. We can now serve the Lord on an individual basis. Jesus was also the only means through which all humanity could be reconciled to God's original plan when He created Adam and Eve.

Today, every individual has the same opportunity to enjoy all the benefits of the covenant the way David did. Like David, we can walk through the valley of the shadow of death and fear no evil (Ps.

23:4-6).

We can be absolutely certain that every experience, every trial, every hurt, every moment of feeling sorry—in short, all our experiences, pleasant and unpleasant—will always work together for our good (cf. Rom. 8:28).

We can rest in the complete assurance that nothing, "neither death, nor life, nor angels, nor principalities, nor powers, nor things present, nor things to come, nor height, nor depth, nor any other creature, shall be able to separate us from the love of God, which is in Christ Jesus our Lord" (Rom. 8:38-39).

We all have the privilege of being partakers of the many benefits of this final covenant. Jesus gave us the key that opens the door to all the blessings in the covenant: "Thou shalt love the Lord thy God with all thy heart, and with all thy soul, and with all thy mind" (Matt. 22:37).

TOPICS FOR NEXT QUARTER

June 1

Obey the Lord
Haggai 1:1-11

June 8

Trust God's Promises
Haggai 1:12; 2:1-9

June 15

Live Pure Lives
Haggai 2:10-19

June 22

Hope for a New Day
Haggai 2:20-23; Zechariah 4:5-14

June 29

A Call to Unity
I Corinthians 1:10-17

July 6

Glorify God with Your Body
I Corinthians 6:12-20

July 13

Love Builds Up
I Corinthians 8:1-13

July 20

Overcoming Temptation
I Corinthians 10:12-22

July 27

Seek the Good of Others
I Corinthians 14:13-26

August 3

Consolation Through Prayer
II Corinthians 1:3-11

August 10

The Need for Forgiveness
II Corinthians 1:23—2:11

August 17

Treasure in Clay Jars
II Corinthians 4:2-15

August 24

An Appeal for Reconciliation
II Corinthians 6:1-13; 7:2

August 31

Sacrificial, Joyful Giving
II Corinthians 8:1-14

PARAGRAPHS ON PLACES AND PEOPLE

SYNAGOGUE

The synagogue in Nazareth was the site of the events related in Luke 4:14-21. After having garnered a reputation for His mighty works, Jesus had returned to Nazareth. After reading from Isaiah 61:1-2 during the synagogue service, Jesus announced to the audience that they were hearing right then the fulfillment of Isaiah's prophecy.

When Jesus went on to talk about God's provision for Gentiles in Israel during the time of Elijah and Elisha, the crowd became enraged, forcibly removed Jesus from the synagogue, and attempted to throw Him from a precipice. Luke records that Jesus simply walked through the crowd and left. Though archaeological evidence of a synagogue in Nazareth has yet to surface, Mount Kedumin, just outside the modern-day town, is supposed by some to mark the spot where the precipice event occurred.

THE MOON

This may seem a bit unusual as a choice for Paragraphs on Places and People, but the moon is, after all, a place. In Psalm 89, the writer extols the permanence of God's covenant with David, comparing it to the sun and moon. The moon is described "as a faithful witness in heaven" (vs. 37). Though the moon gives no light of its own, it faithfully reflects the brilliance of the sun.

The beauty of the full moon has inspired composers, writers, and painters. As the rainbow was a reminder of God's promise to Noah and succeeding generations, so the moon is a steadfast witness of God's faithfulness to David and to all believers. Science has shown that life on earth would not be possible without the moon. In similar fashion, eternal life would not be possible were God ever to revoke His covenants with mankind—which He never will.

MELCHIZEDEK

An enigmatic figure, Melchizedek is mentioned only twice in the Old Testament. He is discussed more extensively by the writer of the book of Hebrews. The name Melchizedek means "legitimate/righteous king"; he is also called "King of peace" (7:2).

Melchizedek lived during a time before any priestly line had been established. As king of Salem (Jerusalem), he met Abram (Abraham) after the slaughter of the kings. He blessed Abram, and Abram, in turn, gave him a tithe. In arguing for the superiority of Christ, the author of Hebrews cited, among other things, the unchanging nature of the Melchizedekian priesthood. Christ, unlike the Levitical priests before Him, will never die.

JOANNA

A New Testament figure who is largely overlooked, Joanna is mentioned only in Luke 8:1-3 and 24:10. Luke notes that she was among a group of women healed by Jesus and that she was the wife of Chuza, the household servant of Herod.

Joanna was probably among the upper classes in Jerusalem, since Luke records that she ministered to the Lord of her own means. Though not mentioned by name, it is likely that Joanna was among the women who returned to the tomb to anoint Jesus' body after His burial. She is listed with those who returned to tell the disciples of that morning's encounter at the empty tomb.

—*James Parry.*

Daily Bible Readings for Home Study and Worship

(Readings are for the week previous to the lesson topics.)

1. March 2.   An Eternal Kingdom
M.—The Lord Is King. Ps. 93:1-5.
T.—You Are My Son. Ps. 2:1-12.
W.—An Eternal Throne. Ps. 45:1-9.
T.—The Lord's Inheritance. Ps. 94:8-15.
F.—A New Song. Ps. 98:1-9.
S.—The Messiah's Eternal Reign. Rev. 11:15-19.
S.—A Throne Established Forever. II Sam. 7:4-16.

2. March 9.   Son of David
M.—A Son Named Emmanuel. Matt. 1:22-25.
T.—The King of the Jews. Matt. 2:1-6.
W.—The Beloved Servant. Matt. 12:15-23.
T.—Hosanna to the Son of David. Matt. 21:12-17.
F.—The Son Whom David Called Lord. Matt. 22:41-45.
S.—Following the Son of David. Mark 10:46-52.
S.—The Son of David. Ps. 89:35-37; Isa. 9:6-7; Matt. 1:18-22.

3. March 16.   An Everlasting King
M.—The Lord Is My Portion. Ps. 16:1-6.
T.—Not Left in the Grave. Ps. 16:7-11.
W.—Freed from the Fear of Death. Heb. 2:14-18.
T.—The Power of the Resurrection. Phil. 3:7-11.
F.—The Heavenly Call of God. Phil. 3:12-16.
S.—Made Both Lord and Messiah. Acts 2:33-36.
S.—Seated on David's Throne. Ps. 110:1-4; Acts 2:22-24, 29-32.

4. March 23.   Worthy Is the Lamb
M.—Sheep Without a Shepherd. Matt. 9:35—10:1.
T.—The One at God's Right Hand. Ps. 80:8-19.
W.—The Lord Defends His Flock. Zech. 10:1-5.
T.—The Wrath of the Lamb. Rev. 6:12-17.
F.—Salvation Belongs to Our God. Rev. 7:9-12.
S.—The Lamb Will Shepherd Them. Rev. 7:13-17.
S.—Worthy Is the Lamb. Rev. 5:6-13.

5. March 30.   The Entrance of the King
M.—The Lord Enthroned as King. Ps. 29:1-11.
T.—The Lord Protects. Zech. 9:10-15.
W.—The Lord Gives Victory. Ps. 20:1-9.
T.—Loud Songs of Joy. Ps. 47:1-9.
F.—Your Salvation Is Near. Isa. 62:8-12.
S.—Coming in the Lord's Name. Ps. 118:21-29.
S.—The Triumphal Entry. Zech. 9:9; Matt. 21:1-11.

6. April 6.   The Cleansing of the Temple
M.—The Holy Temple. Hab. 2:18-20.
T.—The House of the Lord. Ps. 27:1-5.
W.—From His Temple He Hears. Ps. 18:1-6.
T.—Prayer Reaches His Temple. Jonah 2:1-9.
F.—One Greater than the Temple. Matt. 12:1-8.
S.—A Holy Temple in the Lord. Eph. 2:11-22.
S.—A House of Prayer. Isa. 56:6-7; Jer. 7:9-11; Mark 11:15-19.

7. April 13.   The Suffering of the King
M.—A Throne Established Forever. I Chron. 17:7-14.
T.—Light Has Dawned. Matt. 4:12-17.
W.—Seated on the Throne of Glory. Matt. 19:23-30.

T.—The Kingdom of God's Beloved Son. Col. 1:9-14.
F.—A Better Hope. Heb. 7:11-19.
S.—King of Kings, Lord of Lords. Rev. 19:11-16.
S.—Behold the Man! Jer. 23:5-6; Zech. 6:9-15; John 19:1-5.

8. April 20.   The Resurrection of the King (Easter)
M.—Death and Despair. Job 30:20-31.
T.—Redeemed from the Power of Death. Ps. 49:5-15.
W.—Received by God to Glory. Ps. 73:16-28.
T.—Dry Bones Shall Live Again. Ezek. 37:1-14.
F.—The God of the Living. Mark 12:18-27.
S.—Christ Is Risen. I Cor. 15:12-20.
S.—Raised on the Third Day. Hos. 6:1-3; Luke 24:1-12.

9. April 27.   From Suffering to Glory
M.—A Bitter Complaint. Job 23:1-7.
T.—I Will Come Forth as Gold. Job 23:8-14.
W.—A Man of Sorrows. Isa. 52:13—53:4.
T.—Undergoing Great Suffering. Matt. 16:21-28.
F.—Servant of All. Mark 9:30-37.
S.—We Have Seen His Glory. John 1:10-18.
S.—Suffering on Our Behalf. Isa. 53:5-8; Luke 24:25-27, 44-47.

10. May 4.   Victory over Temptation
M.—Character Proved Through Trial. Deut. 8:1-11.
T.—Watch and Pray. Matt. 26:36-41.
W.—Guard Against Temptation. Gal. 6:1-5.
T.—Lead Us Not into Temptation. Matt. 6:9-13.
F.—Kept from the Hour of Trial. Rev. 3:8-13.
S.—Kept Safe in All Your Ways. Ps. 91:1-12.
S.—Serve God Only. Deut. 6:13-16; Matt. 4:4-11.

11. May 11.   Jesus' Mission on Earth
M.—Sent from the Father. John 16:25-33.
T.—Sent to Do God's Will. John 6:35-40.
W.—Sent to Bring Light. John 12:44-50.
T.—Sent to Testify to Truth. John 18:33-38.
F.—Sent to Draw All People. John 12:27-32.
S.—Sent to Give Life. John 10:1-10.
S.—Fulfillment of the Scripture. Luke 4:14-21.

12. May 18.   Jesus' Teaching on the Law
M.—The Precept of Men. Isa. 29:13-19.
T.—The True Fear of God. Exod. 20:12-21.
W.—The Law of Faith. Rom. 3:21-31.
T.—Fulfilling the Law. Matt. 5:14-20.
F.—But I Tell You. Matt. 5:27-37.
S.—What God Requires. Matt. 5:38-48.
S.—What Proceeds from the Heart. Matt. 15:1-11, 18-20.

13. May 25.   The Greatest Commandment
M.—Love and God's Commandments. Deut. 7:7-16.
T.—Serving God with Heart and Soul. Deut. 10:12-21.
W.—Keeping God's Commands Always. Deut. 11:1-7.
T.—Loving Your Neighbor. Lev. 19:11-17.
F.—A Plea for Forgiveness. I Kings 8:31-36.
S.—Marks of the Righteous. Ps. 15:1-5.
S.—The Two Greatest Commands. Lev. 19:18; Deut. 6:4-7; Mark 12:28-34.

REVIEW

What have you learned this quarter? Can you answer these questions?

Jesus' Fulfillment of Scripture

UNIT I: Jesus and the Davidic Covenant

March 2

An Eternal Kingdom

1. Why did David want to build a temple for the Lord? Why was he not the right person to do so?
2. How had God lived among His people before David's time?
3. What did God mean when He promised to make David a house?
4. What work did God say David's heir would accomplish?
5. How was it possible for David's dynasty to be eternal?

March 9

Son of David

1. In what sense is the promised Messiah a "son" (Isa. 9:6)?
2. What names did Isaiah use to describe the Messiah's attributes?
3. Why could Isaiah say that the Messiah's kingdom would be eternal?
4. What does "Jesus" mean? Why was Mary's child to have this name?
5. In what way was the Jews' vision of the Messiah distorted?

March 16

An Everlasting King

1. How can we explain the fact that David called two persons "Lord"?
2. Through what kind of army will the Messiah conquer His enemies?

3. Who was Melchizedek? How did he prefigure Christ's priesthood?
4. What was God's role in Jesus' death, and what was the role of the Jews and the Romans?

March 23

Worthy Is the Lamb

1. What contrasting images of Christ are given in Revelation 5?
2. Why is the slain Lamb alone qualified to open the seals on the book?
3. What does it mean to be redeemed? How was our redemption obtained?
4. What seven qualities did the angels ascribe to the Lamb?
5. What lesson does the whole creation's worship leave for us?

UNIT II: What the Prophets Foretold

March 30

The Entrance of the King

1. What roles did the two animals in Matthew's account have?
2. How will Jesus' demeanor at His second coming differ from what He displayed at the triumphal entry?
3. Why did Jesus weep over Jerusalem on this day?
4. What did the garments and branches on the road signify?

April 6

The Cleansing of the Temple

1. How did the death of Christ affect the Gentiles' access to God?
2. Why had a market been set up in the temple in Jesus' day?
3. What did Jesus do to end this market? Why?
4. How were Gentiles hindered from temple worship in Jesus' day?
5. How did the leaders react to Jesus' purification of the temple?

April 13

The Suffering of the King

1. How will the rule of the Righteous Branch differ from that of the kings of Jeremiah's day?
2. What kind of security will Messiah bring to Judah and Israel?
3. What two offices will the Messiah combine in Himself?
4. Why was Pilate, the Roman procurator, consulted in Jesus' trial?

April 20

The Resurrection of the King (Easter)

1. Why did the women wait until the third day to anoint Jesus' body?
2. What does the question "Why seek ye the living among the dead?" (Luke 24:5) tell us about Jesus?
3. What words of Jesus had the women forgotten?
4. Why had the disciples not taken prophecies of Jesus' death and resurrection to heart?

April 27

From Suffering to Glory

1. Why did Jesus call the disciples on the Emmaus road "fools" (Luke 24:25)?
2. How was these disciples' view of the Messiah flawed?
3. How thorough was Jesus' teaching of the Scriptures about Himself?
4. What major themes did Jesus teach the disciples from Scripture?
5. Where was the outreach to the Gentiles to start? Why?

UNIT III: Jesus' Use of Scripture
May 4

Victory over Temptation

1. What is fear of the Lord? How will it affect one's life?
2. When does God's jealousy lead Him to anger?
3. Why was Jesus especially vulnerable to Satan's first temptation?
4. Should we give credence to everyone who quotes Scripture? Explain.
5. How would Satan's proposition to Jesus have thwarted God's plan?

May 11

Jesus' Mission on Earth

1. What was the early response to Jesus' ministry in Galilee?
2. Where did the power for the Messiah's ministry originate?
3. How did the Year of Jubilee illustrate Jesus' mission?
4. What was Jesus claiming when He said Isaiah's prophecy had been fulfilled by Him?

May 18

Jesus' Teaching on the Law

1. What did the Jews hope to accomplish through ceremonial washing?
2. What is a hypocrite?
3. How did the scribes and Pharisees manifest their hypocrisy? How might we manifest it today?
4. What is the true source of spiritual defilement?
5. How did Jesus treat the law? Why could He set parts of it aside?

May 25

The Greatest Commandment

1. In light of Jesus' teaching, what is a neighbor?
2. How complete is the love the Lord demands of us?
3. In what way did Jesus' answer go beyond the scribe's question?
4. How are love for God and love for one's neighbor related?
5. How did Jesus evaluate the scribe's spiritual condition?